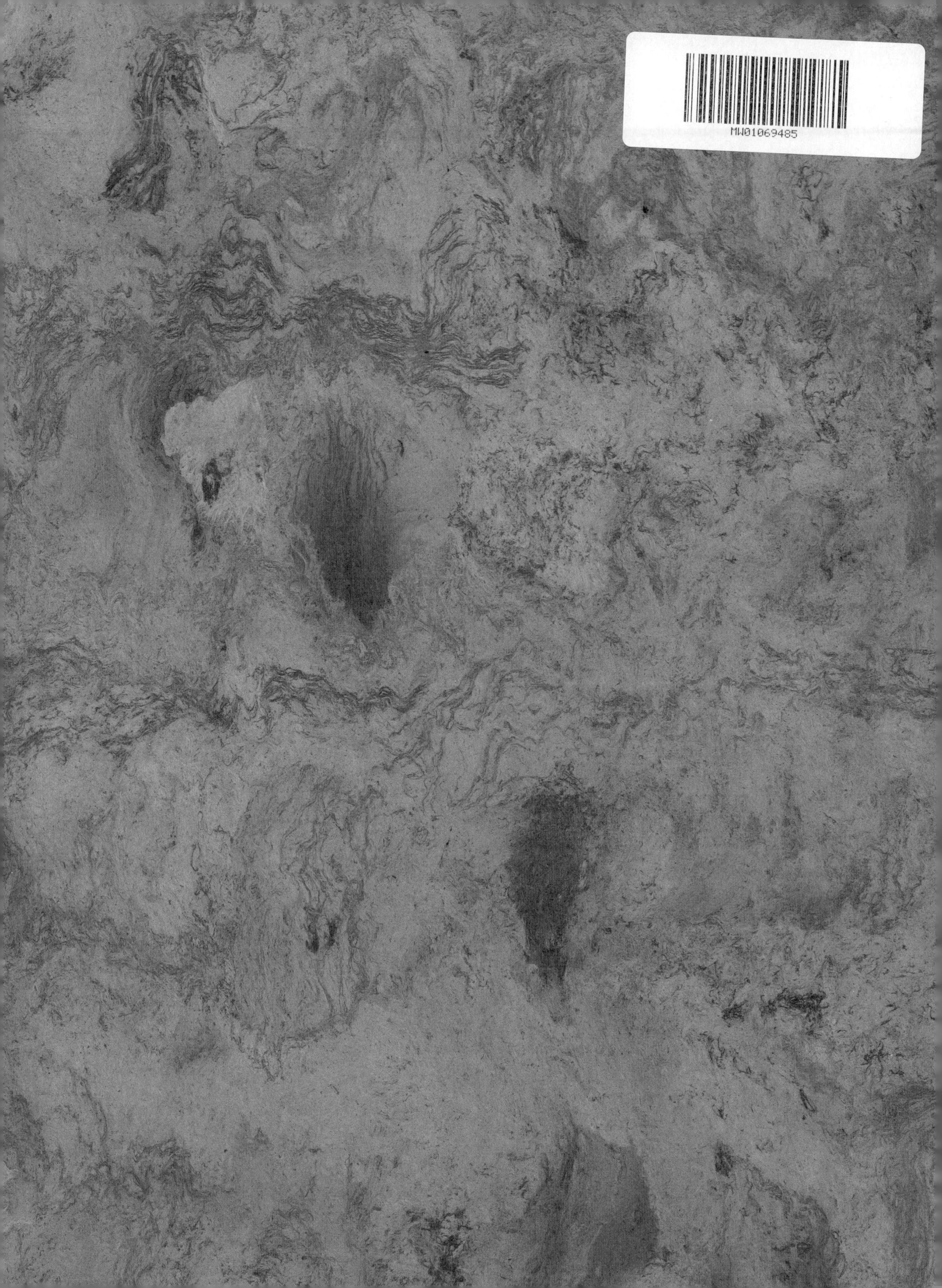
MW01069485

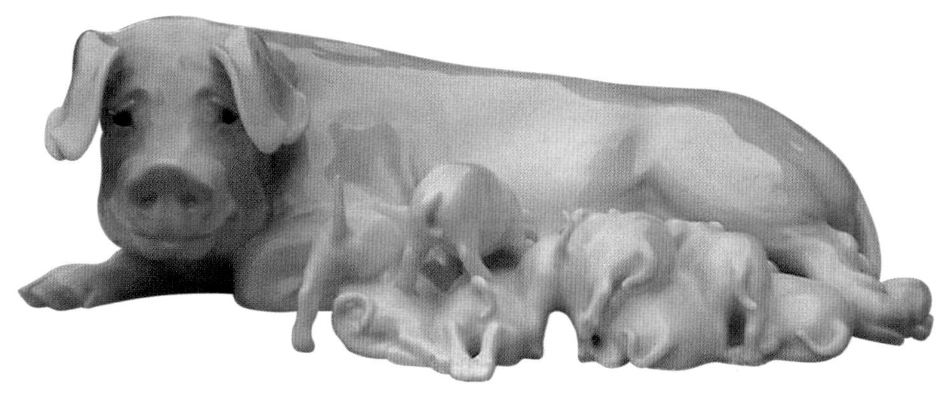

Bing & Grondahl Figurines

Caroline & Nick Pope

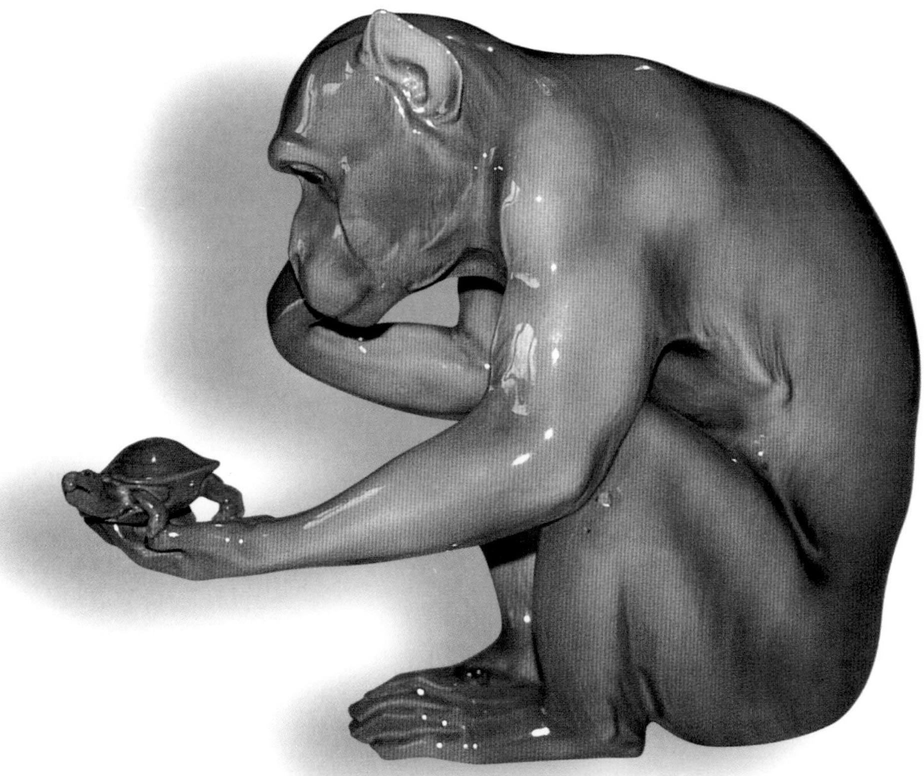

Schiffer Publishing Ltd®

4880 Lower Valley Road, Atglen, PA 19310 USA

To
Phil Anderson

Library of Congress Cataloging-in-Publication Data

Pope, Caroline.
Bing & Grondahl figurines/by Caroline & Nick Pope.
p. cm.
ISBN 0-7643-1698-2 (Hardcover)
1. Bing & Grondahl—Catalogs. 2. Porcelain figures—Collectors and collecting—Denmark—Catalogs. 3. Porcelain, Danish—Collectors and collecting—Catalogs. I. Title: Bing and Grondahl figurines. II. Pope, Nick. III. Title.
NK4210.B49 P66 2003
738.8'2'0948913—dc21
2002014756

Designed by John P. Cheek
Cover design Bruce M. Waters
Type set in Windsor BT/Korinna BT

ISBN: 0-7643-1698-2
Printed in China
1 2 3 4

Published by Schiffer Publishing Ltd.
4880 Lower Valley Road
Atglen, PA 19310
Phone: (610) 593-1777; Fax: (610) 593-2002
E-mail: Schifferbk@aol.com
Please visit our web site catalog at
www.schifferbooks.com
We are always looking for people to write books on new and related subjects. If you have an idea for a book, please contact us at the above address.

This book may be purchased from the publisher. Include $3.95 for shipping. Please try your bookstore first.
You may write for a free catalog.

In Europe, Schiffer books are distributed by
Bushwood Books
6 Marksbury Ave. Kew Gardens
Surrey TW9 4JF England
Phone: 44 (0)20 8392-8585; Fax: 44 (0)20 8392-9876
E-mail: Bushwd@aol.com
Free postage in the UK. Europe: air mail at cost.
Please try your bookstore first.

Contents

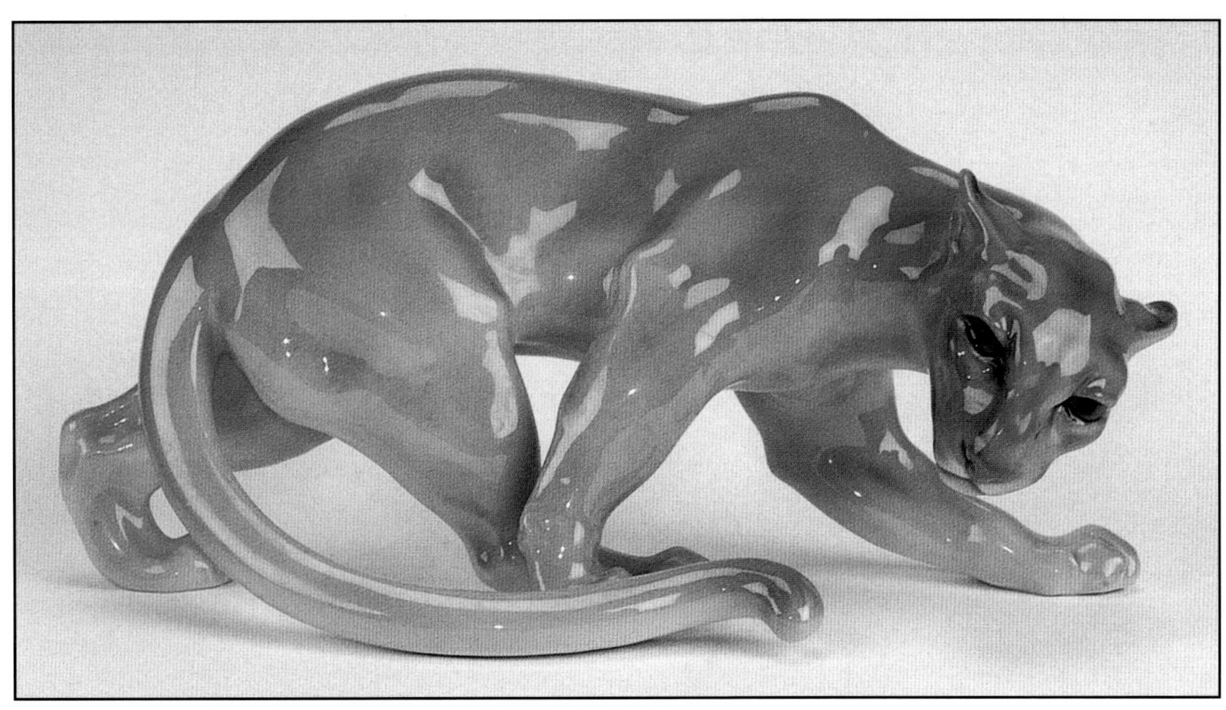

Acknowledgments

With thanks to: Margaret, Dave, Rebecca, and Charlotte.
Betty, John, Melissa Delson, Beatrix Forbes Fine Porcelain, Malcolm & Joan Floyde, Tom & Mabel Hood, Jane the Dane, D.M. Joos de ter Beerst, Kristi, Mark Potterton, Stan & Christine, Stan Tillotson (*www.stan.tillotson.com*), 'Teddies', 'Wiffle', Ian Williams, Willi and Rosi, and the many other dealers and collectors from around the world who have helped us along the way. Special thanks go to Linda H. Purbaugh for her photographs of pieces from the collection of Lawrence Rubin.
En særlig tak rettes til vore danske venner, handlende såvel som samlere og her skal specielt nævnes - Nathalie Geisler, Christian Geisler, Lise Jahn, Ira Hartogsohn, Borg Jensen, Gunnar Jakobsen, Ulla Kayser, Mogens, Peter, Jan Ringsmose, P R Monter (*www.pr.dk*), DPH Trading (*www.dph-trading.dk*) and Else and Anker Dahl-Jensen.

Introduction

The Danish porcelain industry starts and ends, for many collectors, with Royal Copenhagen. Many do not appreciate that the industry was far more wide ranging, with a number of factories producing porcelain of high quality, so far as both artistic merit and manufacturing techniques are concerned.

Bing & Grondahl produced a vast range of products, many of which were designed or sculpted by artists who also worked for Royal Copenhagen. Pre-eminent amongst these was Jens Peter Dahl-Jensen, who subsequently set up his own factory assisted by his son, Georg.

For the sake of simplicity, we have divided the study into two self-contained volumes, this book and its companion volume, *Dahl-Jensen Figurines*. Each has an index, though we have indicated in the listing in the Bing & Grondahl volume interesting similarities in subject, style, or technique between pieces produced by Dahl-Jensen for both factories. In the Dahl-Jensen volume we have also indicated similarities between the factories, for instance Laurits Jensen worked either directly or on commission for all three factories.

Though it should be appreciated that there is little information available on the work of individual sculptors for the Bing & Grondahl factory, we have endeavored to make attributions where possible. We have, however, refrained from making guesses purely on style and subject matter, even when the sculptor's style is virtually unmistakable. A particular instance is the Bing & Grondahl skunk, number 1898, which can be compared to the Royal Copenhagen badger, number 1209.

Bing & Grondahl, 1853-1984

A Short History of the Factory

In the middle of the 19th century, the two brothers, M H and J H Bing, owned a shop in the heart of Copenhagen. It was a fairly large shop offering a variety of merchandise, similar to a present-day department store. A porcelain modeler, F V Grondahl, from The Royal Porcelain Factory, approached the Bing brothers and proposed that they join together in founding a porcelain factory to produce figurines and reliefs, based mainly on the works of the Danish sculptor Thovaldsen, in 'biscuit' (unglazed porcelain).

The Bing & Grondahl Porcelain Factory became a reality in1853. It was situated out in the country, to the west of Copenhagen. The area has since been incorporated as part of the city.

The first workshop, with a wood-firing kiln, soon became too cramped as production of dinnerware increase. A new kiln was constructed that burned coal. People with experience thought the porcelain would become blackened with coal dust, and this proved correct. During experiments to overcome this problem, F V Grondahl died. The Bing brothers continued on with the work, and succeeded only when skilled craftsmen were called in from abroad.

The factory's history can effectively be divided into two periods, with 1900 as a convenient dividing point. In the 19th century, most of the production was decorated over the glaze (overglaze) and dinnerware patterns featured flower bouquets and copious gilding. Large and beautifully decorated vases were produced. Although these demonstrated a high degree of technical knowledge and skill, the factory still sought to establish its own personality.

The factory's first display of the 'Heron' service, designed by Pietro Krohn, at the World Exhibition in Paris in 1889, created a stir, both for the design of the pattern itself and for their first use of decoration under the glaze (underglaze). Eleven years later (1900), at another World Exhibition in Paris, there was universal praise for the advances Bing & Grondahl had made in underglaze technique, through the efforts of J F Willumsen, a painter who took over their artistic direction for several years.

During this period, the company reached new levels of quality in design and technique with the delicate and highly sought-after works of Effie Hegermann-Lindenchrone and Fanny Garde. Bing & Grondahl also applied the new techniques of underglaze decoration to dinnerware, in particular the Seagull pattern designed by Fanny Garde, which is still commonly seen today.

Another innovation by Bing & Grohdahl occurred in 1895, with the production of underglaze Christmas plates. They were conceived by Harald Bing and re mained in production when Royal Copenhagen took over the company in 1987. It was another 13 years (1908) before the Royal Copenhagen factory produced a similar Christmas plate.

The First World War curtailed factory production to a significant degree, since most of the raw and processing materials were imported. However, the factory survived on the sales it made in Denmark itself, and by seeking energy sources other than the coal, which had been imported from England. Sculptor Jean Gauguin, who used various materials to produce pieces for Bing & Grondahl, and often left them unglazed, made a noteworthy display at The Paris Exhibition of 1925.

The factory made great headway over the next few years, but again warfare interrupted their supplies and they continued only by producing dinnerware for the domestic market. Following the Second World War, the American market provided demand for Bing & Grohdahl products, particularly their wide range of figurines. Competition with the Royal Copenhagen factory continued right up until the takeover in 1987, when the companies were combined. Then, many Bing & Grondahl pieces were dropped from production and others were produced only with the Royal Copenhagen mark. The Bing & Grondahl name continues to be used on commemorative and annual pieces, and on some overglaze decorated figurines.

Factory Marks

B&G

1853 – 1895

1895 – 1898

1898 - 1899

1899 – 1902

1902 - 1914

1914 – 1915

1915 - 1948

1948 – 1952

1952 - 1958

1958 – 1962

1962 - 1970

1970 - 1983

1983 – 1984

Materials and Techniques

Types of wares and decorative finishes produced by the Bing & Grondahl factory are presented with brief descriptions to aid identification.

Porcelain

Hard paste porcelain originated in China, but it was not until the middle of the 18th century that European chemists were able to duplicate the quality which the Chinese had been producing for hundreds of years. The particular feature is the high temperature at which the porcelain is fired (around 900°C for first firing and 1440°C during glazing).

Stoneware

Stoneware is made with gray clay, rather than white which is used in hard paste porcelain, and the temperature at which it is first fired is 1250°C, but for glazing is 900°. A wider range of colors can be used under the glaze in stoneware than in hard paste porcelain.

Underglaze Decoration

The porcelain is allowed to dry after being cast and is decorated, usually by hand. After painting, the piece is covered with an opaque glaze which melts in the final firing to become clear. The pigments used only show their color after firing, and decorators have to be extremely skilled since they cannot see shades of color which depend on the thickness of the pigment. Originally, only blue was used for underglaze decoration, but red and green gradually were added, followed by gray and brown. It will be seen that an extraordinary range of colors and effects can be achieved with this technique. As all the figurines are hand painted, there can be considerable variations in the finishes. Generally, the stronger colors seem to be in most demand.

Blanc de Chine

A porcelain with a special glaze which is pure white.

Overglaze Decoration

A wide range of colors are applied on top of a white glaze. The figures are fired at least twice, at 800°C. This technique of lower temperature firing allows for a wider range of around 70 colors. Gold and silver are added before the final firing and are polished by hand.

Cracquelé

First produced in 1910 and perfected about 1920, by C F Ludvigsen at the Royal Copenhagen factory, it is produced by allowing for different rates of shrinkage during the second firing, resulting in a network of cracks being formed during cooling. Color is applied into the cracks and a further protective glaze is applied.

About Seconds and Marks in the Porcelain

When the factory failed to produce perfection, pieces were marked as"seconds" by scratching through the 3-castles mark, either with a diamond cutter or a wheel. There are also pieces known as "thirds", "fourths," etc. From our experience in looking at many seconds, beauty is in the eye of the beholder. The reasons some pieces are seconds are sometimes unclear, ranging from minor color variation to obvious blemishes. Also, older pieces (pre-1935), made when production techniques and quality control were not as stringent as today, are found with glazing or color defects, even though they are not marked as seconds.

If a piece is rare, attractive, or unusual, the fact that it is a second should not dissuade a collector from buying it. If the piece is rare enough, and the blemish does not detract, it is worth buying.

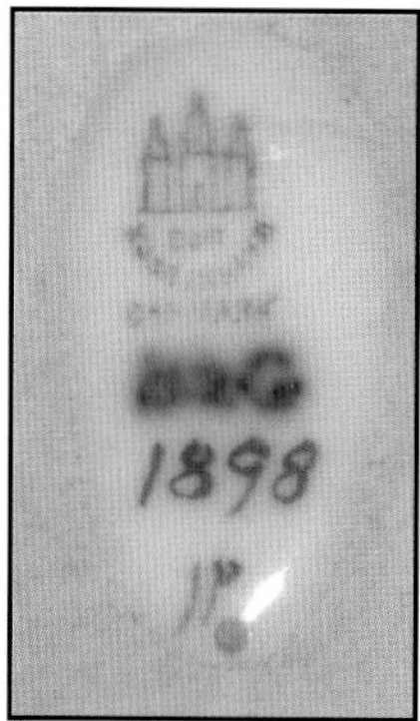

Mark with scratch denoting a second

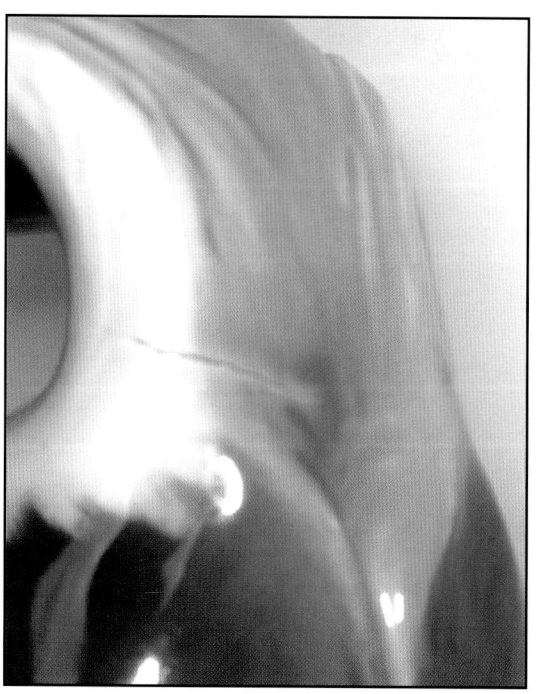

Firing crack

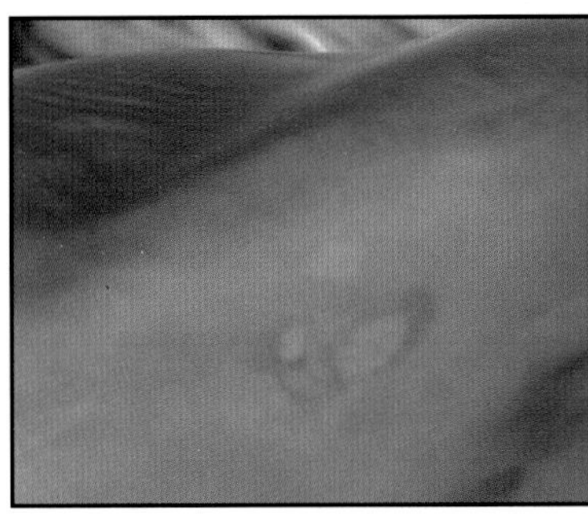

Poorly disguised support mark

Skunk having all three defects

This is a fine example of a rare and attractive piece which is marked as a second, because it has a firing crack in the tail. Since the crack is not visible when the piece is on display, it does not detract significantly from its value. In any other circumstances, a pontil would have been used to support the tail, but the design was such that this was impossible.

Whether or not to buy a second is a personal matter and some collectors will not tolerate seconds.

Support (Pontil) Marks

Some of the larger pieces require additional support during firing, resulting in small circular marks beneath the supported area. It is not possible to eliminate the color variation caused by the support marks, and in our opinion they do not detract from the attractiveness or value of the piece.

Glazing flaws

Porcelain is fired at high temperatures and dark glazes on older pieces tend to be prone to firing defects, particularly to eyes. Small glazing flaws are to be expected on pieces over 80 years old.

Damage and Restoration

As restoration techniques improve, it is more difficult to detect restoration to highly glazed porcelain pieces. Use of a black (ultra-violet) light can help detect restoration, but we have been deceived using one and feel that the best method of detection is your touch. There is no reason to refuse to buy a restored piece, provided the price is right and you like it.

The Sculptors and Their Work

The sculptors are presented alphabetically with their marks and available information of their work. We have added the dates the sculptors lived (in brackets), and also, in **bold type**, the dates they worked at Bing & Grondahl, where we have that information. The bold type initials in brackets are abbreviations we have assigned to the sculptors; they are used for identification throughout this work.

Similarities between certain pieces produced for Bing & Grondahl, Dahl-Jensen, and Royal Copenhagen lead us to believe that many of the sculptors were not employed by the factories directly, but produced pieces when commissioned. This might explain why many of the Bing & Grondahl pieces were not marked by the sculptor.

Agergaard, Jensen **Merete** (b1937 -) **(MA)**

2535 Polar bear cub standing
2536 Polar bear cub feet up
2537 Polar bear cub on back
2538 Polar bear cub lying on back

Ahlmann, Michaela (MAN)

1674 Hen
1759 'Tiny Tot'
1781 Girl with boy
1790 'Two Friends'
1792 Boy with trumpet
1794 'Good toes, bad toes'
1848 Playfellows
2251 'Who is Calling?'
2262 'Happy family'
2273 'My Balloon'
2275 'Help Me, Mum'
2278 Throw down the ball

Andersen, Anders **Valdemar** Peter (1875-1928) **– 1909-1912 (VA)**

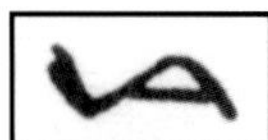

1734 Woman of fashion

Bonfils, Adda Andrea Elisabeth (1883 – 1943) **(AB)**

Adda Bonfils

1995 Girl touching hem of skirt

Bregno, Jens Jakob (1877-1946) **(JJB)** with Hans Teger **(HT)**

8020 Dancing couple
8022 Couple skating
8023 Skater
8024 Restless
8025 Footman with coat
8026 Footman without coat
8027 Skater
8028 Running footman
8029 Jumping footman
8030 Lady with dog
8031 Lady with racket
8032 Girl with racket
8033 Blind Mans Buff
8034 Lady with slippers
8035 Lady without slippers
8036 Rain
8037 Sunshine
8038 Woman watering flowers
8039 Man trimming a box tree
8040 Artist at easel
8041 Dancing couple tumbling
8042 Lady in wind
8043 Man in wind
8044 Lady blowing soap bubbles
8045 Man with apples
8046 'Shepherdess & Chimney Sweep'
8047 'Emperor's New Clothes'
8048 'Little Claus'
8049 'The Nightingale'
8050 'The Swineherd'
8051 'The Tinder Box'
8052 'The Sandman'

Brunoe, Soren (SB)

2532 Boy with raincoat

Dahl-Jensen, Jens Peter (1874-1960) **(1897 – 1925) (DJ)**

1000 Fish shaped covered dish
1500 Snowy Owl
1502 Elephant on knees
1510 Monkey looking at tortoise
1512 Hippopotamus
1515 Woman standing
1525 Woman standing
1531 Falcon
1545 Monkey looking at tortoise
1547 Brahma Bull
1548 Duck
1553 Kitten sitting
1559 Guinea-pigs
1562 Mice - pair on dish
1566 Mice pair
1572 Fox curled
1582 Pig sitting
1583 Sow with eight piglets
1584 Puma
1588 Duckling
1589 Duckling
1596 Rabbit - lop eared
1597 Rabbit - grooming
1599 Rabbit
1605 Bulldog
1610 Magpie
1613 Jaguar
1615 Horse
1619 Kingfisher
1623 Dish with bird on lid
1626 Tapir
1628 Peacock
1629 Polar bear sitting
1630 Pekinese puppies - pair
1631 Pekinese sitting
1633 'Optimist' - titmouse
1635 'Pessimist' - titmouse
1637 Pekinese puppy sitting
1663 Collie lying
1666 Hawk
1670 'Protection'
1675 Crested Tit
1676 Bulldog
1699 Goat
1700 Goat
1707 Finch
1708 Finch group
1714 Crow
1717 Woodpecker
1722 Squirrel
1725 Seagull with fish
1728 Mouse - white
1744 Blackcock (Black grouse)
1752 Dachshund
1755 Dachshund
1764 Wagtail
1770 Cuckoo
1775 Swallow
1776 Flycatcher
1784 Silver pheasant
1795 Eagle - golden
1800 Owl
1801 Mouse gray
1803 Trout
1805 Dachshunds - pair
1808 Gull with fish
1809 Gull crying
1810 Gull

1833 Rabbit
1844 Cat
1846 Owl on base
1850 Goldfinch
1855 Tufted duck
1869 Sparrow with young
1986 Pekinese sitting
1987 Pekinese
1993 Mountain Lion
1998 Terrier
2019 Parrot
2027 Sealyham puppy
2028 Sealyham puppy

Gauguin, Jean René (1881-1961) **(1923 – 1961) (JG)**

1395 'Bed of Roses'
1396 'Silen'
1397 'The Spoils of Europe'
1398 'The Playful Wave'
1399 'The Sea Bull'
2007 Deer - male
2008 Deer - female
2009 Stag

Jensen, Lauritz (1859 – 1935) **(LJ)**

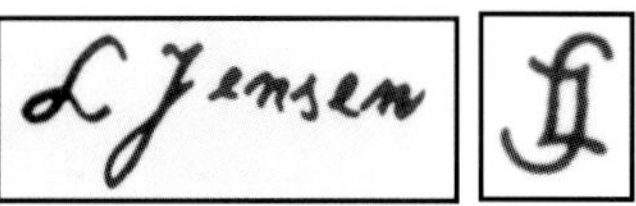

1678 Lioness
1693 Impala
1712 Tiger - snarling
1765 German Shepherd
1773 Great Dane
1789 German Shepherd
1793 Lion
1811 Borzoi lying
1814 Borzoi sitting
1904 Gordon Setter
2015 Setter with bird
2026 Pointer
2038 Great Dane sitting
2044 Pointer lying
2056 Tiger
2060 Pointer pup scratching side
2061 Spaniel
2072 Terrier
2095 Cocker Spaniel
2103 German Shepherd standing
2130 Skye Terrier
2161 Cow licking side
2179 Sealyham
2268 Lioness & cub
2279 Lion & Lioness

Jespersen, Svend Olfert Neumann **(1895-1985)** (SJ)

S.J.

2141 Hare
2144 Sea Scorpion
2145 Roach
2168 Calf
2169 Trout
2171 Lamb
2172 Cocker Spaniel
2173 Herring
2174 Perch
2177 Squirrel
2178 Cockatoo
2189 Great Dane sitting
2190 Great Dane lying
2192 Cock
2193 Hen
2194 Chick
2197 German Shepherd
2210 Budgerigar - blue
2212 Boxer
2217 Polar bear sitting
2218 Polar bear
2234 Belgian Stallion
2242 Finch
2256 Cat sitting
2269 Fish (pair) & crab
2304 'Merete'
2306 'The Little Builder'
2308 Siamese cat
2310 Robin
2311 Robin on twig
2312 'Gentleman'
2313 'Ruth'
2317 Girl buttoning shoe
2318 'Vanity'
2322 Chaffinch
2323 Great Titmouse
2324 'Up to Mom'
2328 Hunter with dog
2335 Foundry worker
2339 Carpenter
2341 Budgerigar - green
2342 Guardsman
2347 White eye -robin?
2359 Lily pad
2360 Lily pad
2370 Old fisherman
2377 Dish with anchor
2379 Nurse

2384 Puffin
2386 Partridge
2389 Cock pheasant

Jesperson, Svend, Jointly with Ebbe Sadolin:

2264 Sea boy with shell
2265 Sea boy with starfish
2266 Sea boy with Sea-weed
2267 Sea girl
2298 Ida's flowers
2314 Sea girl lying
2315 Sea boy resting
2332 Madonna
2353 Pierrot
2354 Harlequin
2355 Columbine
2378 'Thumbelina' on tray
2394 Child with sea horse
2395 Child with sea horse
2396 Child with sea horse
2397 Child with sea horse
2408 Hamlet
2409 Ophelia

Jorgensen, Agnete (b. 1918) **(1967-1976) (AJ)**

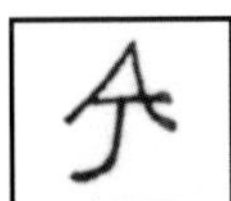

4200 Horses large pair
4201 Cats - pair
4202 Swan
4203 Rams - pair
4204 Geese - three
4205 Penguins - pair
4206 Cows - three
4207 Horses - three
4208 Horses small - pair
4209 Llamas - pair

Kristoffersen, Karl (KAK)

2410 Greenlander lifting stone
2413 Greenlander sitting
2414 Greenlandic woman
2415 Greenlander standing
2416 Greenlandic woman with bucket
2417 Greenlander - angry

Kyhn, Knud Carl Edvard (1880-1969)
(1908-1915 & 1933-1935) (KK)

1823 Lion with lioness
1826 Calf scratching ear
1852 Sparrow - fledgling
1853 Wren
1857 Polar bear

Lausham, Mathias (ML)

2411 Greenlander standing

Lindhart, Svend William Peder (1898-1989) **(SL)**

SV. LINDHART

2126 Woman with eggs
2127 Boy with bucket
2206 Headache
2207 Toothache
2208 Tummyache
2209 Earache
2229 'So big'
2230 'Eve'
2231 'Adam'
2232 'Fright'

Locher, Axel Thilson (1879 – 1941) **(1897-1900) (AL)**

AXEL LOCHER 

1734 Woman of fashion
Actors - Poulsen & Mantzius
2004 Actor
2010 Shepherdess
2017 Dairy maid
2025 Fisher family
2036 Woman with fishing net
2043 Shepherd Boy
2059 Penguin on rock
2180 Girl with goat
2181 Girl with milk can
2220 Poultry girl
2223 Baker
2225 Smith
2228 Cobbler
2233 'Fish Market'
2237 Woman with pig
2254 Goose girl
2263 Farmer with pig
2270 Girl with calves
2272 Girl with cow and goose

Lykke Madsen, Sten (b.1937 -) **(1962-1987)(SLM)**

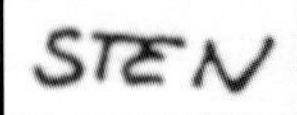

7041 Abstract figurine
7042 Abstract figurine
7043 Abstract figurine
7044 Abstract figurine
7045 Abstract figurine
7046 Abstract figurine
7047 Abstract figurine
7048 Abstract figurine
7049 Abstract figurine
7051 Abstract figurine
7052 Abstract figurine
7053 Abstract figurine

Madsen, Sveistrup (1883 – 1946) **(SM)**

1821 Penguin
1822 Penguin - Blackfoot
2114 Japanese Chin standing
2121 Bull

Moller, Knud Max (1879-1965)
(1909-1912 & 1914-1921) (KM)

1733 Seal
1925 Eagle
1952 Pheasants - pair
1953 Gerfalcon
1980 Peewit

Mortensen, Laurits **Carl** Nicolaj (1861-1945) **(CM)**

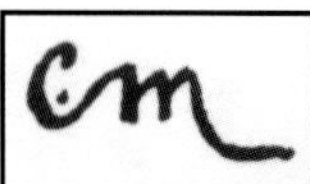

1551 Duck
1590 Crucian carp - pair
1593 Goose
1607 Sparrow
1608 Bream
1645 Carp

Nielsen, Kai (1882-1924) **(KN)**

1702 Danish Fisherwoman
4020 Mare lying
4021 Man with grapes
4022 Woman with grapes
4023 Man & woman
4024 Man with grapes sitting
4025 Man with grapes
4026 Man, horse & child
4027 Faun with grapes
4028 Nude, children, man
4029 Woman lying
4030 Neptune, woman
4031 Woman standing
4032 Woman bending
4033 Children
4034 Child with dolphin
4035 Child with dolphin
4036 Boy on fish
4037 Child with dolphin
4038 Girl with dolphin
4055 Mother Nile
4056 Girl riding dolphin
4057 Girl riding dolphin
4058 Girl with dolphin
4059 Girl with dolphin
4060 Girl with dolphin
4061 Girl with dolphin
4108 Eve & Apple
4109 Mother & child
4110 Mother & child
4111 Mother & child

Nielsen, Niels (1872 – 1921) **(1915-1921) (NN)**

1692 Polar bear sniffing
1785 Polar bear walking
1786 Mason
1874 Rabbit
1875 Rabbits sitting
1878 Cat
1880 Starling
1885 Kingfisher
1887 Linnet
1888 Sparrow on base
1892 Sparrow Hawk
1902 Goose
1906 Foxes - pair
1909 Bullfinch
1911 Pigeon
1926 St Bernard puppy
1929 Deer on base
1954 Polar bear

Petersen, Armand

2235 Blue Ara

Petersen, Emil (EP)

2366 Salmon trout
2405 Blackbird
2406 Nuthatch

Platen-Hallermund, Francis Valdemar von (1875 – 1965) **(PH)**

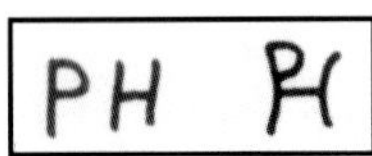

2020 Linnet

Plockross-Irminger, Ingeborg (1872-1962) **(1897-1900) (IP)**

1524 Monkey - pair
1526 Little girl
1552 'Mother Love'
1567 Children reading
1568 Children playing
1574 'Else'
1581 Monkey family - four
1587 Man & Woman talking on bench
1600 Mandolin player
1614 'Love refused'
1617 'Kaj'
1636 'Dickie'
1642 'Dickie's Mama'
1644 Woman with children
1648 'Tom & Willy'
1655 'The Little Match Girl'
1656 'Grethe'
1661 'Merry Sailor'
1667 Monkey
1671 Boy sitting looking down
1684 Woman with guitar
1694 Girl
1696 'Peter'
1713 'Victor'
1715 Skater
1721 'Mary'
1742 'School's Out'
1745 'Only one drop'
1747 'Ole'
1757 'Paddling About'
1761 Girls standing
1779 'Little Mother'
1780 Girl
1783 Boy in coat/hat (formal)
1841 Girl sitting
1845 'Dancing School'
1870 Boy with crab
1871 Sisters
1876 Cat sitting
1879 Girl sitting
1897 Flute player
Boy with dog
2013 Graduate

Sadolin, Ebbe (1900 – 1982) **(EBS)**

2264 Sea boy with shell
2265 Sea boy with starfish
2266 Sea boy with Sea-weed
2267 Sea girl
2298 Ida's flowers
2314 Sea girl lying
2315 Sea boy resting
2332 Madonna
2353 Pierrot
2354 Harlequin
2355 Columbine
2378 'Thumbelina' on tray
2394 Child with sea horse
2395 Child with sea horse
2396 Child with sea horse
2397 Child with sea horse
2408 Hamlet
2409 Ophelia

Seidelin, Henning (1904 –1987) **(1943-1951) (HES)**

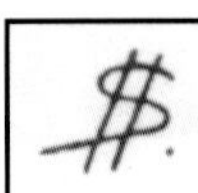

2037 Hans Christian Andersen
2055 'The Sandman'

Tegner, Hans Christian Harald (1853-1932) **(1907-1932) (HT) with Jens Jakob Bregno (JJB)**

8020 Dancing couple
8022 Couple skating
8023 Skater
8024 Restless
8025 Footman with coat
8026 Footman without coat
8027 Skater
8028 Running footman
8029 Jumping footman
8030 Lady with dog
8031 Lady with racket
8032 Girl with racket

8033 Blind Mans Buff
8034 Lady with slippers
8035 Lady without slippers
8036 Rain
8037 Sunshine
8038 Woman watering flowers
8039 Man trimming a box tree
8040 Artist at easel
8041 Dancing couple tumbling
8042 Lady in wind
8043 Man in wind
8044 Lady blowing soap bubbles
8045 Man with apples
8046 'Shepherdess & Chimney Sweep'
8047 'Emperor's New Clothes'
8048 'Little Claus'
8049 'The Nightingale'
8050 'The Swineherd'
8051 'The Tinder Box'
8052 'The Sandman'

Thymann, Vita Birgitte (1925 -) **(VT)**

2316 Girl with puppy
2321 'Little Sailor'
2325 Ballet dancer
2326 'Little Gardener'
2327 'Little Hunter'
2329 'Birgite'
2333 'Make friends'
2334 'Must I be washed?'
2336 Girl with kid goat
2338 Boy with fish & net
2340 Girl feeding dove
2344 Boy playing flute
2345 Girl with garland
2346 Boy holding Flowers
2350 'The Little Painter'
2351 'Skating Girl'
2356 Girl
2358 Boy with skis
2364 Tennis player - female
2367 'Hairdresser'
2369 Horsewoman
2375 Footballer

Vangedal. Erling (EV)

2366 Salmon trout

Weiss, Claire (1906 -) **(CW)**

CLAIRE WEISS

2162 'Youthful boldness'
2163 Girl with dog
2175 'Unfair Treatment'
2201 Boy with scottie
2246 'Spilt milk'
2247 'First Book'
2249 'Friends'
2372 'Pardon me'
2373 'Marianne'
2374 'Erik'
2380 Boy with sailing boat
2381 'Anne'
2385 Dancing couple
2387 'Miss Charming'
2388 Girl with bricks
2390 Boy with flowers
2391 Girl with ball
2392 'Cathrine'
2393 'Jacob'
2398 'Congratulations Mama'
2399 'I am coming now'
2400 'Children's Hour'
2401 'Jorgen'
2402 'The Little Player'
2403 Boy with ball
2404 Girl singing

Numerical List

1395 'Bed of Roses' JG
1396 'Silen' JG
1397 'The Spoils of Europe' JG
1398 'The Playful Wave' JG
1399 'The Sea Bull' JG
1500 Snowy Owl DJ
1501 Owl on dish
1502 Elephant on knees DJ
1504 Seagull
1506 Cow
1509 Bear with tree stump
1510 Monkey looking at tortoise DJ
1512 Hippopotamus DJ
1513 Great Dane on base
1515 Woman standing DJ
1516 Nude lying on base
1519 Finch
1521 Pigeon
1524 Monkey - pair IPI
1525 Woman standing DJ
1526 Little girl IPI
1529 Cat
1530 Deer sitting
1531 Falcon DJ
1532 'Meditation'
1533 Woman looking into pool
1534 Woman standing
1535 Duck preening
1536 Snail
1537 Duck
1540 Crucian carp - pair
1543 Child kneeling
1544 Parrot on base
1545 Monkey looking at tortoise DJ
1546 Bust of woman
1547 Brahma Bull DJ
1548 Duck DJ
1550 Woman standing
1551 Duck CM
1552 'Mother Love' IPI
1553 Kitten sitting DJ
1554 Nude on base
1555 Cat with ball
1556 Woman kneeling (matchstick holders)
1557 Candlestick with figurines on base
1558 Guinea-pig
1559 Guinea-pigs – three DJ
1560 Children (Naked)
1561 Mouse with matchstick holder
1562 Mice - pair on dish DJ
1565 Dog
1566 Mice – pair DJ
1567 Children reading IPI
1568 Children playing IPI
1570 Bloodhound
1571 Man
1572 Fox curled DJ
1573 Stoat
1574 'Else' IPI
1575 Pigeon
1576 Owl
1577 Budgie on base
1578 Woman
1579 Dachshund
1580 Woman reading on chair
1581 Monkey family - four IPI
1582 Pig sitting DJ
1583 Sow with eight piglets DJ
1584 Puma DJ
1585 Llama
1586 Lady painting porcelain
1587 Man & woman talking on bench IPI
1588 Duckling DJ
1589 Duckling DJ
1590 Crucian carp - pair CM
1591 Cockerel
1592 Woman carrying baby on back
1593 Goose CM
1594 Lovers on bench
1595 Rabbit
1596 Rabbit - lop eared DJ
1597 Rabbit - grooming DJ
1598 Finch?
1599 Rabbit DJ

1600 Mandolin player IPI
1601 Elephant
1602 Donkey
1603 Dachshund begging
1604 'Maud' (bust)
1605 Bulldog DJ
1606 Bird ?
1607 Sparrow CM
1608 Bream CM
1609 Woman sitting
1610 Magpie DJ
1611 Woman sitting pensive
1612 Bust of boy
1613 Jaguar DJ
1614 'Love refused' IPI
1615 Horse DJ
1617 'Kaj' IPI
1618 Man & woman
1619 Kingfisher DJ
1620 Partridge
1621 Partridge - three
1623 Dish with bird on lid DJ
1624 'Good Morning'
1625 Woman & Child
1626 Tapir DJ
1627 Woman on bench
1628 Peacock DJ
1629 Polar bear sitting DJ
1630 Pekinese puppies - pair DJ
1631 Pekinese sitting DJ
1632 Guillemot
1633 'Optimist' - titmouse DJ
1634 Eel
1635 'Pessimist' - titmouse DJ
1636 'Dickie' IPI
1637 Pekinese puppy sitting DJ
1638 Mackerel - pair
1639 Dish- figurine on lid (mouse?)
1640 Mouse
1641 Horse lying
1642 'Dickie's Mama' IPI
1643 Mandarin duck
1644 Woman with children IPI
1645 Carp CM
1646 Monkey
1647 Monkeys - pair
1648 'Tom & Willy' IPI
1649 Baby on base
1650 Boy on seat
1651 Girl sitting?
1652 Girl standing
1653 Bowl with child sitting on lid
1654 Hound standing
1655 'The Little Match Girl' IPI
1656 'Grethe' IPI
1657 Birds - pair
1658 Pigeon
1659 Carpenter
1660 Boy - naked on tray
1661 'Merry Sailor' IPI
1662 Chick on base
1663 Collie lying DJ
1664 Serval
1665 Duck
1666 Hawk DJ
1667 MonkeyIPI
1668 Lion on rock
1669 Boy sitting
1670 'Protection' DJ
1671 Boy sitting looking down IPI
1672 Bison
1673 Cockerel
1674 Hen MAN
1675 Crested Tit DJ
1676 Bulldog DJ
1677 Lion
1678 LionessLJ
1679 Boy, nude on dish
1680 Teenage lovers
1681 Children sitting
1683 Owl
1684 Woman with guitar IPI
1685 Woman washing floor
1686 Cat
1687 Girl writing
1688 Stoat
1689 Coati Mundi
1690 German Shepherd seated
1691 Dachshund sitting
1692 Polar bear sniffing NN
1693 Impala LJ
1694 Girl IPI
1695 Woman seated
1696 'Peter' IPI
1697 Bust
1698 Bear on base
1699 Goat DJ
1700 Goat DJ
1702 Danish Fisherwoman KN
1703 Woman in coat & large hat
1705 Girl in cloak
1706 Woman sitting
1707 Finch DJ
1708 Finch group DJ
1709 Woman standing
1710 Woman doing hair
1711 Woman sitting
1712 Tiger - snarling LJ

1713 'Victor' IPI
1714 Crow DJ
1715 Skater IPI
1716 Pointer sitting
1717 Woodpecker DJ
1718 Mouse
1719 Fox
1720 Boy in cloak
1721 'Mary' IPI
1722 Squirrel DJ
1723 Pointer playing
1724 Man in uniform
1725 Seagull with fish DJ
1726 Seagull
1727 Seagull
1728 Mouse - white DJ
1729 Violinist
1730 Bird
1732 Mouse
1733 Seal KM
1734 Woman of fashion VA
1735 Guinea Fowl
1736 Woman with washing
1737 Children on toboggan
1738 Duck
1739 Toucan
1740 Cockatoo on base
1741 Rabbit
1742 'School's Out' IPI
1743 Boy sitting
1744 Blackcock (Black grouse) DJ
1745 'Only one drop' IPI
1746 Dachshund sitting
1747 'Ole' IPI
1749 Cockerel
1750 Hen
1751 Duck
1752 Dachshund DJ
1753 Puppy sitting
1754 Cat
1755 Dachshund DJ
1756 Man carrying box
1757 'Paddling About' IPI
1758 Girl
1759 'Tiny Tot' MAN
1760 Jay
1761 Girls standing IPI
1762a Bear sitting
1762b Bear sitting on base
1763 Donkey?
1764 Wagtail DJ
1765 German Shepherd LJ
1766 Woman standing
1767 Squirrel on branch
1768 Butterfly
1769 Cow
1770 Cuckoo DJ
1771 Finch?
1772 Hunter
1773 Great Dane LJ
1775 Swallow DJ
1776 Flycatcher DJ
1777 Bird?
1778 Birds on base
1779 'Little Mother' IPI
1780 Girl IPI
1781 Girl with boy MAN
1782 Boy standing
1783 Boy in coat/hat (formal) IPI
1784 Silver pheasant DJ
1785 Polar bear walking NN
1786 Mason NN
1787 Boy standing
1788 Pointer sitting
1789 German Shepherd LJ
1790 'Two Friends' MAN
1791 Llama?
1792 Boy with trumpet MAN
1793 Lion LJ
1794 'Good toes, bad toes' MAN
1795 Eagle - golden DJ
1796 Baby sitting
1797 Panther
1798 Girl standing
1799 Cat playing with ball
1800 Owl DJ
1801 Mouse gray DJ
1802 Collie standing
1803 Trout DJ
1804 Bear walking
1805 Dachshunds - pair DJ
1806 Elephant
1807 Cat sitting
1808 Gull with fish DJ
1809 Gull crying DJ
1810 Gull DJ
1811 Borzoi lying LJ
1812 Guinea-pig
1813 Elephant
1814 Borzoi sitting LJ
1815 Pointer puppies playing - three?
1816 Bears playing
1817 Swan
1818 Swan
1821 Penguin SM
1822 Penguin - Blackfoot SM
1823 Lion with lioness KK
1824 Bear brown

1825 Bears playing
1826 Calf scratching ear KK
1827 Boy standing
1828 Brother and sister
1829 Mother with baby
1830 Rabbits - lying
1831 Rabbit - lying
1832 Rabbit
1833 Rabbit DJ
1834 Cat curled
1835 Elephants - pair
1836 Boy lying
1837 Cat with ball
1838 Ballet dancer
1839 Girl with toy
1841 Girl sitting IPI
1842 Pigs pair
1843 Boy standing
1844 Cat DJ
1845 'Dancing School' IPI
1846 Owl on base DJ
1847 Girl sitting
1848 Playfellows MAN
1849 Boys playing with bricks
1850 Goldfinch DJ
1851 Lovebird
1852 Sparrow - fledgling KK
1853 Wren KK
1854 German Shepherd
1855 Tufted duck DJ
1856 Bird
1857 Polar bear KK
1858 Elephant and Mahout
1859 Bird
1860 Turkey chick
1861 Dachshunds - pair
1862 Crab?
1863 Mice?
1864 Sparrow fledglings
1865 Mice - pair
1866 Red Cross Nurse
1867 Red Cross Nurse
1868 Lemur
1869 Sparrow with young DJ
1870 Boy with crab IPI
1871 Sisters IPI
1872 Polar bear cub
1873 Polar bear cub
1874 Rabbit NN
1875 Rabbits sitting NN
1876 Cat sitting IPI
1878 Cat NN
1879 Girl sitting IPI
1880 StarlingNN

1881 Pig
1882 Pig
1885 Kingfisher NN
1887 Linnet NN
1888 Sparrow on base NN
1889 Cat curled
1890 Dog standing
1891 Cat drinking from bowl
1892 Sparrow Hawk NN
1893 French Bulldog
1894 Kangaroo
1895 Pug sitting
1897 Flute player IPI
1898 Skunk
1899a Boy standing
1899b Boy standing
1900 Rabbit
1901 Boy in raincoat
1902 Goose NN
1903 Pug sitting
1904 Gordon Setter LJ
1905 Fox sitting
1906 Foxes - pair NN
1907 Lynx
1908 Schoolgirl
1909 Bullfinch NN
1910 Mother with two girls
1911 Pigeon NN
1913 Schoolboy
1914 Cairn terrier sitting
1915 Bear
1916 St Bernard
1917 Dog standing
1918 Poodle sitting
1919 Fox cub?
1920 Boy with kitten and cat
1921 Terrier standing
1922 Dog standing
1923 Lion Cub
1924 Bird?
1925 Eagle KM
1926 St Bernard puppy NN
1927 Seal pup
1928 Goat
1929 Deer on base NN
1930 Deer
1931 Bird on base
1932 Eider duck
1934 Ostrich
1936 Stoat
1938 Graduate
1939 Duck
1940 Puffin
1941 Peahen

1946 Bear with cub - lying
1948 Tiger with cub
1949 Chaffinch
1950 Girl with accordion
1951 Boy with dog IPI
1952 Pheasants - pair KM
1953 Gerfalcon KM
1954 Polar bear NN
1958 Fox sitting
1962 Dachshund
1969 Otter with fish
1973 Girl with dog
1980 Peewit KM
1983 Bulldog puppy
1986 Pekinese sitting DJ
1987 Pekinese DJ
1990 Pekinese puppies
1992 Bulldog
1993 Mountain Lion DJ
1995 Girl touching hem of skirt AB
1997 Actors - Poulsen & Mantzius AL
1998 Terrier DJ
2000 French Bull Terrier
2002 Mother, toddler & baby
2004 Actor AL
2006 Pointer
2007 Deer - buck JG
2008 Deer - doe JG
2009 Stag JG
2010 Shepherdess AL
2011 Scottish Terrier
2012 'Little Match Girl'
2013 Graduate IPI
2015 Setter with bird LJ
2017 Dairy maid AL
2018 German Shepherd standing
2019 Parrot DJ
2020 Linnet PH
2022 Mother & two children
2025 Fisher family AL
2026 Pointer LJ
2027 Sealyham puppy DJ
2028 Sealyham puppy DJ
2030 Terrier
2032 Cellist
2035 Cavalier King Charles Spaniel
2036 Woman with fishing net AL
2037 Hans Christian Andersen HS
2038 Great Dane sitting LJ
2039 Leopard
2041 Dachshund standing
2043 Shepherd Boy AL
2044 Pointer lying LJ
2049 Harvest Man
2050 Girl with rake
2051 Lioness grooming
2052 Lion standing
2053 Ape
2055 'The Sandman' HS
2056 Tiger LJ
2057 Lion on rock
2059 Penguin on rock AL
2060 Pointer pup scratching side LJ
2061 Spaniel LJ
2062 English Setter
2069 Scottish Terrier standing
2071 Sealyham
2072 Terrier LJ
2073 Scottish Terrier
2075 Pointer standing
2076 Greyhound standing
2077 Scottish Terrier lying
2078 Greyhound
2079 Greyhound, lying
2080 Hare sitting up
2081 Hare sitting
2082 Bulldog
2083 Bulldog sitting
2084 Bloodhound sniffing
2085 Scottish Terrier standing
2086 Terrier standing
2089 Schnauzer
2090 Chow Chow
2091 Schnauzer
2092 Pomeranian
2095 Cocker Spaniel LJ
2098 Bear sitting - bookend
2099 Airedale Terrier
2101 Pekinese
2103 German Shepherd standing LJ
2104 Sisyphus
2105 Tinderbox Dog
2108 Mastiff
2110 English Bulldog
2111 Pointer bitch & pups
2114 Japanese Chin standing SM
2115 Borzoi
2116 Old English Sheepdog
2117 Scottish Terrier
2118 Scottish Terrier
2119 Farmer with two horses
2120 Irish Wolfhound
2121 Bull SM
2122 Dalmatian
2123 Japanese Chin
2124 Great Dane standing
2125 Girl with butterfly
2126 Woman with eggs SL

2127 Boy with bucket SL
2128 Green Elephant with Howdah
2130 Skye Terrier LJ
2132 Swimmer - female
2133 Skye Terrier
2134 Swimmer - male
2136 Wild Boar
2137 Skye Terrier
2138 Eel
2139 Pelican
2140 Elephant calf
2141 Hare SJ
2142 Kitten
2143 Kitten
2144 Sea Scorpion SJ
2145 Roach SJ
2146 Horse
2148 Boy with papers
2161 Cow licking side LJ
2162 'Youthful boldness' CW
2163 Girl with dog CW
2166 Penguin
2167 Scottish Terrier standing
2168 Calf SJ
2169 Trout SJ
2170 Scottish Terrier sitting
2171 Lamb SJ
2172 Cocker Spaniel SJ
2173 Herring SJ
2174 Perch SJ
2175 'Unfair Treatment' CW
2177 Squirrel SJ
2178 Cockatoo SJ
2179 Sealyham LJ
2180 Girl with goat AL
2181 Girl with milkcan AL
2182 Girl comforting boy
2183 Boy & girl
2184 'Little Artist'
2185 Girl with doll
2187 Puma
2188 Boy & girl singing
2189 Great Dane sitting SJ
2190 Great Dane lying SJ
2191 Girl with doll
2192 Cock SJ
2193 Hen SJ
2194 Chick SJ
2195 Boy with foal
2196 Mother with children
2197 German Shepherd SJ
2198 German Shepherd lying
2199 Boy taking off sock
2200 Mother with baby
2201 Boy with scottie CW
2202 Girl with puppy
2204 Bear
2205 Deer
2206 Headache SL
2207 Toothache SL
2208 Tummyache SL
2209 Earache SL
2210 Budgerigar - blue SJ
2211 Deer standing
2212 Boxer SJ
2213 Bear, walking
2214 Tiger cub
2215 Camel lying
2217 Polar bear sitting SJ
2218 Polar bear SJ
2219 Washer woman
2220 Poultry girl AL
2221 Monkey
2222 Soccer player
2223 Baker AL
2224 Girl in swimsuit
2225 Smith AL
2226 Nurse
2227 Boxer
2228 Cobbler AL
2229 'So big' SL
2230 'Eve' SL
2231 'Adam' SL
2232 'Fright' SL
2233 'Fish Market' AL
2234 Belgian Stallion SJ
2235 Blue Ara AP
2236 Cat lying
2237 Woman with pig AL
2238 Bowling
2239 Polar bear with cub
2240 Owl
2241 Tailor
2242 Finch SJ
2244 Chihuahua
2246 'Spilt milk' CW
2247 'First Book' CW
2249 'Friends' CW
2250 Girl & baby
2251 'Who is Calling?' MAN
2253 Greenlander
2254 Goose girl AL
2255 Mother & child
2256 Cat sitting SJ
2257 Girl braiding hair
2258 Girl on footstool
2259 Horse
2261 'Offended'

2262 'Happy family' MAN
2263 Farmer with pig AL
2264 Sea boy with shell ES/SJ
2265 Sea boy with starfish ES/SJ
2266 Sea boy with sea-weed ES/SJ
2267 Sea girl ES/SJ
2268 Lioness & cub LJ
2269 Fish (pair) & crab SJ
2270 Girl with calves AL
2271 Arabian horse
2272 Girl with cow & goose AL
2273 'My Balloon' MAN
2274 Boy
2275 'Help Me, Mum' MAN
2276 Girl with kittens
2277 Mother, child on knee looking at tortoise
2278 Throw down the ball MAN
2279 Lion & lioness LJ
2280 Greenland girl sitting
2281 Greenland girl sitting
2282 Greenland girl standing
2283 Nude kneeling
2285 Girl with starfish
2293 Shire Horse
2296 Girl potter
2298 Ida's flowers ES/SJ
2300 Ballet girl
2301 'Guess who?'
2302 Nude on steps
2303 My horse
2304 'Merete' SJ
2305 'Christmas Meal'
2306 'The Little Builder' SJ
2307 Motherly care
2308 Siamese cat SJ
2309 Cat sleeping
2310 Robin SJ
2311 Robin on twig SJ
2312 'Gentleman' SJ
2313 'Ruth' SJ
2314 Sea girl- lying ES/SJ
2315 Sea boy- resting ES/SJ
2316 Girl with puppy VT
2317 Girl buttoning shoe SJ
2318 'Vanity' SJ
2319 Child with rabbit
2320 Boy with toy car
2321 'Little Sailor' VT
2322 Chaffinch SJ
2323 Great Titmouse SJ
2324 'Up to Mom' SJ
2325 Ballet dancer VT
2326 'Little Gardener' VT
2327 'Little Hunter' VT
2328 Hunter with dog SJ
2329 'Birgite' VT
2330 Boston Terrier
2331 Boy with dog
2332 Madonna ES/SJ
2333 'Make friends' VT
2334 'Must I be washed?' VT
2335 Foundry worker SJ
2336 Girl with kid goat VT
2337 Boy sitting
2338 Boy with fish & net VT
2339 Carpenter SJ
2340 Girl feeding dove VT
2341 Budgerigar - green SJ
2342 Guardsman SJ
2344 Boy playing flute VT
2345 Girl with garland VT
2346 Boy holding flowers VT
2347 White eye -robin SJ
2348 Finch
2350 'The Little Painter' VT
2351 'Skating Girl' VT
2353 Pierrot ES/SJ
2354 Harlequin ES/SJ
2355 Columbine ES/SJ
2356 Girl VT
2357 Youth with basket
2358 Boy with skis VT
2359 Lily pad SJ
2360 Lily pad SJ
2361 Bird preening tail -Chaffinch ?
2362 Finch
2364 Tennis player - female VT
2366 Salmon trout EV
2367 'Hairdresser' VT
2368 'Aalborg'
2369 Horsewoman VT
2370 Old fisherman SJ
2371 Anchor
2372 'Pardon me' CW
2373 'Marianne' CW
2374 'Erik' CW
2375 Footballer VT
2377 Dish with anchor SJ
2378 'Thumbelina' on tray ES/SJ
2379 Nurse SJ
2380 Boy with sailing boat CW
2381 'Anne' CW
2384 Puffin SJ
2385 Dancing couple CW
2386 Partridge SJ
2387 'Miss Charming' CW
2388 Girl with bricks CW
2389 Cock pheasant SJ

2390 Boy with flowers CW
2391 Girl with ball CW
2392 'Cathrine' CW
2393 'Jacob' CW
2394 Child with sea horse ES/SJ
2395 Child with sea horse ES/SJ
2396 Child with sea horse ES/SJ
2397 Child with sea horse ES/SJ
2398 'Congratulations Mama' CW
2399 'I am coming now' CW
2400 'Children's Hour' CW
2401 'Jorgen'CW
2402 'The Little Player' CW
2403 Boy with ball CW
2404 Girl singing CW
2405 Blackbird EP
2406 Nuthatch EP
2408 Hamlet ES/SJ
2409 Ophelia ES/SJ
2410 Greenlander lifting stone KAK
2411 Greenlander standing ML
2412 Greenlander with child SK
2413 Greenlander sitting KAK
2414 Greenlandic woman KAK
2415 Greenlander standing KAK
2416 Greenlandic woman with bucket KAK
2417 Greenlander - angry KAK
2419 Potter
2421 Rabbit - lying
2422 Rabbit - sitting
2423 Rabbit - standing
2424 Little owl
2425 Turkey cock
2426 Turkey hen
2428 Electrician
2429 Baker
2431 House painter
2432 Pipe fitter
2433 Butcher
2434 Carpenter
2435 'Thirst'
2436 Policeman
2439 Grebe & chicks
2441 Rabbit lying - white
2442 Rabbit, sitting - white
2443 Rabbit, standing - white
2444 Gunner - Army
2445 Pilot
2446 Sailor - Navy
2451 Postman
2452 Cat - gray
2453 Cat - white
2454 Cat - gray
2455 Goldcrest
2458 Kinglet
2459 Bird preening
2461 Bird preening
2463 Blue Tit on base
2464 Siamese cat - white
2465 Cat - gray
2466 Cat sitting
2467 Frog
2468 Seal
2469 Owl
2470 Girl with ice lolly
2471 Seal on back
2472 Seal
2473 Vagabond
2474 Squirrel
2475 Snowy Owl
2476 Cat - white
2478 Vagabond with bottle
2479 Guinea-pig - sitting
2480 Guinea-pig - lying
2481 Titmouse spread wings
2482 Titmouse
2483 Titmouse
2484 Titmouse
2485 Titmouse
2486 Sailor
2487 Girl bowling
2489 Guinea-pig - sitting
2490 Guinea-pig - lying
2491 Sparrow wings spread
2492 Sparrow - Swollen
2493 Sparrow - head left
2494 Sparrow - raised tail
2495 Sparrow
2496 Do not hear
2497 Do not see
2498 Do not speak
2499 Guinea-pig - sitting
2500 Guinea-pig - lying
2501 Titmouse with chain
2502 Parliament attendant
2504 Kitten lying - white
2505 Kitten sitting - white
2506 Kitten standing - white
2507 Kitten tail up - white
2508 Clown
2509 Clown hands at sides
2510 Clown hands in pockets
2511 Clown hands on braces
2512 Girl in long dress
2514 Kitten lying - gray
2515 Kitten sitting - gray
2516 Kitten standing - gray
2517 Kitten tail up - gray

2525 'The Tea Party'
2526 'The Magical Tea Party'
2527 Cat
2528 Lion cub
2529 Lion cub
2530 Lion cub
2531 Lion cub
2532 Boy with raincoat SB
2533 Girl - dressed up
2535 Polar bear cub standing MA
2536 Polar bear cub feet up MA
2537 Polar bear cub on backMA
2538 Polar bear cub lying on back MA
2539 Pigeon
2540 Pigeon
2541 'A Joyful Flight'
2544 Boy - dressed up
2546 'The Little Gardner'
2547 Spaniel - white
2548 Gipsy girl
2549 Witch
2551 Billy
2556 Lapwing
2558 Lamb sleeping
2559 Lamb
2560 Lamb
2562 Lamb
2563 'Wash Day'
2563 Children's Day figurine 88
2564 Beagle - standing
2565 Beagle - lying
2571 Girl with teddy
2573 Elephant
2575 Elephant
2576 Elephant
2581 Kid on rock
2586 See my dress
2631 Bird head back
2807 Kitten
2917 Cat
2995 Mercury BT
2996 Venus BT
2997 Ballerina BT
3027 Girl carrying serving dish
3028 Dolls head
3188 Budgie stoneware
4020 Woman with grapes KN
4021 Man with grapes KN
4022 Woman with grapes KN
4023 Man & woman KN
4024 Man with grapes sittingKN
4025 Man with grapes KN
4026 Man, horse & child KN
4027 Faun with grapes KN
4028 Nude, children, man KN
4029 Woman lying KN
4030 Neptune, woman KN
4031 Woman standing KN
4032 Woman bending KN
4033 Children KN
4034 Child with dolphin KN
4035 Child with dolphin KN
4036 Boy on fish KN
4037 Child with dolphin KN
4038 Girl with dolphin KN
4055 Mother Nile KN
4056 Girl riding dolphin KN
4057 Girl riding dolphin KN
4058 Girl with dolphin KN
4059 Girl with dolphin KN
4060 Girl with dolphin KN
4061 Girl with dolphin KN
4108 Eve & Apple KN
4109 Mother & child KN
4110 Mother & child KN
4111 Mother & child KN
4200 Horses - large pair AJ
4201 Cats - pair AJ
4202 Swan AJ
4203 Rams - pair AJ
4204 Geese - three AJ
4205 Penguins - pair AJ
4206 Cows - three AJ
4207 Horses - three AJ
4208 Horses small - pair AJ
4209 Llamas AJ
7016 Africa
7029 Grizzly Bear
7031 Ravens
7032 Mountain Goat
7034 Thrush
7036 Pigeon
7041 Abstract figurine SLM
7042 Abstract figurine SLM
7043 Abstract figurine SLM
7044 Abstract figurine SLM
7045 Abstract figurine SLM
7046 Abstract figurine SLM
7047 Abstract figurine SLM
7048 Abstract figurine SLM
7049 Abstract figurine SLM
7051 Abstract figurine SLM
7052 Abstract figurine SLM
7053 Abstract figurine SLM
7054 Bison
7055 Ram's head
7212 Horse
8020 Dancing couple JJB/HT

8022 Couple skating JJB/HT
8023 Skater JJB/HT
8024 Restless JJB/HT
8025 Footman with coat JJB/HT
8026 Footman without coat JJB/HT
8027 Skater JJB/HT
8028 Running footman JJB/HT
8029 Jumping footman JJB/HT
8030 Lady with dog JJB/HT
8031 Lady with racket JJB/HT
8032 Girl with racket JJB/HT
8033 Blind Mans Buff JJB/HT
8034 Lady with slippers JJB/HT
8035 Lady without slippers JJB/HT
8036 Rain JJB/HT
8037 Sunshine JJB/HT

8038 Woman watering flowers JJB/HT
8039 Man trimming a box tree JJB/HT
8040 Artist at easel JJB/HT
8041 Dancing couple tumbling JJB/HT
8042 Lady in wind JJB/HT
8043 Man in wind JJB/HT
8044 Lady blowing soap bubbles JJB/HT
8045 Man with apples JJB/HT
8046 'Shepherdess & Chimney Sweep' JJB/HT
8047 'Emperor's New Clothes' JJB/HT
8048 'Little Claus' JJB/HT
8049 'The Nightingale' JJB/HT
8050 'The Swineherd' JJB/HT
8051 'The Tinder Box' JJB/HT
8052 'The Sandman' JJB/HT

Categories List

Abstract and Modernist Figurines

1395 'Bed of Roses' JG
1396 'Silen' JG
1397 'The Spoils of Europe' JG
1398 'The Playful Wave' JG
1399 'The Sea Bull' JG
7041 Abstract figurine SLM
7042 Abstract figurine SLM
7043 Abstract figurine SLM
7044 Abstract figurine SLM
7045 Abstract figurine SLM
7046 Abstract figurine SLM
7047 Abstract figurine SLM
7048 Abstract figurine SLM
7049 Abstract figurine SLM
7051 Abstract figurine SLM
7052 Abstract figurine SLM
7053 Abstract figurine SLM

Birds

Birds of Prey

1531 Falcon DJ
1666 Hawk DJ
1795 Eagle - golden DJ
1892 Sparrow Hawk NN
1925 Eagle KM
1953 Gerfalcon KM
1975 Eagle

Exotic Birds

1544 Parrot on base
1577 Budgie on base
1628 Peacock DJ
1739 Toucan
1740 Cockatoo on base
1784 Silver pheasant DJ
1851 Lovebird
1931 Bird on base
1934 Ostrich
1941 Peahen
2019 Parrot DJ
2139 Pelican
2178 Cockatoo SJ
2210 Budgerigar - blue SJ
2235 Blue Ara AP
2341 Budgerigar - green SJ
3188 Budgie stoneware

Game Birds

1620 Partridge
1621 Partridge - three
1744 Blackcock (Black grouse) DJ
1952 Pheasants - pair KM
2386 Partridge SJ
2389 Cock pheasant SJ

Garden Birds

1519 Finch
1598 Finch?
1607 Sparrow CM
1623 Bird on lid DJ
1633 'Optimist' - titmouse DJ
1635 'Pessimist' - titmouse DJ
1657 Birds - pair
1670 'Protection' DJ
1675 Crested Tit DJ
1707 Finch DJ
1708 Finch group DJ
1764 Wagtail DJ
1771 Finch?
1778 Bird on base
1850 Goldfinch DJ
1852 Sparrow - fledgling KK
1853 Wren KK
1856 Bird
1864 Sparrow fledglings
1869 Sparrow with young DJ
1880 StarlingNN
1888 Sparrow on base NN
1909 Bullfinch NN
1949 Chaffinch
2242 Finch SJ
2310 Robin SJ
2311 Robin on twig SJ

2322 Chaffinch SJ
2323 Great Titmouse SJ
2347 White eye -robin? SJ
2348 Finch
2361 Bird preening tail -Chaffinch ?
2362 Finch
2405 Blackbird EP
2406 Nuthatch EP
2455 Goldcrest
2463 Blue Tit on base
2481 Titmouse spread wings
2482 Titmouse
2483 Titmouse
2484 Titmouse
2485 Titmouse
2491 Sparrow wings spread
2492 Sparrow - Swollen
2493 Sparrow - head left
2494 Sparrow - raised tail
2495 Sparrow
2631 Bird head back
7034 Thrush

Owls
1500 Snowy Owl DJ
1501 Owl on dish
1576 Owl
1683 Owl
1800 Owl DJ
1846 Owl on base DJ
2240 Owl
2424 Little owl
2469 Owl
2475 Snowy Owl

Penguins
1821 Penguin SM
1822 Penguin - Blackfoot SM
2059 Penguin on rock AL
2166 Penguin

Sea Birds
1504 Seagull
1632 Guillemot
1725 Seagull with fish DJ
1726 Seagull
1727 Seagull
1808 Gull with fish DJ
1809 Gull crying DJ
1810 Gull DJ
1940 Puffin
2384 Puffin SJ
4205 Penguins - pair AJ
6250 Seagull

Water Birds
1535 Duck preening
1537 Duck
1548 Duck DJ
1551 Duck CM
1588 Duckling DJ
1589 Duckling DJ
1593 Goose CM
1619 Kingfisher DJ
1643 Mandarin duck
1665 Duck
1738 Duck
1751 Duck
1817 Swan
1818 Swan
1855 Tufted duck DJ
1885 Kingfisher NN
1902 Goose NN
1932 Eider duck
1939 Duck
2439 Grebe & chicks
4202 Swan AJ
4204 Geese - three AJ

Wild Birds
1521 Pigeon
1575 Pigeon
1606 Bird ?
1610 Magpie DJ
1658 Pigeon
1714 Crow DJ
1717 Woodpecker DJ
1730 Bird
1760 Jay
1770 Cuckoo DJ
1775 Swallow DJ
1776 Flycatcher DJ
1777 Bird?
1859 Bird
1887 Linnet NN
1911 Pigeon NN
1924 Bird?
1980 Peewit KM
2020 Linnet PH
2458 Kinglet
2459 Bird preening
2461 Bird preening
2539 Pigeon
2540 Pigeon
2556 Lapwing
7031 Ravens
7036 Pigeon

Cats

1529 Cat
1553 Kitten sitting DJ
1555 Cat with ball
1686 Cat
1754 Cat
1799 Cat playing with ball
1807 Cat sitting
1834 Cat curled
1837 Cat with ball
1844 Cat DJ
1876 Cat sitting IPI
1878 Cat NN
1889 Cat curled
1891 Cat drinking from bowl
2142 Kitten
2143 Kitten
2236 Cat lying
2256 Cat sitting SJ
2308 Siamese cat SJ
2309 Cat sleeping
2452 Cat - gray
2453 Cat - white
2454 Cat - gray
2464 Siamese cat - white
2465 Cat - gray
2466 Cat sitting
2476 Cat - white
2504 Kitten lying - white
2505 Kitten sitting - white
2506 Kitten standing - white
2507 Kitten tail up - white
2514 Kitten lying - gray
2515 Kitten sitting - gray
2516 Kitten standing - gray
2517 Kitten tail up - gray
2527 Cat
2807 Kitten
2917 Cat
4201 Cats - pair AJ

Dogs

Gun Dogs
1716 Pointer sitting
1723 Pointer playing
1788 Pointer sitting
1815 Pointer puppies playing - three?
1904 Gordon Setter LJ
2006 Pointer
2015 Setter with bird LJ
2026 Pointer LJ
2044 Pointer lying LJ
2060 Pointer pup scratching side LJ
2061 Spaniel LJ
2062 English Setter
2075 Pointer standing
2095 Cocker Spaniel LJ
2111 Pointer Bitch & pups
2172 Cocker Spaniel SJ
2547 Spaniel – white

Hounds
1565 Dog
1570 Bloodhound
1579 Dachshund
1603 Dachshund begging
1654 Hound standing
1691 Dachshund sitting
1746 Dachshund sitting
1752 Dachshund DJ
1753 Puppy sitting
1755 Dachshund DJ
1805 Dachshunds - pair DJ
1811 Borzoi lying LJ
1814 Borzoi sitting LJ
1861 Dachshunds - pair
1890 Dog standing
1917 Dog standing
1962 Dachshund
2041 Dachshund standing
2076 Greyhound standing
2078 Greyhound
2079 Greyhound, lying
2084 Bloodhound sniffing
2115 Borzoi
2120 Irish Wolfhound
2564 Beagle - standing
2565 Beagle – lying

Terriers
1914 Cairn terrier sitting
1921 Terrier standing
1998 Terrier DJ
2000 French Bull Terrier
2011 Scottish Terrier
2027 Sealyham puppy DJ
2028 Sealyham puppy DJ
2030 Terrier
2069 Scottish Terrier standing
2071 Sealyham
2072 Terrier LJ
2073 Scottish Terrier
2077 Scottish Terrier lying
2085 Scottish Terrier standing

2086 Terrier standing
2099 Airedale Terrier
2117 Scottish Terrier
2118 Scottish Terrier
2130 Skye Terrier LJ
2133 Skye Terrier
2137 Skye Terrier
2167 Scottish Terrier standing
2170 Scottish Terrier sitting
2179 Sealyham LJ

Toy Dogs
1630 Pekinese puppies - pair DJ
1631 Pekinese sitting DJ
1637 Pekinese puppy sitting DJ
1895 Pug sitting
1903 Pug sitting
1986 Pekinese sitting DJ
1987 Pekinese DJ
1990 Pekinese puppies
2035 Cavalier King Charles Spaniel
2092 Pomeranian
2101 Pekinese
2114 Japanese Chin standing SM
2123 Japanese Chin
2244 Chihuahua

Utility Dogs
1605 Bulldog DJ
1676 Bulldog DJ
1893 French Bulldog
1918 Poodle sitting
1983 Bulldog puppy
1992 Bulldog
2082 Bulldog
2083 Bulldog sitting
2090 Chow Chow
2110 English Bulldog
2122 Dalmatian
2330 Boston Terrier

Working Dogs
1513 Great Dane on base
1663 Collie lying DJ
1690 German Shepherd seated
1765 German Shepherd LJ
1773 Great Dane LJ
1789 German Shepherd LJ
1802 Collie standing
1854 German Shepherd
1916 St Bernard
1922 Dog standing
1926 St Bernard puppy NN
2018 German Shepherd standing
2038 Great Dane sitting LJ
2089 Schnauzer
2091 Schnauzer
2103 German Shepherd standing LJ
2108 Mastiff
2116 Old English Sheepdog
2124 Great Dane standing
2189 Great Dane sitting SJ
2190 Great Dane lying SJ
2197 German Shepherd SJ
2198 German Shepherd lying
2212 Boxer SJ
2227 Boxer

Farm and Domestic Animals

Cattle
1547 Brahma Bull DJ
2121 Bull SM
1506 Cow
1769 Cow
1826 Calf scratching ear KK
2161 Cow licking side LJ
2168 Calf SJ
4206 Cows - three AJ

Donkeys
1602 Donkey
1763 Donkey?

Fowl
1591 Cockerel
1662 Chick on base
1673 Cockerel
1674 Hen MA
1735 Guinea Fowl
1749 Cockerel
1750 Hen
1860 Turkey chick
2192 Cock SJ
2193 Hen SJ
2194 Chick SJ
2425 Turkey cock
2426 Turkey hen

Goats/Sheep
1699 Goat DJ
1700 Goat DJ
1928 Goat
2171 Lamb SJ
2558 Lamb sleeping
2559 Lamb
2560 Lamb
2562 Lamb
2581 Kid on rock
4203 Rams - pair AJ
7055 Ram's head

Horses
1615 Horse DJ
1641 Horse lying
2146 Horse
2234 Belgian Stallion SJ
2259 Horse
2271 Arabian horse
2293 Shire Horse
4020 Mare lying KN
4200 Horses - large pair AJ
4207 Horses - three AJ
4208 Horses small - pair AJ
7212 Horse

Pigs
1582 Pig sitting DJ
1583 Sow with eight piglets DJ
1842 Pigs pair
1881 Pig
1882 Pig

Figurines

Adults Alone
1515 Woman standing DJ
1516 Nude lying on base
1525 Woman DJ
1534 Woman standing
1550 Woman standing
1554 Nude on base
1556 Woman kneeling (matchstick holders)
1571 Man
1578 Woman
1580 Woman reading on chair
1587 Man & woman talking on bench IPI
1594 Lovers on bench
1609 Woman sitting
1611 Woman sitting pensive
1618 Man & woman
1627 Woman on bench
1680 Teenage lovers
1695 Woman seated
1703 Woman in coat & large hat
1706 Woman sitting
1709 Woman standing
1710 Woman doing hair
1711 Woman sitting
1734 Woman of fashion VA
1756 Man carrying box
1766 Woman standing
1938 Graduate
2219 Washer Woman
2283 Nude kneeling
2302 Nude on steps
2435 'Thirst'
2473 Vagabond
2478 Vagabond with bottle
2997 Ballerina
7016 'Africa'
8030 Lady with dog JJB/HT
8042 Lady in wind JJB/HT

Adults with children
1552 'Mother Love' IPI
1592 Woman carrying baby on back
1625 Woman & Child
1642 'Dickie's Mama' IPI
1644 Woman with children IPI
1829 Mother with baby
1910 Mothcr with two girls
2002 Mother, toddler & baby
2022 Mother & two children
2025 Fisher family AL
2196 Mother with children
2200 Mother with baby
2255 Mother & child
2262 'Happy family' MA
2277 Mother, child on knee looking at tortoise

Biblical
2332 Madonna EB/SJ
4108 Eve & Apple KN

Busts
1546 Bust of woman
1612 Bust of boy
1697 Bust
3028 Dolls head

Children
1523 Children reading
1526 Little girl IPI
1543 Child kneeling
1567 Children reading IPI
1568 Children playing IPI
1574 'Else' IPI
1614 'Love refused' IPI
1617 'Kaj' IPI
1624 'Good Morning'
1636 'Dickie' IPI
1648 'Tom & Willy' IPI
1650 Boy on seat
1651 Girl sitting?
1652 Girl standing
1656 'Grethe' IPI
1660 Boy - naked on tray
1661 'Merry Sailor' IPI
1669 Boy sitting
1671 Boy sitting looking down IPI
1681 Children sitting

1687 Girl writing
1694 Girl IPI
1696 'Peter' IPI
1705 Girl in cloak
1713 'Victor' IPI
1720 Boy in cloak
1721 'Mary' IPI
1737 Children on toboggan
1742 'School's Out' IPI
1743 Boy sitting
1757 'Paddling About' IPI
1758 Girl
1759 'Tiny Tot' MA
1761 Girls standing IPI
1780 Girl IPI
1781 Girl with boy MA
1782 Boy standing
1783 Boy in coat/hat (formal) IPI
1787 Boy standing
1792 Boy with trumpet MA
1794 'Good toes, bad toes' MA
1796 Baby sitting
1798 Girl standing
1827 Boy standing
1828 Brother and sister
1836 Boy lying
1839 Girl with toy
1841 Girl sitting IPI
1843 Boy standing
1845 'Dancing School' IPI
1847 Girl sitting
1848 Playfellows MA
1849 Boys playing with bricks
1870 Boy with crab IPI
1871 Sisters
1879 Girl sitting IPI
1897 Flute player IPI
1899a Boy standing
1899b Boy standing
1901 Boy in raincoat
1908 Schoolgirl
1913 Schoolboy
1950 Girl with accordion
1995 Girl touching hem of skirt AB
2127 Boy with bucket SL
2148 Boy with papers
2162 'Youthful boldness' CW
2175 'Unfair Treatment' CW
2182 Girl comforting boy
2183 Boy & girl
2184 'Little Artist'
2185 Girl with doll
2188 Boy & girl singing
2191 Girl with doll
2199 Boy taking off sock
2206 Headache SL
2207 Toothache SL
2208 Tummyache SL
2209 Earache SL
2229 'So big' SL
2230 'Eve' SL
2231 'Adam' SL
2232 'Fright' SL
2246 'Spilt milk' CW
2247 'First Book' CW
2250 Girl & baby
2251 'Who is Calling?' MA
2257 Girl braiding hair
2258 Girl on footstool
2261 'Offended'
2267 Sea girl EB/SJ
2273 'My Balloon' MA
2274 Boy
2275 'Help Me, Mum' MA
2278 Throw down the ball MA
2296 Girl potter
2298 Ida's flowers EB/SJ
2301 'Guess who?'
2303 My horse
2304 'Merete' SJ
2306 'The Little Builder' SJ
2307 Motherly care
2312 'Gentleman' SJ
2313 'Ruth' SJ
2317 Girl buttoning shoe SJ
2318 'Vanity' SJ
2320 Boy with toy car
2321 'Little Sailor' VT
2324 'Up to Mom' SJ
2325 Ballet dancer VT
2326 'Little Gardener' VT
2327 'Little Hunter' VT
2337 Boy sitting
2344 Boy playing flute VT
2345 Girl with garland VT
2346 Boy holding flowers VT
2350 'The Little Painter' VT
2351 'Skating Girl' VT
2356 Girl VT
2357 Youth with basket
2358 Boy with skis VT
2367 'Hairdresser' VT
2372 'Pardon me' CW
2373 'Marianne' CW
2374 'Erik' CW
2375 Footballer VT
2380 Boy with sailing boat CW
2381 'Anne' CW
2385 Dancing couple CW
2387 'Miss Charming' CW
2388 Girl with bricks CW

2390 Boy with flowers CW
2391 Girl with ball CW
2392 'Cathrine' CW
2393 'Jacob' CW
2398 'Congratulations Mama' CW
2399 'I am coming now' CW
2400 'Children's Hour' CW
2401 'Jorgen' CW
2402 'The Little Player' CW
2403 Boy with ball CW
2404 Girl singing CW
2470 Girl with ice lolly
2487 Girl bowling
2496 Do not hear
2497 Do not see
2498 Do not speak
2512 Girl in long dress
2525 'The Tea Party'
2526 'The Magical Tea Party'
2532 Boy with raincoat SB
2533 Girl - dressed up
2541 'A Joyful Flight'
2544 Boy - dressed up
2546 'The Little Gardner'
2548 Gipsy girl
2549 Witch
2551 Billy
2563 'Wash Day'
2563 Children's Day figurine 88
2571 Girl with teddy
2586 See my dress
3027 Girl carrying serving dish

Children with animals

1745 'Only one drop' IPI
1747 'Ole' IPI
1779 'Little Mother' IPI
1790 'Two Friends' MA
1920 Boy with kitten and cat
1951 Boy with dog IPI
1973 Girl with dog
2125 Girl with butterfly
2163 Girl with dog CW
2195 Boy with foal
2201 Boy with scottie CW
2202 Girl with puppy
2249 'Friends' CW
2276 Girl with kittens
2316 Girl with puppy VT
2319 Child with rabbit
2329 'Birgite' VT
2331 Boy with dog
2333 'Make friends' VT
2334 'Must I be washed? VT'
2336 Girl with kid goat VT
2338 Boy with fish & net VT
2340 Girl feeding dove VT

Clowns

2508 Clown
2509 Clown hands at sides
2510 Clown hands in pockets
2511 Clown hands on braces

Fairytale/Fictional Figurines

1655 'The Little Match Girl' IPI
2012 'Little Match Girl'
2037 Hans Christian Andersen HS
2055 'The Sandman' HS
2104 Sisyphus
2105 Tinderbox Dog
2107 Tinderbox Dog
2264 Sea boy with shell EB/SJ
2265 Sea boy with starfish EB/SJ
2266 Sea boy with Sea-weed EB/SJ
2285 Girl with starfish
2305 'Christmas Meal'
2314 Sea gir- lyingl EB/SJ
2315 Sea boy- resting EB/SJ
2353 Pierrot EB/SJ
2354 Harlequin EB/SJ
2355 Columbine EB/SJ
2368 'Aalborg'
2394 Child with sea horse EB/SJ
2395 Child with sea horse EB/SJ
2396 Child with sea horse EB/SJ
2397 Child with sea horse EB/SJ
2408 Hamlet EB/SJ
2409 Ophelia EB/SJ
2995 Mercury
2996 Venus
4021 Man with grapes KN
4022 Woman with grapes KN
4023 Man & woman KN
4024 Man with grapes sitting KN
4025 Man with grapes KN
4026 Man, horse & child KN
4027 Faun with grapes KN
4028 Nude, children, man KN
4029 Woman lying KN
4030 Neptune, woman KN
4031 Woman standing KN
4032 Woman bending KN
4033 Children KN
4034 Child with dolphin KN
4035 Child with dolphin KN
4036 Boy on fish KN
4037 Child with dolphin KN
4038 Girl with dolphin KN
4055 Mother Nile KN

4056 Girl riding dolphin KN
4057 Girl riding dolphin KN
4058 Girl with dolphin KN
4059 Girl with dolphin KN
4060 Girl with dolphin KN
4061 Girl with dolphin KN
4109 Mother & child KN
4110 Mother & child KN
4111 Mother & child KN
8046 'Shepherdess & Chimney Sweep' JJB/HT
8047 'Emperor's New Clothes' JJB/HT
8048 'Little Claus' JJB/HT
8049 'The Nightingale' JJB/HT
8051 'The Tinder Box' JJB/HT
8052 'The Sandman' JJB/HT

Greenlanders

2280 Greenland girl sitting
2281 Greenland girl sitting
2282 Greenland girl standing
2410 Greenlander lifting stone KAK
2411 Greenlander standing ML
2412 Greenlander with child SK
2413 Greenlander sitting KAK
2414 Greenland woman KAK
2415 Greenlander standing KAK
2416 Greenland woman with bucket KAK
2417 Greenlander - angry KAK

Occupations

1586 Lady painting porcelain
1659 Carpenter
1685 Woman washing floor
1702 Danish Fisherwoman KN
1724 Man in uniform
1736 Woman with washing
1786 Mason NN
1866 Red Cross Nurse
1867 Red Cross Nurse
1997 Actors - Poulsen & Mantzius AL
2004 Actor AL
2010 Shepherdess AL
2017 Dairy maid AL
2036 Woman with fishing net AL
2043 Shepherd Boy AL
2049 Harvest Man
2050 Girl with rake
2119 Farmer with two horses
2126 Woman with eggs SL
2180 Girl with goat AL
2181 Girl with milkcan AL
2220 Poultry girl AL
2223 Baker AL
2225 Smith AL
2226 Nurse
2228 Cobbler AL
2233 'Fish Market' AL
2237 Woman with pig AL
2241 Tailor
2254 Goose girl AL
2263 Farmer with pig AL
2270 Girl with calves AL
2272 Girl with cow & goose AL
2335 Foundry worker SJ
2339 Carpenter SJ
2342 Guardsman SJ
2370 Old fisherman SJ
2379 Nurse SJ
2419 Potter
2428 Electrician
2429 Baker
2431 House painter
2432 Pipe fitter
2433 Butcher
2434 Carpenter
2436 Policeman
2444 Gunner - Army
2445 Pilot
2446 Sailor - Navy
2451 Postman
2486 Sailor
2502 Parliament attendant
8050 'The Swineherd' JJB/HT

Overglaze figurines

8020 Dancing couple JJB/HT
8022 Couple skating JJB/HT
8023 Skater JJB/HT
8024 Restless JJB/HT
8025 Footman with coat JJB/HT
8026 Footman without coat JJB/HT
8027 Skater JJB/HT
8028 Running footman JJB/HT
8029 Jumping footman JJB/HT
8033 Blind Mans Buff JJB/HT
8034 Lady with slippers JJB/HT
8035 Lady without slippers JJB/HT
8036 Rain JJB/HT
8037 Sunshine JJB/HT
8038 Woman watering flowers JJB/HT
8039 Man trimming a box tree JJB/HT
8040 Artist at easel JJB/HT
8041 Dancing couple tumbling JJB/HT
8043 Man in wind JJB/HT
8044 Lady blowing soap bubbles JJB/HT
8045 Man with apples JJB/HT

Sports/Leisure Figurines

1600 Mandolin player IPI
1684 Woman with guitar IPI

1715 Skater IPI
1729 Violinist
1772 Hunter
1838 Ballet dancer
2032 Cellist
2132 Swimmer - female
2134 Swimmer - male
2222 Soccer player
2224 Girl in swimsuit
2238 Bowling
2300 Ballet girl
2328 Hunter with dog SJ
2364 Tennis player - female VT
2369 Horsewoman VT
8031 Lady with racket JJB/HT
8032 Girl with racket JJB/HT

Fish

1111 Hermit crab dish
1540 Crucian carp - pair
1590 Crucian carp - pair CM
1608 Bream CM
1634 Eel
1638 Mackerel - pair
1645 Carp CM
1803 Trout DJ
1862 Crab?
2138 Eel
2144 Sea Scorpion SJ
2145 Roach SJ
2169 Trout SJ
2173 Herring SJ
2174 Perch SJ
2366 Salmon trout EV

Rodents

Guinea-pigs

1558 Guinea-pig
1559 Guinea-pigs – three DJ
1812 Guinea-pig
2479 Guinea-pig - sitting
2480 Guinea-pig - lying
2489 Guinea-pig - sitting
2490 Guinea-pig - lying
2499 Guinea-pig - sitting
2500 Guinea-pig – lying

Hares

2080 Hare sitting up
2081 Hare sitting
2141 Hare SJ

Mice

1561 Mouse with matchstick holder
1562 Mice - pair on dish DJ
1566 Mice – pair DJ
1639 Dishe with figurine on lid (mouse?)
1640 Mouse
1718 Mouse
1728 Mouse - white DJ
1732 Mouse
1801 Mouse gray DJ
1863 Mice?
1865 Mice – pair

Rabbits

1595 Rabbit
1596 Rabbit - lop eared DJ
1597 Rabbit - grooming DJ
1599 Rabbit DJ
1741 Rabbit
1830 Rabbits - lying
1831 Rabbit - lying
1832 Rabbit
1833 Rabbit DJ
1874 Rabbit NN
1875 Rabbits sitting NN
1900 Rabbit
2421 Rabbit - lying
2422 Rabbit - sitting
2423 Rabbit - standing
2441 Rabbit lying - white
2442 Rabbit, sitting - white
2443 Rabbit, standing - white

Wildlife

Bears

1509 Bear with tree stump
1698 Bear on base
1762a Bear sitting
1762b Bear sitting on base
1804 Bear walking
1816 Bears playing
1824 Bear brown
1825 Bears playing
1915 Bear
1946 Bear with cub - lying
2098 Bear sitting - bookend
2204 Bear
2213 Brown bear, walking
7029 Grizzly Bear

Bison

1672 Bison
7054 Bison

Camels/Llamas
1585 Llama
1791 Llama?
2215 Camel lying
4209 Llamas- pair

Cat family
1584 Puma DJ
1613 Jaguar DJ
1664 Serval
1668 Lion on rock
1677 Lion
1678 LionessLJ
1712 Tiger - snarling LJ
1793 Lion LJ
1797 Panther
1823 Lion with lioness KK
1907 Lynx
1923 Lion Cub
1948 Tiger with cub
1993 Mountain Lion DJ
2039 Leopard
2051 Lioness grooming
2052 Lion standing
2056 Tiger LJ
2057 Lion on rock
2187 Puma
2214 Tiger cub
2268 Lioness & cub LJ
2279 Lion & lioness LJ
2528 Lion cub
2529 Lion cub
2530 Lion cub
2531 Lion cub

Coati Mundi
1689 Coati Mundi

Deer
1530 Deer sitting
1929 Deer on base NN
1930 Deer
2007 Deer - male JG
2008 Deer - female JG
2009 Stag JG
2205 Deer
2211 Deer standing

Elephants
1502 Elephant on knees DJ
1601 Elephant
1806 Elephant
1813 Elephant
1835 Elephants - pair
1858 Elephant and Mahout
2128 Green Elephant with Howdah
2140 Elephant calf
2573 Elephant
2575 Elephant
2576 Elephant

Foxes
1572 Fox curled DJ
1719 Fox
1905 Fox sitting
1906 Foxes - pair NN
1919 Fox cub?
1958 Fox sitting

Frogs and Snails
1050 Bowl with frog on lid
1536 Snail
2467 Frog

Goats
7032 Mountain Goat

Hippopotamus
1512 Hippopotamus DJ

Impala
1693 Impala LJ

Kangaroo
1894 Kangaroo

Lemur
1868 Lemur

Primates
1510 Monkey looking at tortoise DJ
1524 Monkey - pair IPI
1545 Monkey looking at tortoise DJ
1581 Monkey family - four IPI
1646 Monkey
1647 Monkeys - pair
1667 MonkeyIPI
2221 Monkey

Otter
1969 Otter with fish

Polar Bears
1629 Polar bear sitting DJ
1692 Polar bear sniffing NN
1785 Polar bear walking NN

1857 Polar bear KK
1872 Polar bear cub
1873 Polar bear cub
1954 Polar bear NN
2217 Polar bear sitting SJ
2218 Polar bear SJ
2239 Polar bear with cub
2535 Polar bear cub standing MA
2536 Polar bear cub feet up MA
2537 Polar bear cub on backMA
2538 Polar bear cub lying on back MA

Seals
1733 Seal KM
1927 Seal pup
2468 Seal
2471 Seal on back
2472 Seal

Skunk
1898 Skunk

Squirrels
1722 Squirrel DJ
1767 Squirrel on branch
2177 Squirrel SJ
2474 Squirrel

Stoat
1573 Stoat
1688 Stoat
1936 Stoat

Tapir
1626 Tapir DJ

Wild Boar
2136 Wild Boar

The Figurines

The figures are listed here in numerical order. The majority are underglaze decorated porcelain, though some are porcelain decorated overglaze, stoneware, or blanc-de-chine. Where possible, comprehensive information has been given (see below), but in a number of cases the reference material gives only the barest detail. The information is provided in the following order:

Piece Number – followed by the current Royal Copenhagen number where applicable. Charts of the modern Royal Copenhagen production numbers are provided in the Appendix.

Description – a simple description of the piece or the Bing & Grondahl title. Some reference material was so indistinct that guesses have had to be made as to the subject and a ? has been inserted where appropriate. Many of the animals are difficult to identify and some of the dogs may owe more to imagination than reality.

Sculptor – in some cases the sculptor is known but there are a number of pieces produced jointly by two sculptors.

Size – a guide only can be given. Size can vary significantly on each piece during production. Where a size is given, this is normally the height. All sizes are in centimeters.

Rating – this is very subjective, based on experience in the world market and trends in value and demand.

* In production by Royal Copenhagen.

** Piece not in production, easily obtainable.

*** Piece not in production and sometimes difficult to find.

**** Rare and/or older pieces but with limited appeal.

***** Rare, highly desirable subject matter

Comments – observations and further information.

Value – in most cases a fairly wide range has been given because the factors affecting value can make significant differences. All prices are based on the piece being perfect. In particular age, quality of decoration and availability influence prices. Sale prices at collectors fairs, auctions and on the internet have been analyzed over a long period and prices for the same piece can vary by as much as 500%. In addition some subjects for instance dogs, cats, fish and fauns appeal to a wider market not limited to Danish porcelain collectors. If a piece is still in production under the Royal Copenhagen mark the MSRP (Manufacturer's Suggested Retail Price) figure is the 'new' cost in the US at December 2001. Overglaze and stoneware have not been valued as the market is smaller and less reliable information is available. Suffice to say that when they were new, overglaze figurines were considerably more expensive and this is reflected in second hand prices.

Research indicates that the numbering of underglaze figurines starts at 1500 (the exceptions being some dishes and bowls with figurines and the Jean Gauguin sculptural pieces) and as they appear to be consecutive we believe that if there is a number for which we have no indication it is likely to be a figurine. We have found that the vases, dishes, bowls, etc. tend to be numbered between 1 and 1499.

1050
Bowl with frog on lid

1395
'Bed of Roses'
Jean Gauguin
46cms

1396
'Silen'
Jean Gauguin
48.5cms

1397
'The Spoils of Europe'
Jean Gauguin
74cms

1398
'The Playful Wave'
Jean Gauguin
59cms

1399
'The Sea Bull'
Jean Gauguin
68cms

1500
Snowy Owl
Dahl-Jensen
44cms
**
In production 1988
$550-800

1501
Owl on dish
14
***
$75-150

1502
Elephant on knees
Dahl-Jensen
29cms
***
$400-650

1504
Seagull
43cms
****
$300-450

1506
Cow
23cms
****
$200-300

1509
Bear with tree stump
20cms
*****
$300-450

1510
Monkey looking at tortoise
Dahl-Jensen
13cms
**
Also available in stoneware. In production 1984
$125-225

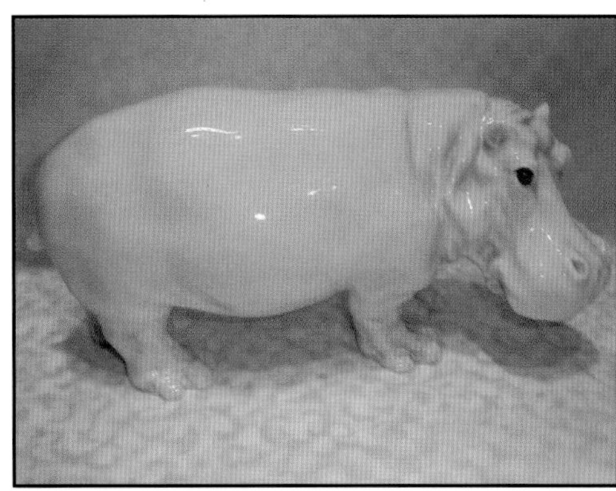

1512
Hippopotamus
Dahl-Jensen
34cms
*****
$750-1000

1513
Great Dane on base
20cms
*****
$300-450

1515
Woman standing
Dahl-Jensen
24cms
****
$125-225

1516
Nude lying on base
16cms
****
$100-200

1519
Finch
13cms
***
$100-175

1521
Pigeon
22cms
****
$100-150

1523
Children
10cms
****
$100-200

1524
Monkey - pair
Ingeborg Plockross Irminger
8cms
**
In production 1984
$75-150

1525
Woman
Dahl-Jensen
27cms
****
Also produced as lamp base
$300-400

1526 RC number 400
Little girl
Ingeborg Plockross Irminger
11cms
*
$75-150 MSRP $195

1529
Cat
34cms
****
$450-600

1530
Deer sitting
16cms
****
$125-225

1531
Falcon
Dahl-Jensen
38cms
**
In production 1984
$700-1000

1532
Meditation
20cms
***
$100-200

1536
Snail
11cms
*****
$100-250

1533
Woman looking into pool
22cms
****
$125-225

1534
Woman standing
18cms
****
$200-300

1535
Duck preening
27cms
*****
$200-300

1537
Duck
11cms
**
In production 1988
$40-75

1540
Crucian carp - pair
11
***
$100-200

1543
Child kneeling
9cms
****
$100-200

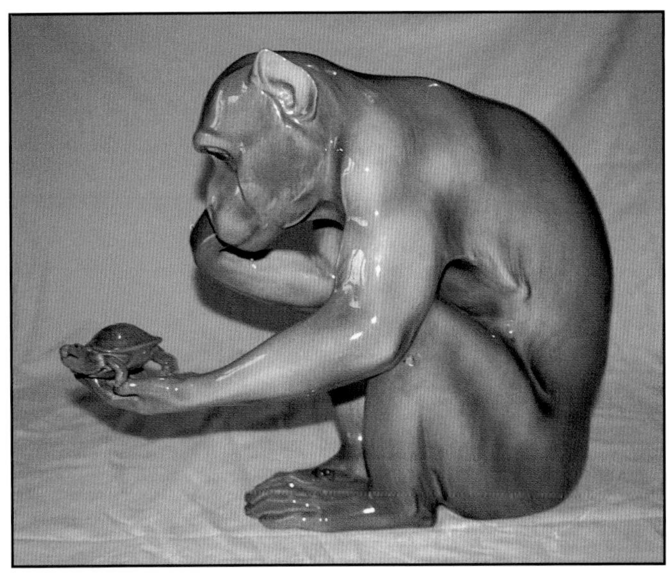

1545
Monkey looking at tortoise
Dahl-Jensen
34cms
****
In production 1984
$1250-2000

1546
Bust of woman
43cms
****
$300-400

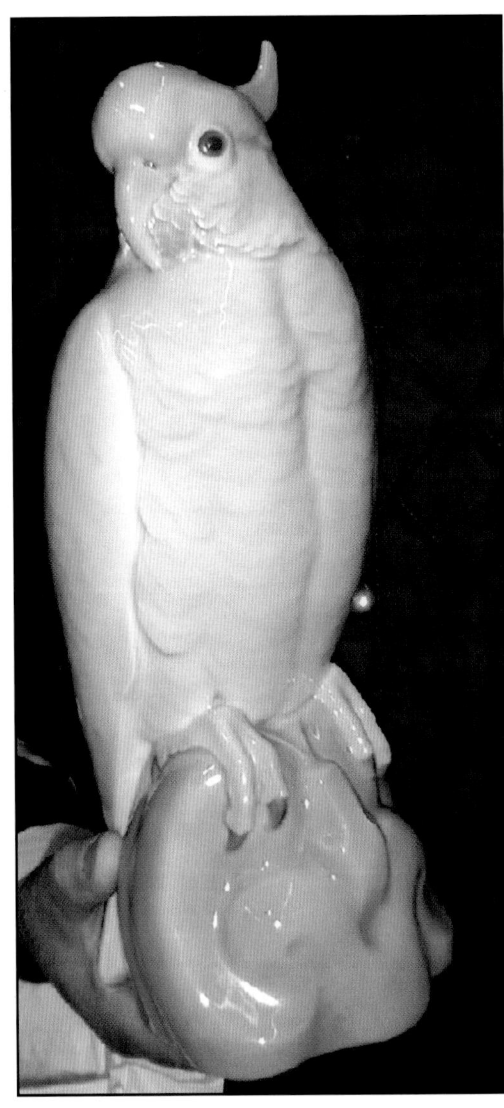

1544
Parrot on base
33cms
****
$400-650

1547
Brahma Bull
Dahl-Jensen
38cms
*****
$750-950

1548
Duck
Dahl-Jensen
Compare Dahl-Jensen 1029
8cms
**
In production 1988
$40-60

1550
Woman standing
36cms
****
$450-550

1551
Duck
C Mortensen
25cms
*****
$400-500

1552 RC number 401
'Mother Love'
Ingeborg Plockross Irminger
28cms
*
$350-500 MSRP $1,150

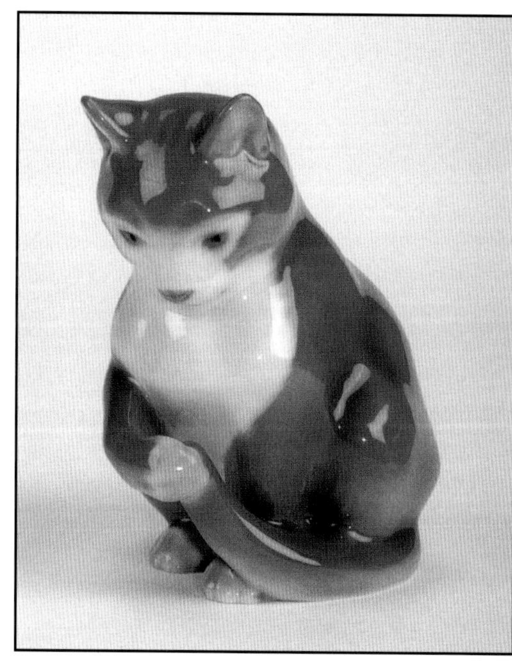

1553
Kitten sitting
Dahl-Jensen
10cms
**
In production 1972
$75-150

1554
Nude on base
15cms
***
$100-200

1555
Cat with ball
17cms
*****
$250-400

1556
Woman kneeling (matchstick holders)
17cms
*****
$250-350

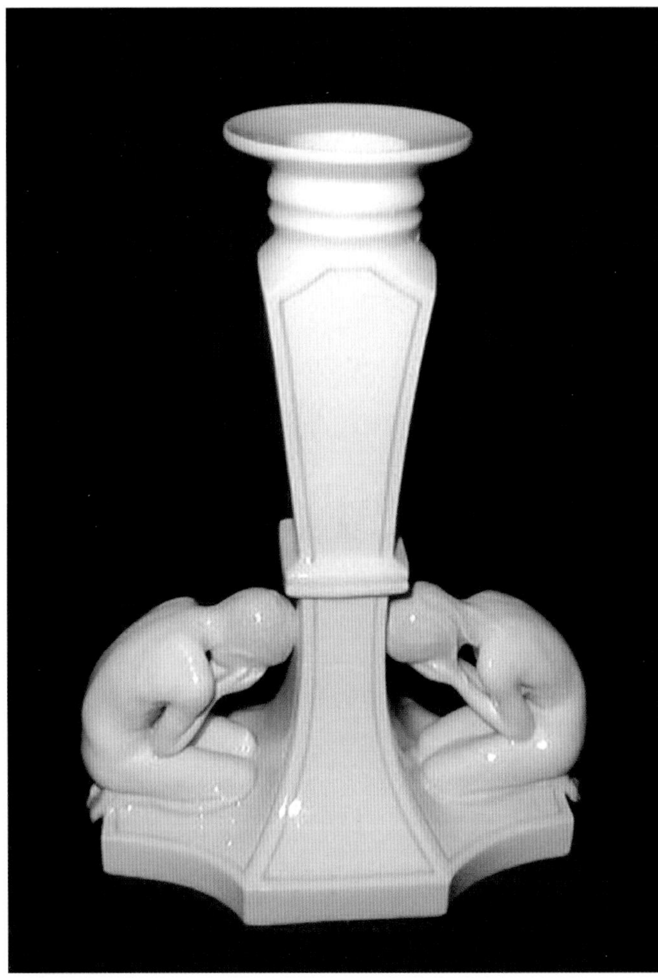

1557
Candlestick with figurines on base
19cms
*****
$200-300

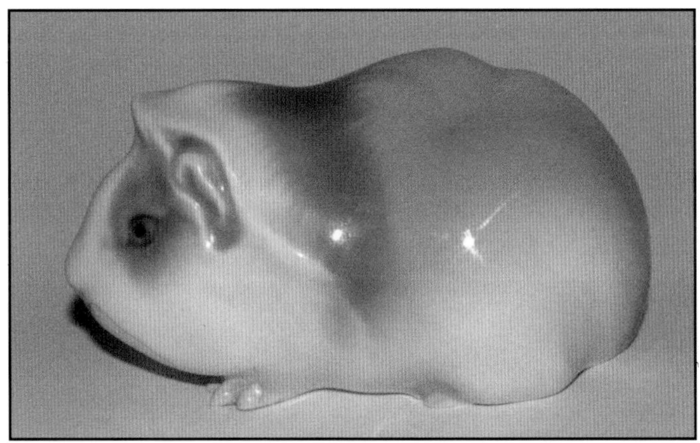

1558
Guinea-pig
10cms
*****
$200-300

1559
Guinea-pigs – three
Dahl-Jensen
12cms
*****
$350-450

1560
Children (Naked)
17cms
*****
$200-300

1561
Mouse with matchstick holder
12cms
*****
$150-250

1562
Mice - pair on dish
Dahl-Jensen
Compare Dahl-Jensen 1011
14cms
*****
$250-400

1565
Dog
22cms
*****
$400-550

1566
Mice – pair
Dahl-Jensen
7cms
*****
$125-225

1568 RC number 403
Children playing
Ingeborg Plockross Irminger
12cms
*
$75-210 MSRP $245

1567 RC number 402
Children reading
Ingeborg Plockross Irminger
10cms
*
$75-210 MSRP $225

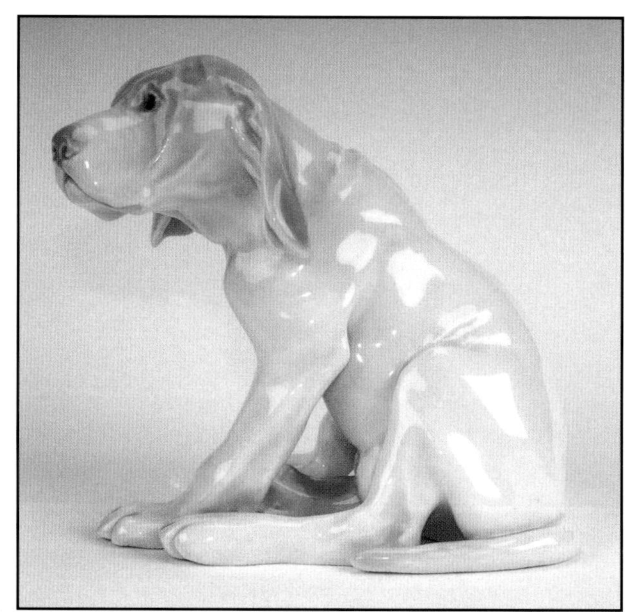

1570
Bloodhound
13cms
*****
$300-400

1571
Man
38cms
****
$200-300

1572
Fox curled
Dahl-Jensen
17cms
*****
$150-350

1573
Stoat
18cms
****
$250-350

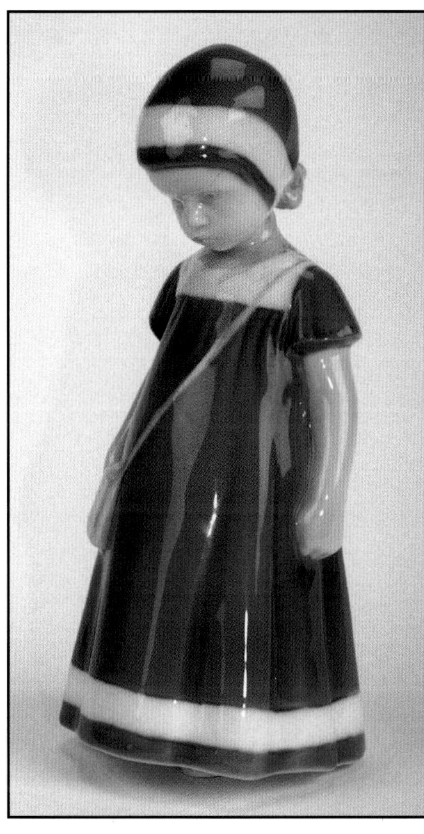

1574 RC number 404
'Else'
Ingeborg Plockross Irminger
17cms
*
Available with blue or white dress
$100-175 MSRP $225

1575
Pigeon
15cms
***
$125-200

1576
Owl
11cms
***
$75-150

1577
Budgie on base
16cms
****
$100-150

1578
Woman
22cms
****
$100-200

1579
Dachshund
20cms
****
$250-400

1580
Woman reading on chair
15cms
****
$200-300

1581
Monkey family - four
Ingeborg Plockross Irminger
13cms
**
In production 1984
$100-250

1582 RC number 405
Pig sitting
Dahl-Jensen
12cms
*
$75-125

1583
Sow with eight piglets
Dahl-Jensen
28cms
*****
$600-750

1584
Puma
Dahl-Jensen
Compare Dahl-Jensen 1019
26cms
****
$500-800

1585
Llama
28cms
*****
$500-750

1586
Lady painting porcelain
21cms
***
$200-300

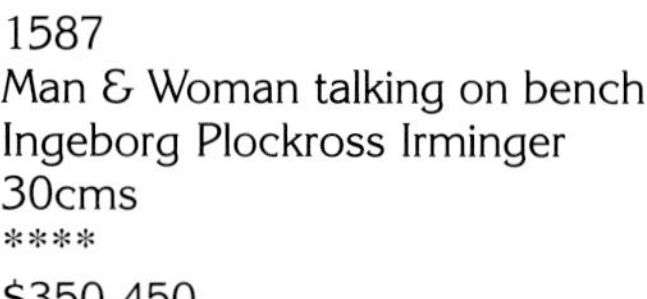

1587
Man & Woman talking on bench
Ingeborg Plockross Irminger
30cms
****
$350-450

1588
Duckling
Dahl-Jensen
Compare Dahl-Jensen 1054
10cms
***
$40-100

1589
Duckling
Dahl-Jensen
Compare Dahl-Jensen 1054
11cms
***
$50-125

1590
Crucial carp - pair
C Mortensen
14cms
***
$75-125

1591
Cockerel
21cms
****
$250-350

1592
Woman carrying baby on back
30cms
****
$200-300

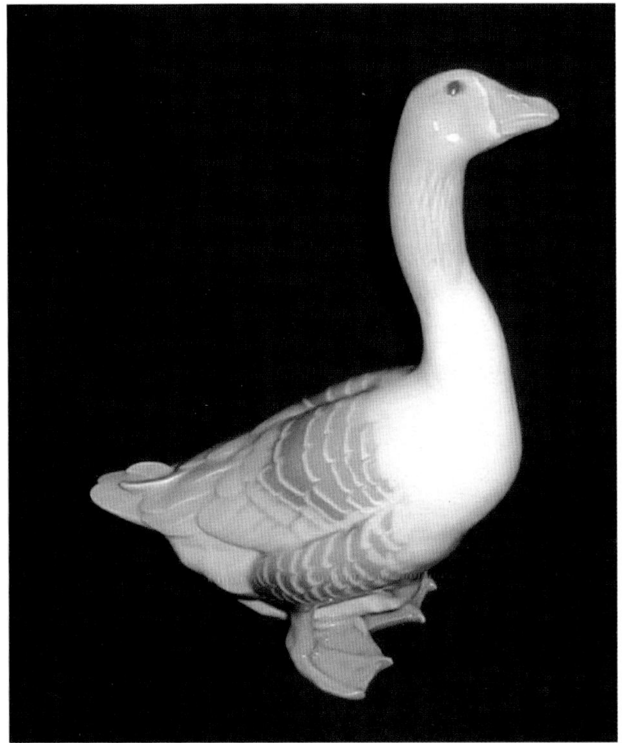

1593
Goose
Carl Mortensen
26cms
****
$150-250

1594
Lovers on bench
23cms
****
$250-350

1595
Rabbit
29cms
*****
$250-350

1596
Rabbit - lop eared
Dahl-Jensen
11cms
***
$75-125

1597
Rabbit - grooming
Dahl-Jensen
Compare Dahl-Jensen 1045
11cms
***
$75-125

1598
Finch?
8cms
****
$75-125

1599
Rabbit
Dahl-Jensen
Compare Dahl-Jensen 1045
9cms
***
$75-125

1600
Mandolin player
Ingeborg Plockross Irminger
28cms
**
In production 1984
$150-300

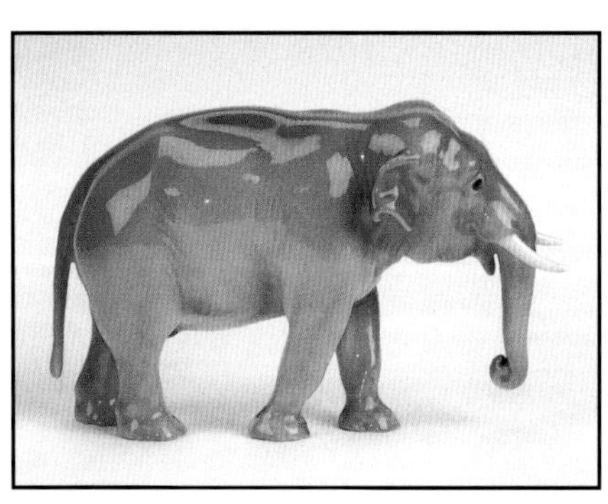

1601
Elephant
18cms
***
$100-250

1602
Donkey
19cms
*****
$200-300

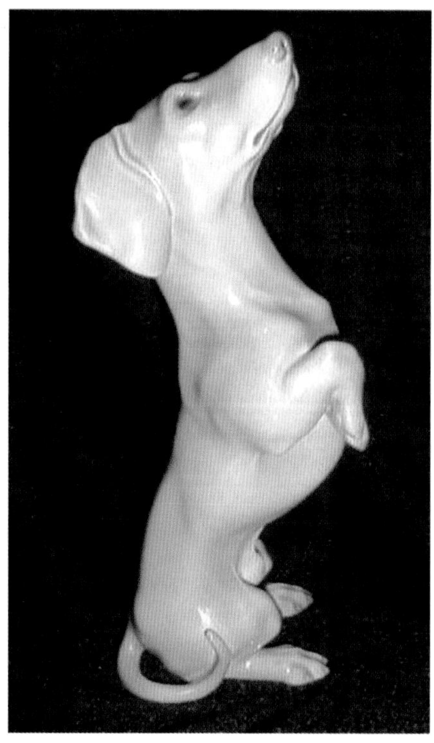

1603
Dachshund begging
19cms
***
$150-325

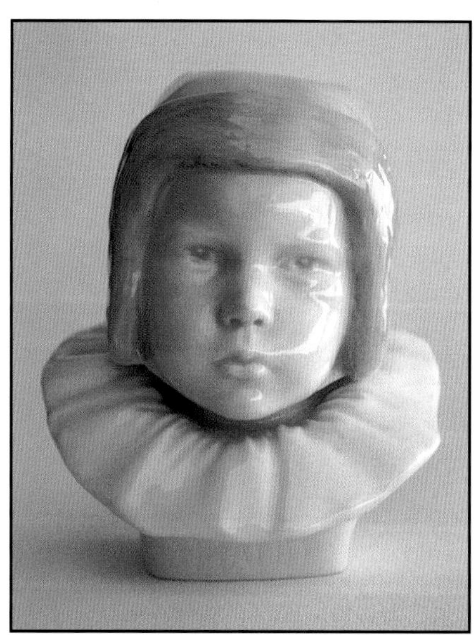

1604
'Maud' (bust)
16cms
***
$200-300

1605
Bulldog
Dahl-Jensen
24cms
*****
With tail
$350-500

1606
Bird ?
11cms
****
$75-125

1607
Sparrow
C Mortensen
13cms
**
Stoneware 1984
$50-125

1608
Bream
C Mortensen
28cms
***
$125-225

1609
Woman sitting
24cms
****
$175-275

1610
Magpie
Dahl-Jensen
33cms
****
$100-175

1611
Woman sitting pensive
22cms
***
$250-350

1612
Bust of boy
23cms
****
$150-250

1613
Jaguar
Dahl-Jensen
Compare Dahl-Jensen 1020
47cms
***
$500-850

1614 RC number 406
'Love refused'
Ingeborg Plockross Irminger
17cms
*
$75-275 MSRP $395

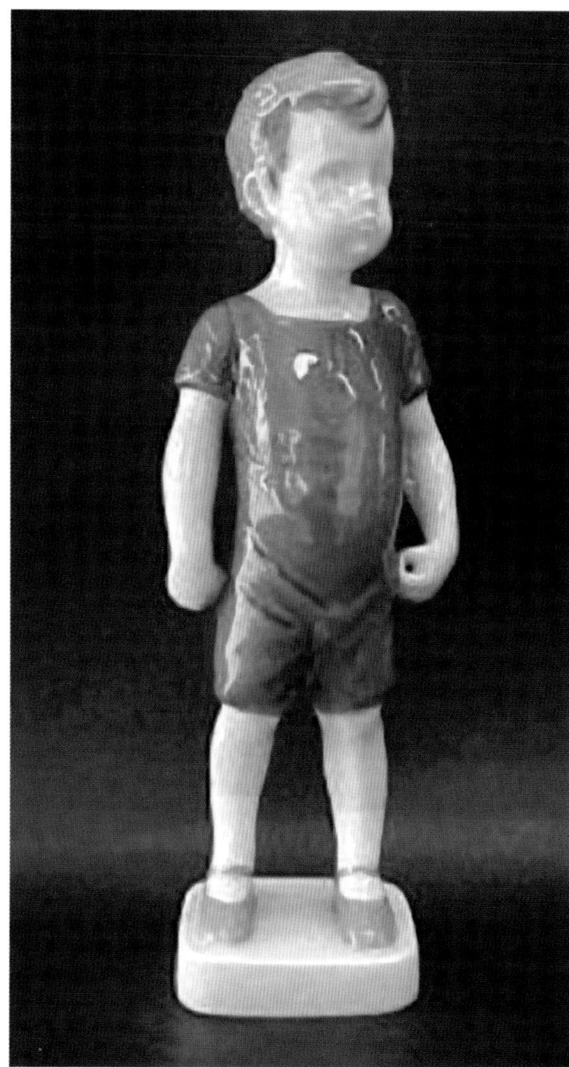

1617
'Kaj'
Ingeborg Plockross Irminger
20cms
**
In production 1988
$75-150

1618
Man & woman
30cms
****
$350-450

1615
Horse
Dahl-Jensen
26cms
*****
$350-450

1619 RC number 407
Kingfisher
Dahl-Jensen
Compare Dahl-Jensen 1049
11cms
*
Also available in stoneware
$75-150 MSRP $145

1620
Partridge
16cms
****
$125-225

1621
Partridge - three
14cms
*****
$225-325

1623
Dish with bird on lid
Dahl-Jensen
12cms
**
In production 1984
$100-200

1624 RC number 408
'Good Morning'
20cms
*
$75-150 MSRP $160

1625
Woman & Child
23cms
*****
$225-325

1626
Tapir
Dahl-Jensen
25cms
*****
$250-500

1627
Woman on bench
18c,s
****
$200-300

1628
Peacock
Dahl-Jensen
40cms
**
1984
$500-650

1629 RC number 409
Polar bear sitting
Dahl-Jensen
19cms
*
$75-125 MSRP $195

1630
Pekinese puppies - pair
Dahl-Jensen
15cms
****
$300-500

1631
Pekinese sitting
Dahl-Jensen
Compare Dahl-Jensen 1003
9cms
***
$100-200

1632
Guillemot
19cms
*****
$150-250

1633 RC number 410
'Optimist' - titmouse
Dahl-Jensen
Compare Dahl-Jensen 1030
13cms
*
Also available in stoneware
$75-125 MSRP $115

1634
Eel
19cms
*****
$125-200

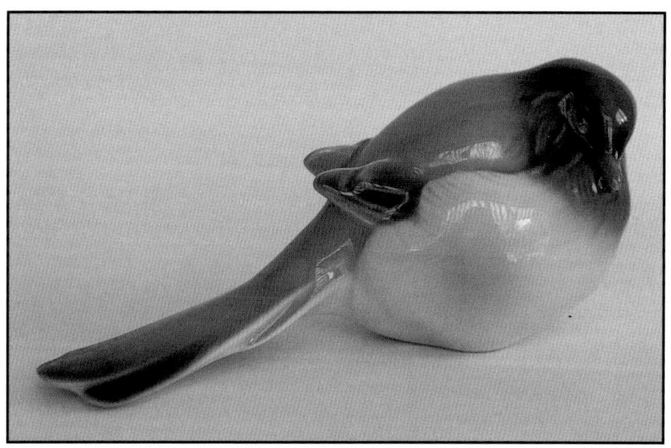

1635 RC number 411
'Pessimist' - titmouse
Dahl-Jensen
13cms
*
Also available in stoneware
$75-125 MSRP $115

1637
Pekinese puppy sitting
Dahl-Jensen
Compare Dahl-Jensen 1003
16cms
***
$350-450

1636 RC number 412
'Dickie'
Ingeborg Plockross Irminger
12cms
*
$75-150 MSRP $225

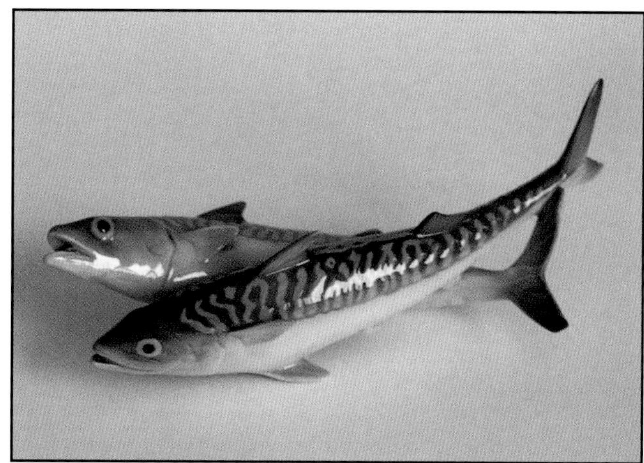

1638
Mackerel - pair
21cms
***
$125-225

1639
Dish with figurine on lid (mouse?)
11cms
****

1640
Mouse
7cms
*****
$75-150

1641
Horse lying
22cms
*****
$225-325

1642 RC number 413
'Dickie's Mama'
Ingeborg Plockross Irminger
22cms
*
$250-450 MSRP $595

1644
Woman with children
Ingeborg Plockross Irminger
28cms
***
$250-450

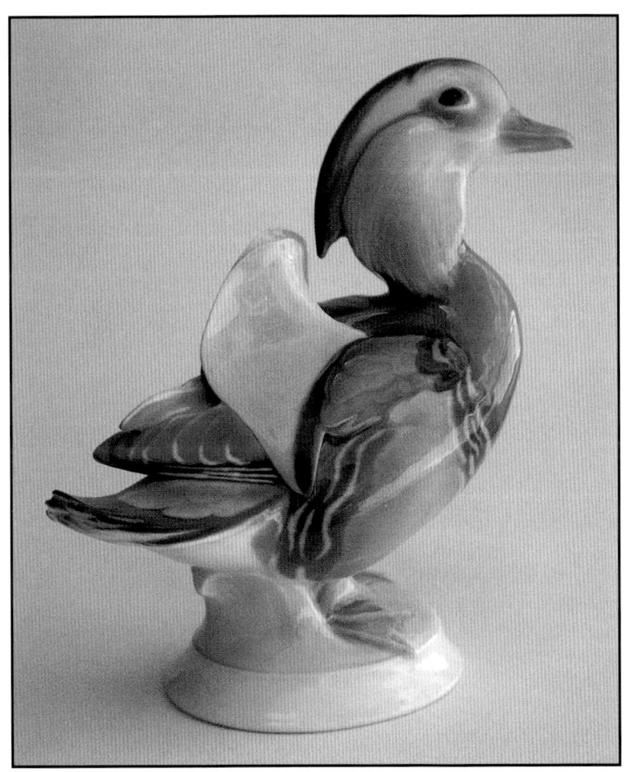

1643
Mandarin duck
26cms
*****
$200-300

1646
Monkey
17cms
***
$150-300

1645
Carp
C Mortensen
22cms
**
In production 1984
$100-200

1647
Monkeys - pair
15cms
*****
$200-400

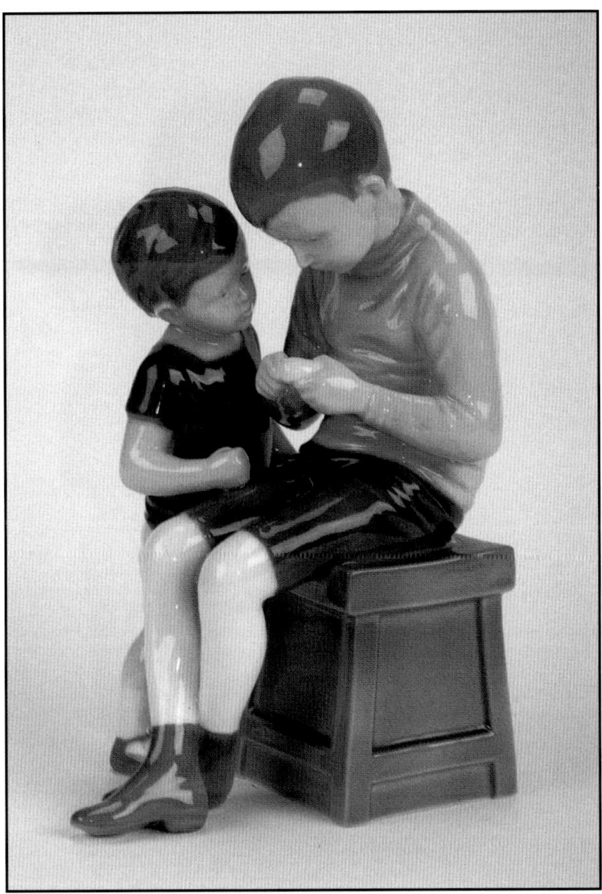

1648
'Tom & Willy'
Ingeborg Plockross Irminger
19cms
**
In production 1988
$125-200

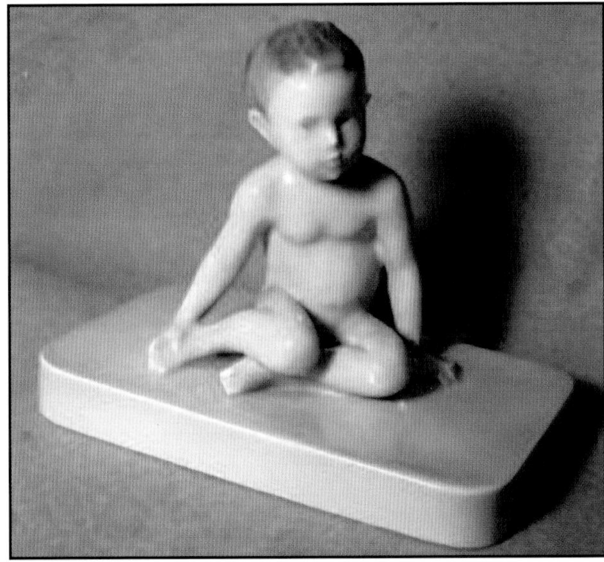

1649
Baby on base
11cms
***
$100-200

1650
Boy on seat
19cms
****
$100-200

1651
Girl sitting?
12cms
****
$100-200

1652
Girl standing
16cms
****
$125-225

1653
Bowl with child sitting on lid
*****

1654
Hound standing
18cms
*****
$200-350

1655
'The Little Match Girl'
Ingeborg Plockross Irminger
14cms
**
In production 1984
$100-200

1660
Boy - naked on tray
22cms
***
$100-200

1656 RC number 414
'Grethe'
Ingeborg Plockross Irminger
17cms
*
$100-175 MSRP $250

1657
Birds - pair
15cms
****
$100-150

1658
Pigeon
9cms
****
$50-100

1659
Carpenter
17cms
****
$300-400

1661
'Merry Sailor'
Ingeborg Plockross Irminger
22cms
**
In production 1988
$150-300

1662
Chick on base
8cms
****
$75-125

1664
Serval
13cms
*****
$250-400

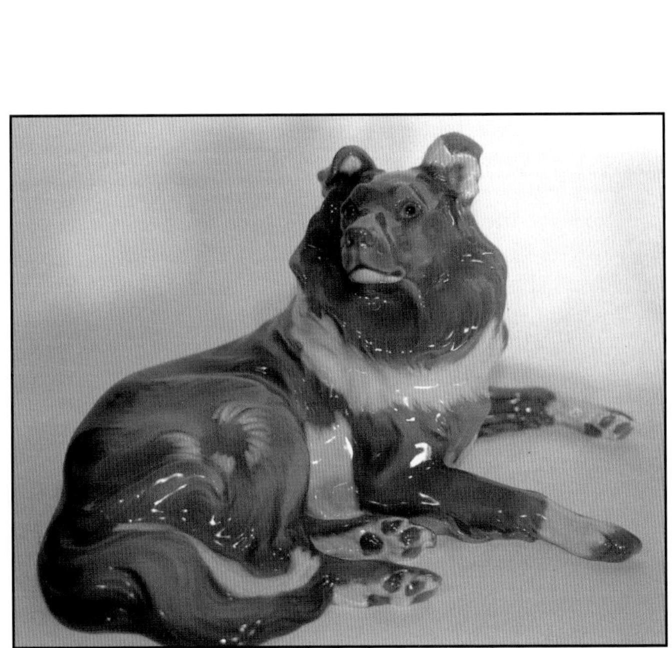

1663
Collie lying
Dahl-Jensen
29cms
***
$350-550

1665
Duck
16cms
***
$50-125

1666
Hawk
Dahl-Jensen
26cms
**
In production 1984
$400-600

1668
Lion on rock
30cms
****
$350-450

1669
Boy sitting
18cms
****
$100-200

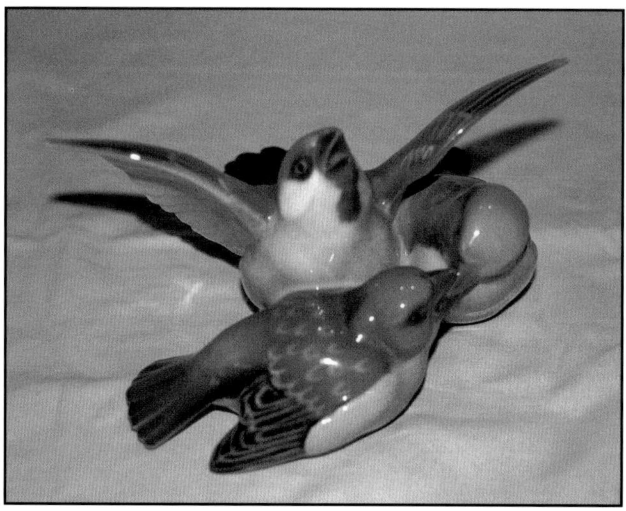

1670 RC number 415
'Protection'
Dahl-Jensen
18cms
*
Also available in stoneware
$100-200 MSRP $275

1667
Monkey
Ingeborg Plockross Irminger
8cms
**
In production 1984
$75-175

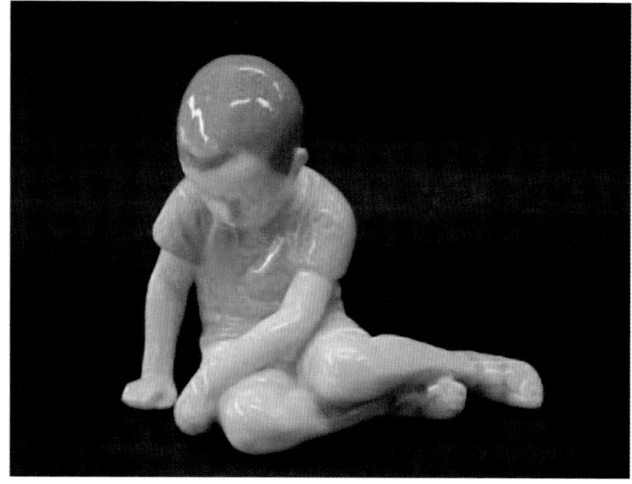

1671
Boy sitting looking down
Ingeborg Plockross Irminger
12cms
**
In production 1984
$50-125

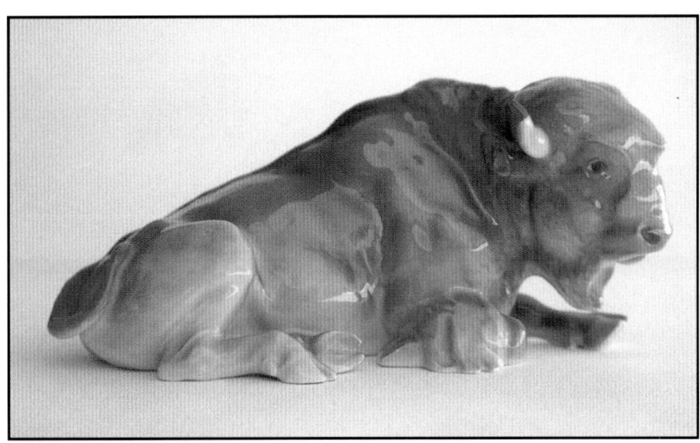

1672
Bison
23cms
*****
$500-800

1673
Cockerel
21cms
****
(see 1749)
$150-250

1675
Crested Tit
Dahl-Jensen
Compare Dahl-Jensen 1050
9cms
**
In production 1984
$75-125

1674
Hen
Michaela Ahlmann
19cms
****
(see 1750)
$150-250

1676
Bulldog
Dahl-Jensen
Compare Dahl-Jensen 1135
11cms
**
In production 1984
$75-175

1677
Lion
30cms
***
$350-450

1678
Lioness
Laurits Jensen
Compare Dahl-Jensen 804
30cms
**
In production 1984
$300-450

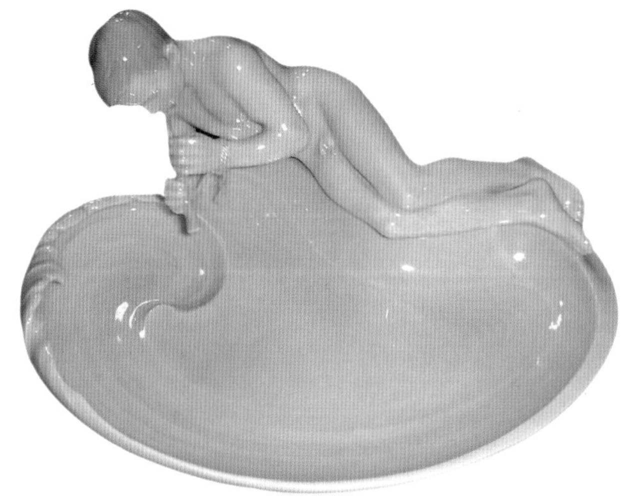

1679
Boy, nude on dish
22cms
****
$100-200

1680
Teenage lovers
31cms
****
$200-300

1681
Children sitting
20cms
****
$100-200

1683
Owl
25cms
*****
$250-350

1687
Girl writing
20cms
****
$100-200

1684 RC number 416
Woman with guitar
Ingeborg Plockross Irminger
24cms
*
$200-300 MSRP $495

1685
Woman washing floor
15cms
****
$200-300

1686
Cat
19
*****
$250-350

1688
Stoat
11cms
*****
$150-250

1689
Coati Mundi
20cms
*****
$300-550

1690
German Shepherd seated
29cms
*****
$450-650

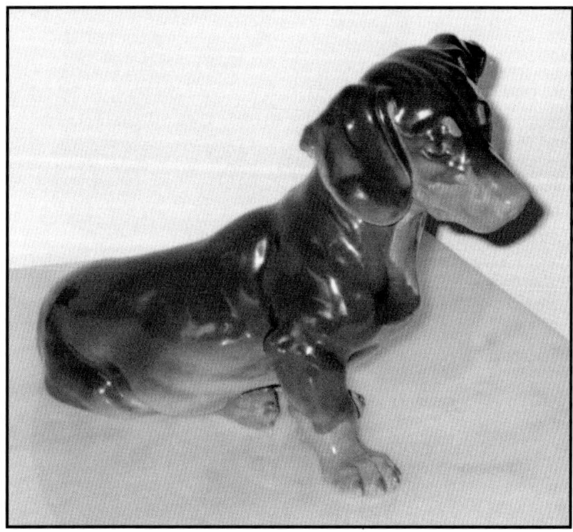

1691
Dachshund sitting
33cms
*****
$450-650

1692 RC number 417
Polar bear sniffing
Niels Nielsen
19cms
*
$75-150 MSRP $195

1693
Impala
Laurits Jensen
23cms
**
In production 1984
$125-250

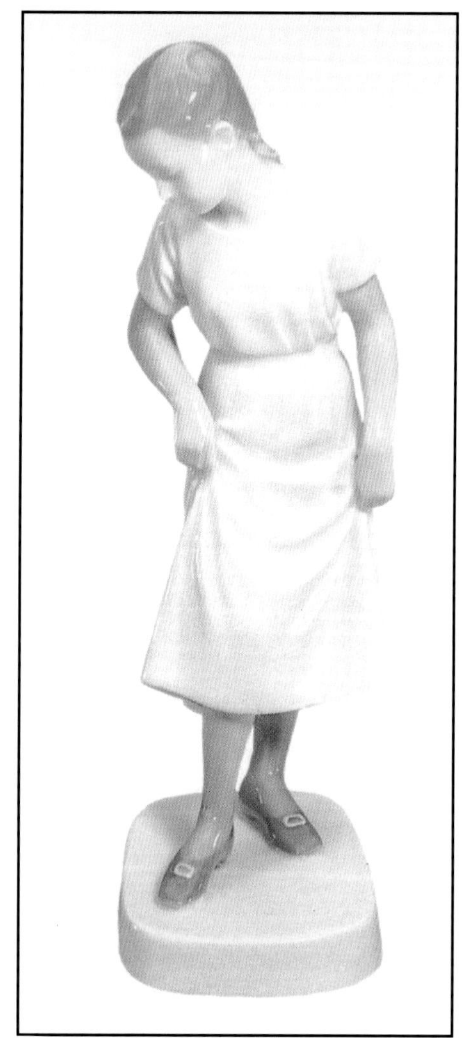

1694
Girl
Ingeborg Plockross Irminger
23cms
****
$100-200

1695
Woman seated
14cms
****
$125-225

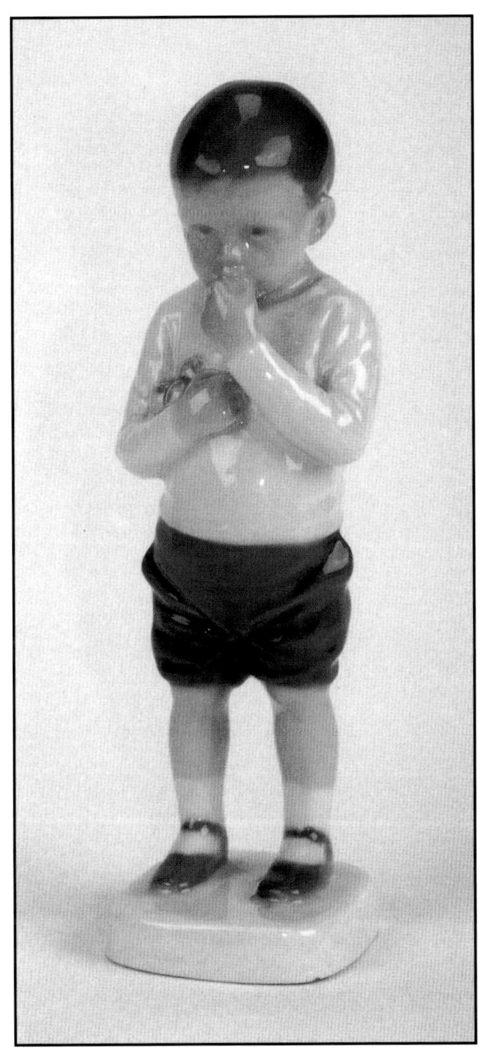

1696
'Peter'
Ingeborg Plockross Irminger
19cms
**
In production 1988
$75-150

1697
Bust
27cms
****
$300-400

1698
Bear on base
8cms
*****
$100-250

1699
Goat
Dahl-Jensen
17cms
**
Also available in stoneware. In production 1984
$75-150

Goat
Dahl-Jensen
16cms
**
Also available in stoneware. In production 1984
$75-150

1703
Woman in coat & large hat
29cms
****
$350-550

1702
Danish Fisherwoman
Kai Nielsen
28cms
**
In production 1984
$175-275

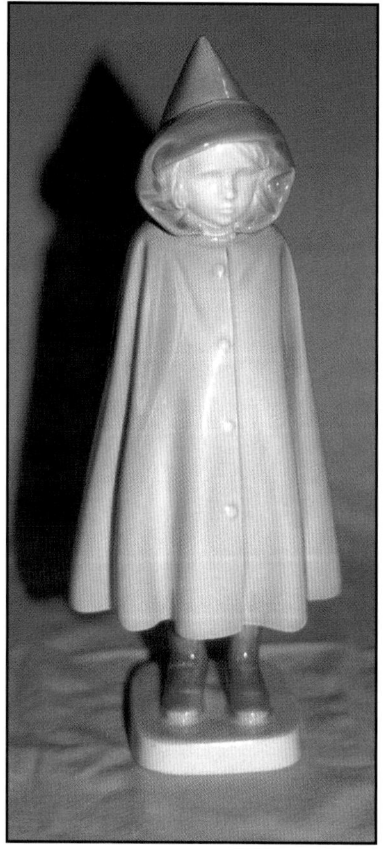

1705
Girl in cloak
24cms
****
$300-475

1706
Woman sitting
20cms
***
$300-500

1707
Finch
Dahl-Jensen
11cms
**
In production 1984
$50-100

1708
Finch group
Dahl-Jensen
12cms
**
In production 1988
$75-125

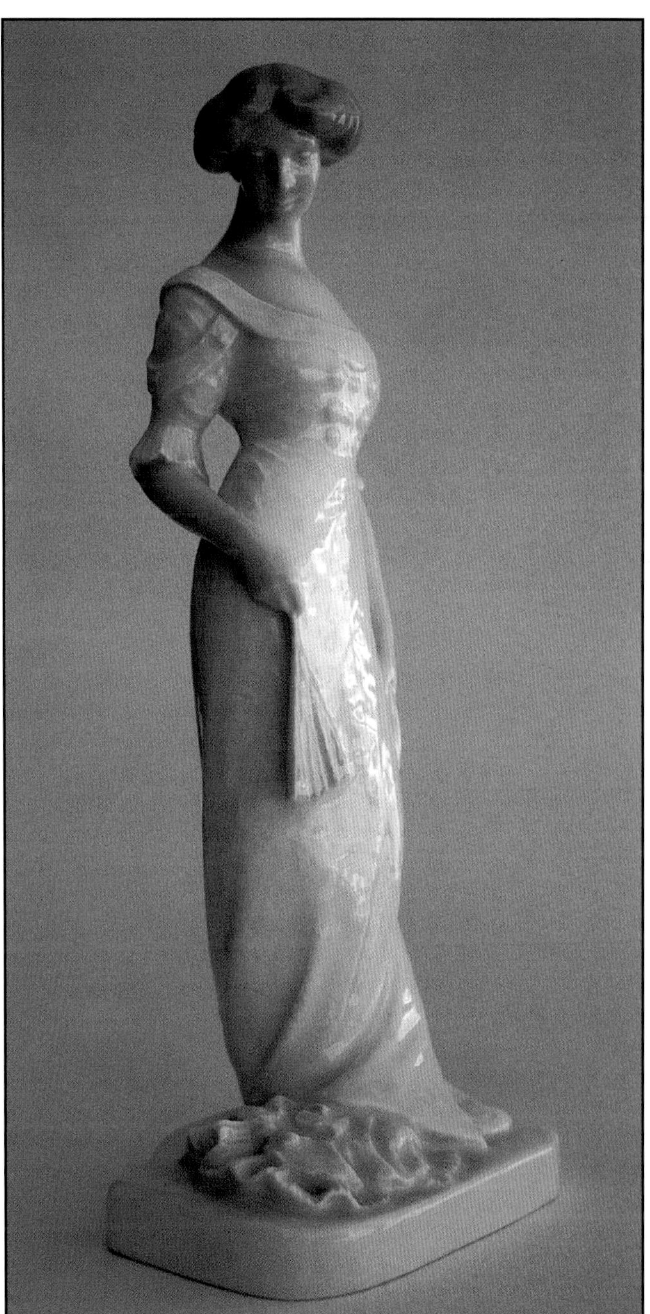

1709
Woman standing
29cms
****
$325-500

1710
Woman doing hair
22cms
****
$325-500

1711
Woman sitting
19cms
****
$300-500

1712
Tiger - snarling
Laurits Jensen
Compare Dahl-Jensen 1246 and 1285
29cms
**
In production 1984
$550-900

1714
Crow
Dahl-Jensen
33cms
**
Also available in stoneware. In production 1984
$125-225

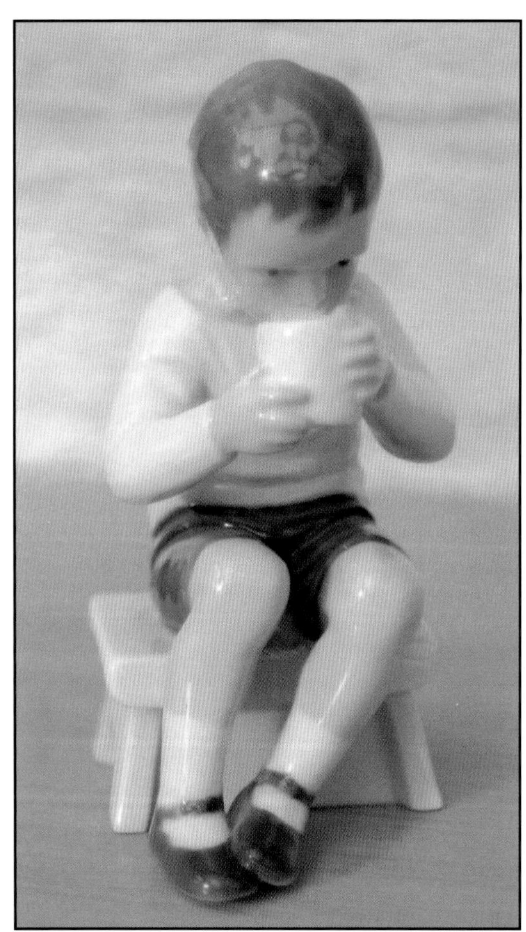

1713 RC number 418
'Victor'
Ingeborg Plockross Irminger
13cms
*
$100-175 MSRP $250

1715
Skater
Ingeborg Plockross Irminger
18.5cms
****
$250-350

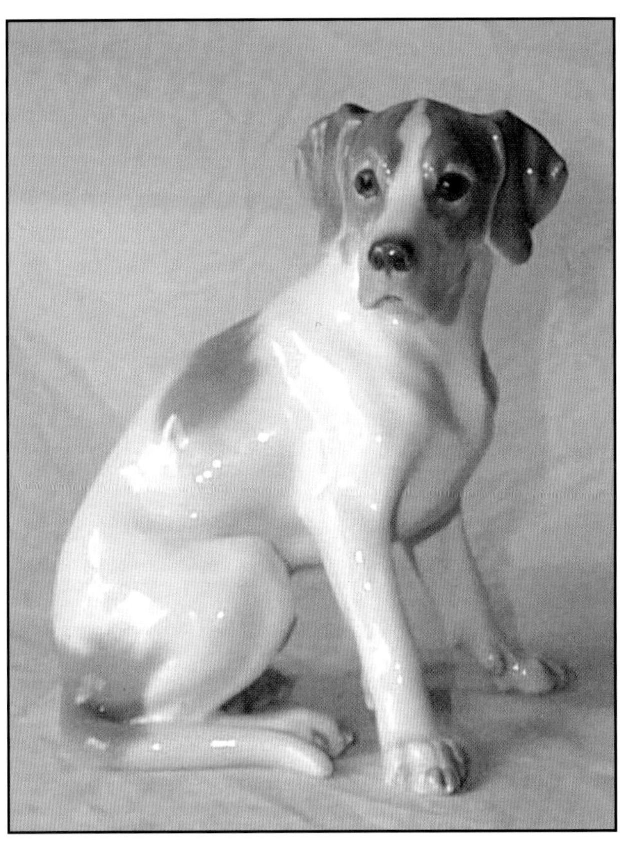

1716
Pointer sitting
18cms
***
$200-350

1718
Mouse
7.5cms
***
$175-300

1719
Fox
30cms
***
$300-550

1720
Boy in cloak
21cms
****
$175-300

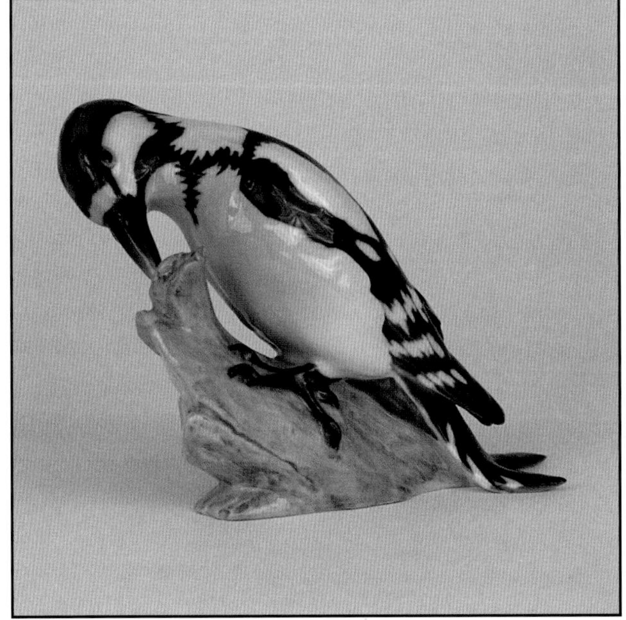

1717
Woodpecker
Dahl-Jensen
Compare Dahl-Jensen 1343
19cms
**
In production 1984
$75-175

1721 RC number 561
'Mary'
Ingeborg Plockross Irminger
19
*
Available with blue or spotted dress and also as a doll
$75-150

1722
Squirrel
Dahl Jensen
17cms
*****
$250-450

1723
Pointer playing
30cms
****
$400-650

1724
Man in uniform
28cms
****
$350-450

1725
Seagull with fish
Dahl-Jensen
37cms
**
In production 1988
$100-200

1726
Seagull
35cms
***
$75-125

1727
Seagull
27cms
***
$100-200

1728 RC number 419
Mouse - white
Dahl-Jensen
Compare Dahl-Jensen 1010
5cms
*
See 1801
$30-60 MSRP $65

1729
Violinist
23cms
****
$350-450

1730
Bird
13cms
****
$75-150

1732
Mouse
14cms
*****
$100-200

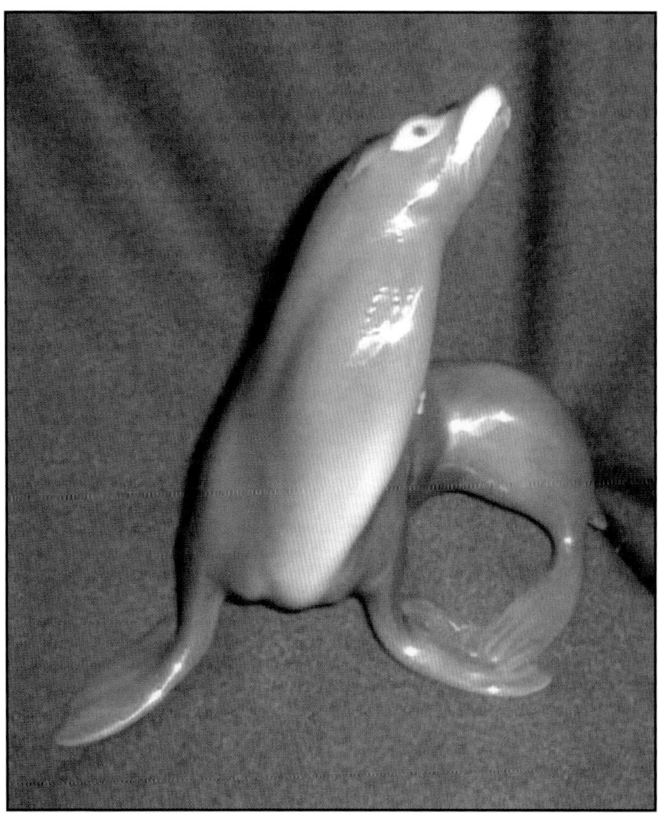

1733
Seal
Knud Moller
19cms
**
In production 1984
$100-200

1734 →
Woman of fashion
Valdemar Andersen
30cms
****
Available in various colors
$350-450

1735
Guinea Fowl
26cms
****
$100-200

1736
Woman with washing
26cms
****
$300-400

1737
Children on toboggan
17cms
****
$100-200

1738
Duck
10cms
****
$50-100

1739
Toucan
18cms
****
$200-300

1740
Cockatoo on base
33cms
****
$200-300

1741
Rabbit
30cms
*****
$225-325

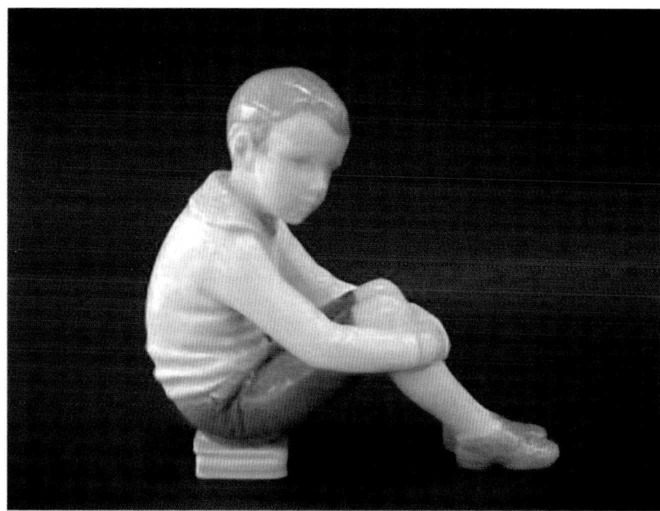

1742
'School's Out'
Ingeborg Plockross Irminger
13cms
**
In production 1984
$75-150

1743
Boy sitting
17cms
****
$100-200

1744 RC number 420
Blackcock (Black grouse)
Dahl-Jensen
41cms
*
$700-850

1745 RC number 421
'Only one drop'
Ingeborg Plockross Irminger
15cms
*
$125-245 MSRP $350

1746
Dachshund sitting
19cms
*****
$300-500

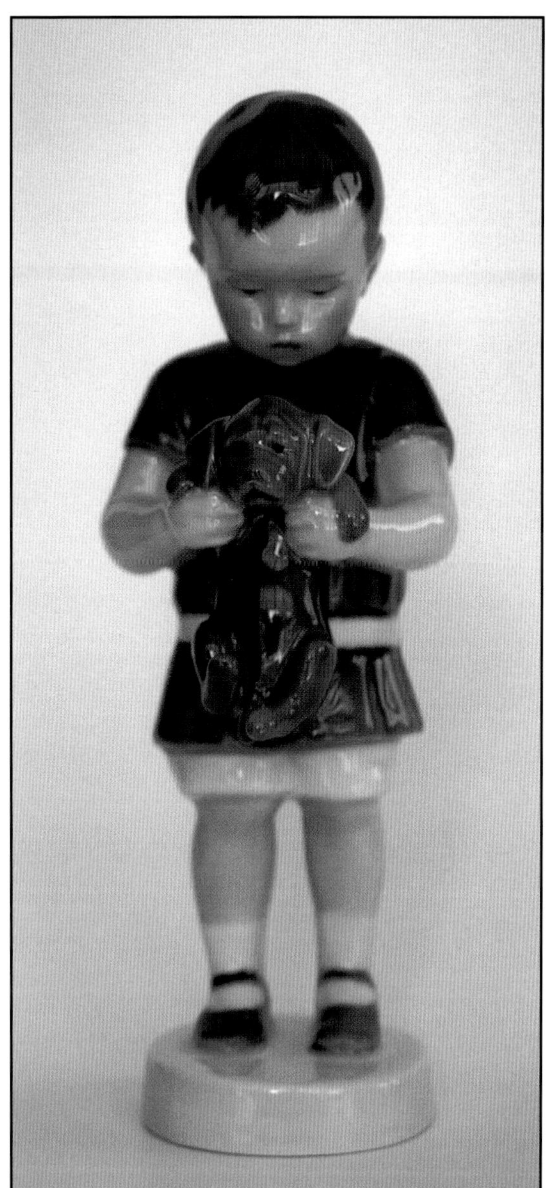

1747 RC number 422
'Ole'
Ingeborg Plockross Irminger
17cms
*
$125-225 MSRP $275

1749
Cockerel
21cms
****
(see 1673)
$150-250

1750
Hen
19cms
****
(see 1674)
$150-250

1751
Duck
25cms
*****
$225-325

1752
Dachshund
Dahl-Jensen
19cms
***
$150-300

1753
Puppy sitting
18cms
*****
$300-450

1754
Cat
23cms
*****
$300-400

1755
Dachshund
Dahl-Jensen
7cms
**
In production 1984
$50-150

1756
Man carrying box
28cms
****
$250-350

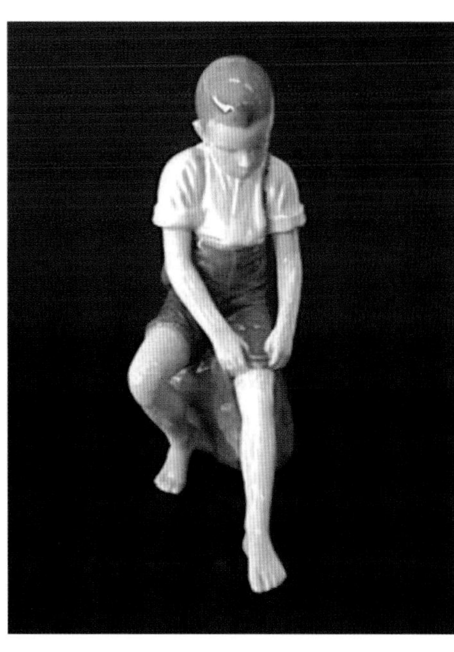

1757
'Paddling About'
Ingeborg Plockross Irminger
20cms
**
In production 1984
$125-200

1758
Girl
14cms
****
$100-200

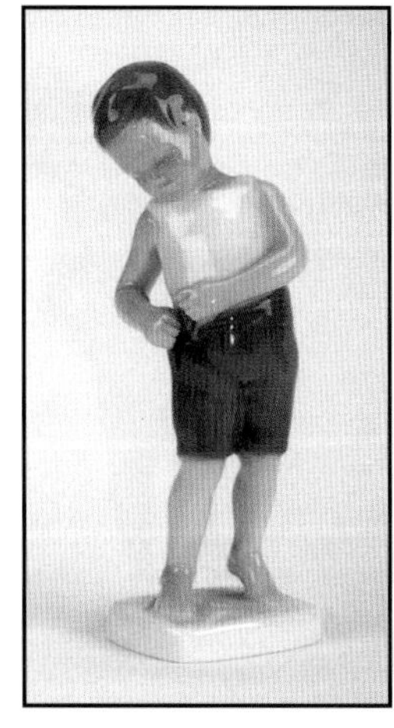

1759
'Tiny Tot'
Michaela Ahlmann
15cms
**
In production 1984
$50-150

1764
Wagtail
Dahl-Jensen
Compare Dahl-Jensen 1233 and 1248
14cms
**
In production 1984
$75-150

1760
Jay
21cms
***
$75-175

1761
Girls standing
Ingeborg Plockross Irminger
23cms
****
$150-250

1762a
Bear sitting
15cms
*****
$250-400

1762b
Bear sitting on base
19cms
*****
$300-450

1763
Donkey?
20cms
*****

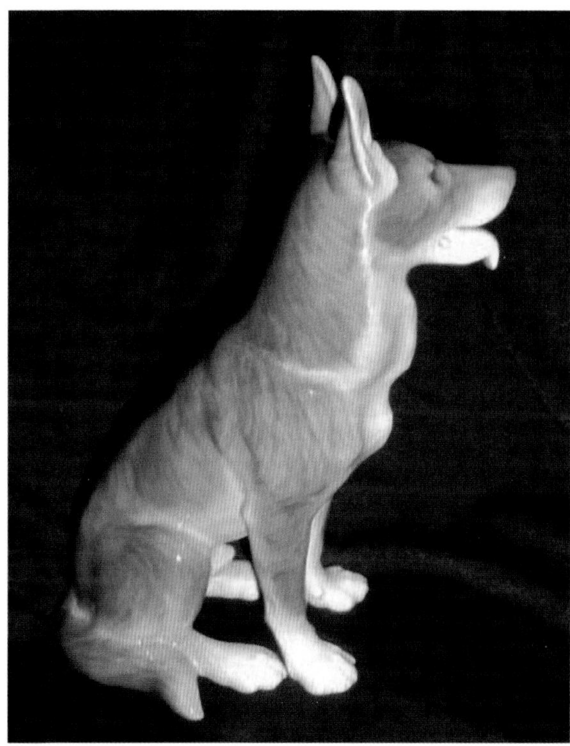

1765
German Shepherd
Laurits Jensen
22cms
**
In production 1984
$300-450

1766
Woman standing
28cms
****
$300-400

1770 RC number 423
Cuckoo
Dahl-Jensen
Compare Dahl-Jensen 1314
24cms
*
Stoneware
$150-300 MSRP $495

1771
Finch?
9cms
***
$75-150

1772
Hunter
30cms
****
$200-300

1767
Squirrel on branch
20cms
*****
$250-400

1768
Butterfly
5cms
*****
$100-200

1769
Cow
21cms
****
$150-250

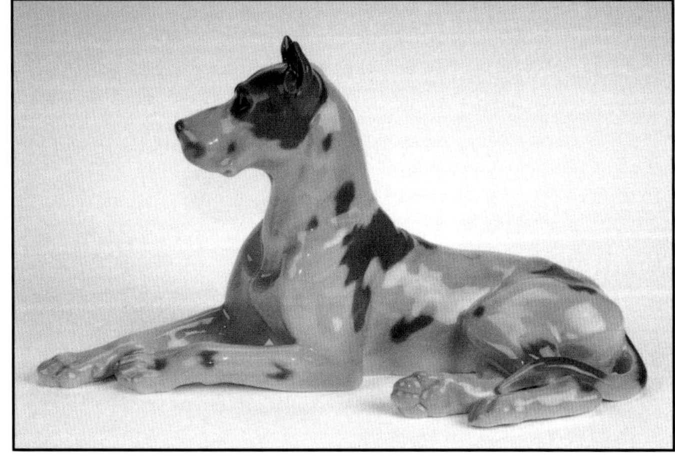

1773
Great Dane
Laurits Jensen
29cms
**
In production 1984
$300-450

1775
Swallow
Dahl-Jensen
14cms
**
Also available in stoneware. In production 1984
$75-150

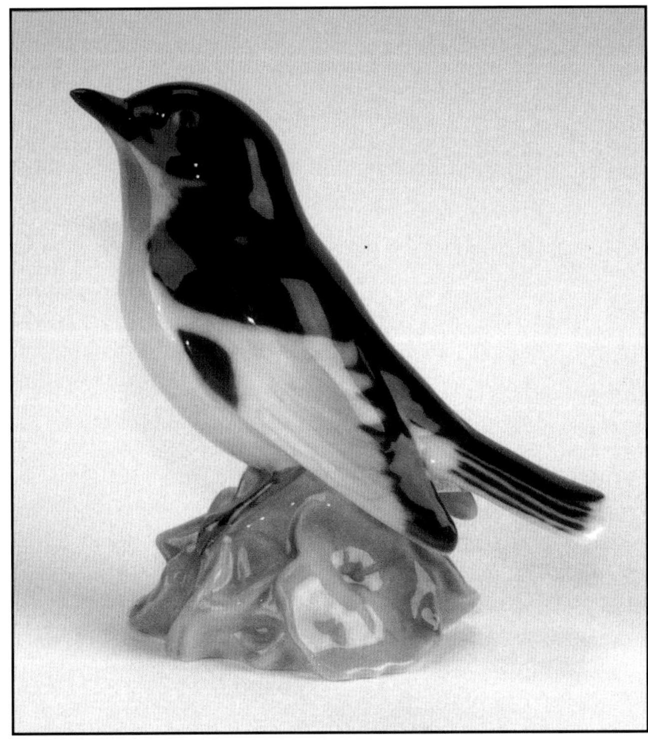

1776
Flycatcher
Dahl-Jensen
10cms
**
In production 1984
$75-125

1777
Bird?
14cms
****
$75-150

1778
Birds on base
9cms
****
$75-150

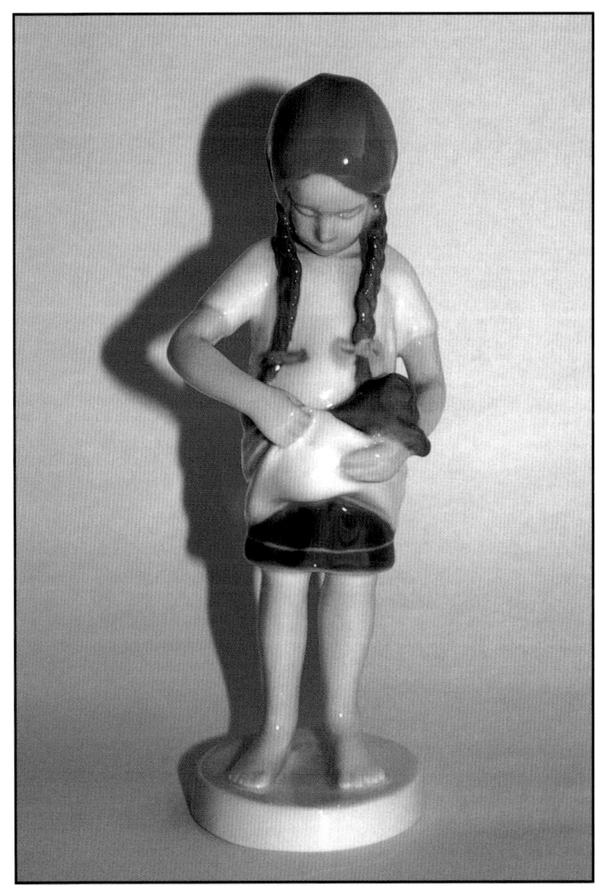

1779 RC number 424
'Little Mother'
Ingeborg Plockross Irminger
17cms
*
$100-175 MSRP $240

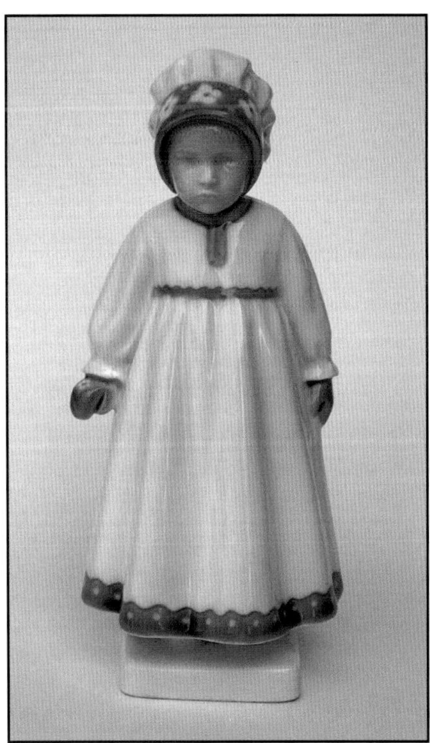

1780
Girl
Ingeborg Plockross Irminger
21cms
****
$150-250

1781
Girl with boy
Michaela Ahlmann
21cms
**
In production 1984
$125-225

1782
Boy standing
20cms
****
$100-200

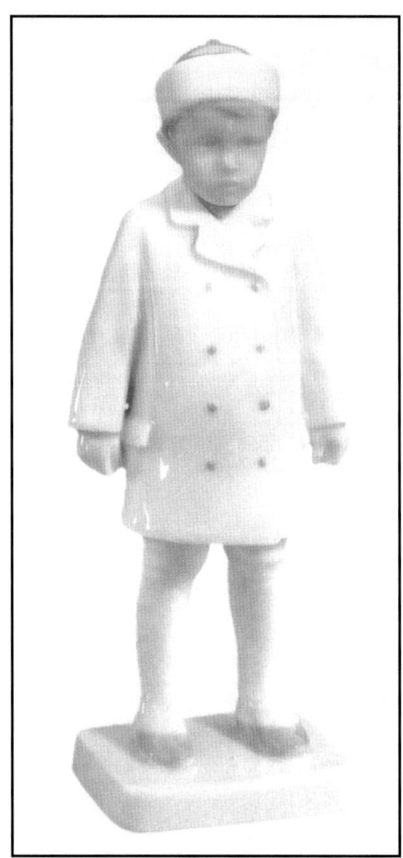

1783
Boy in coat/hat (formal)
Ingeborg Plockross Irminger
21cms
****
$125-225

1784
Silver pheasant
Dahl-Jensen
43cms
**
In production 1988
$700-850

1785 RC number 425
Polar bear walking
Niels Nielsen
30cms
*
See 2218
$125-300 MSRP $285

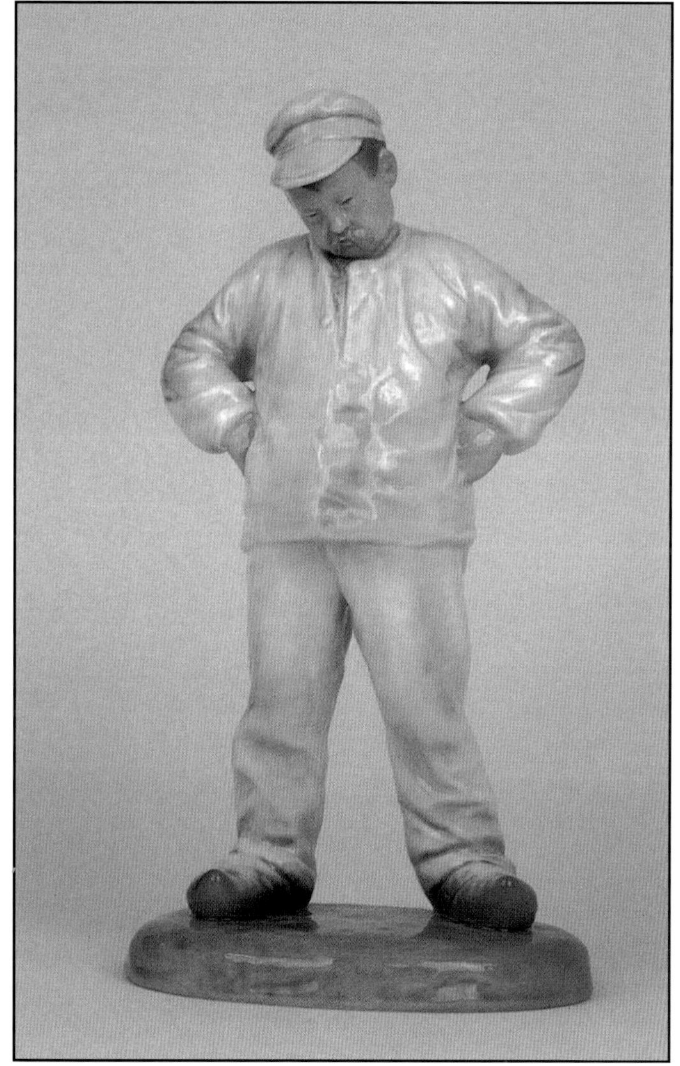

1786 RC number 426
Mason
Niels Nielsen
29cms
*
$200-300 MSRP $775

1787
Boy standing
20cms
****
$100-200

1788
Pointer sitting
20cms
***
$300-450

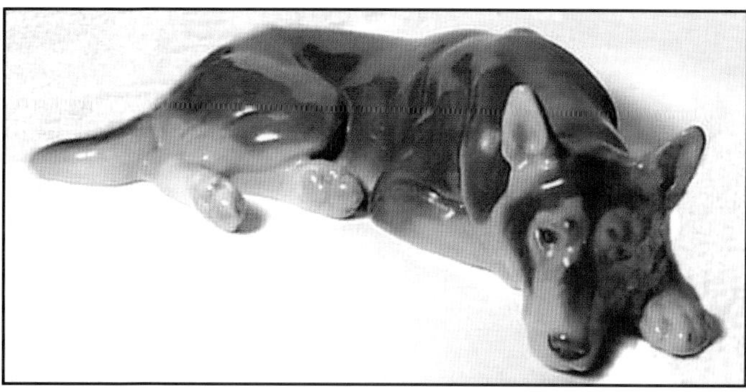

1789
German Shepherd
Laurits Jensen
24cms
***
$300-450

1790 RC number 427
'Two Friends'
Michaela Ahlmann
12cms
*
$100-200 MSRP $350

1791
Llama?
13cms
*****
$150-300

1793
Lion
Laurits Jensen
Compare Dahl-Jensen 1286
34cms
**
In production 1984.
$600-900

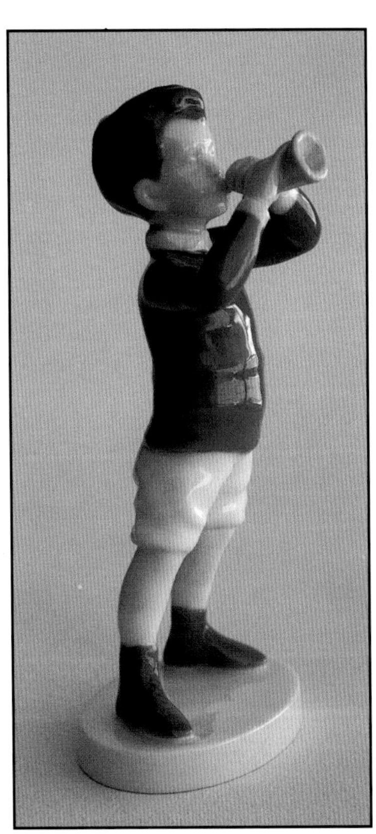

1792
Boy with trumpet
Michaela Ahlmann
18cms
**
In production 1984
$75-125

1794
'Good toes, bad toes'
Michaela Ahlmann
20cms
**
In production 1984
$100-175

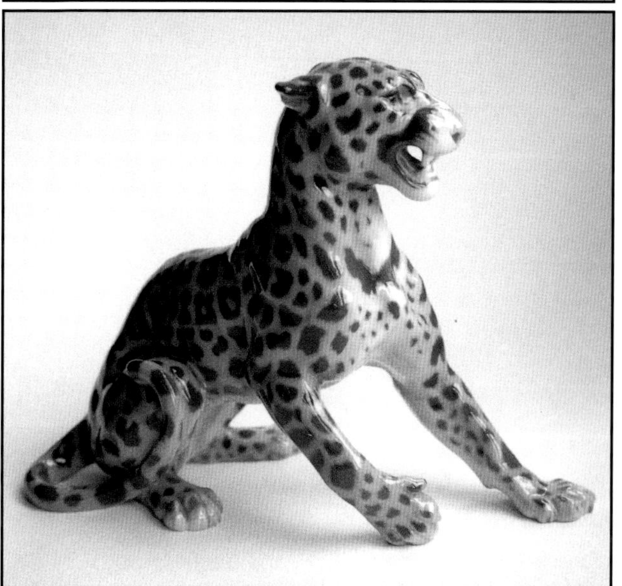

1795
Eagle - golden
Dahl-Jensen
51cms
**
In production 1988
$1750-2750

1796
Baby sitting
15cms
*****
$100-200

1797
Panther
27cms
****
$500-850

1798
Girl standing
21cms
****
$100-200

1799
Cat playing with ball
25cms
*****
$150-250

1801
Mouse gray
Dahl-Jensen
Compare Dahl-Jensen 1010
5cms
**
See 1728. In production 1988
$30-70

1800
Owl
Dahl-Jensen
Compare Dahl-Jensen 1389
11cms
**
In production 1988
$50-100

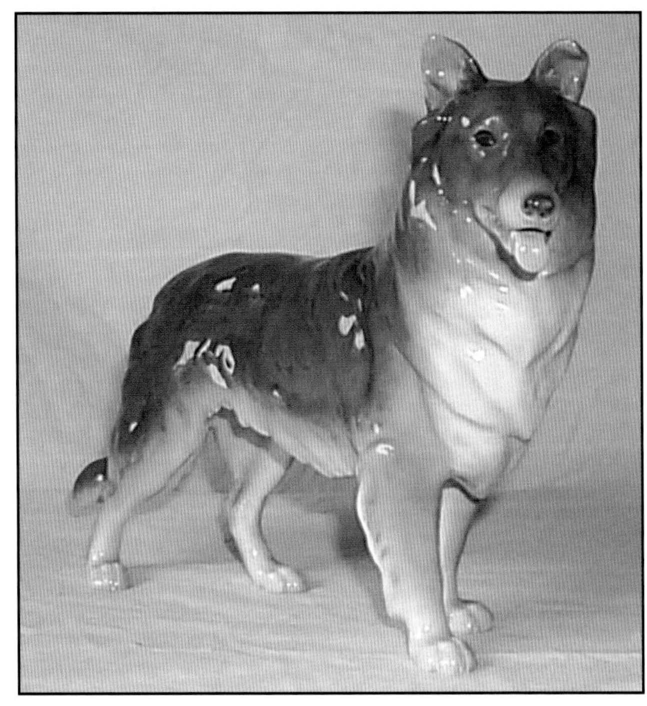

1802
Collie standing
28cms
*****
$500-750

1803
Trout
Dahl-Jensen
22cms
**
In production 1984
$75-125

1804
Bear walking
16cms
***
$75-125

1805
Dachshunds - pair
Dahl-Jensen
10cms
***
$150-200

1806
Elephant
18cms
***
$200-300

1807
Cat sitting
20cms
****
$300-400

1808 RC number 428
Gull with fish
Dahl-Jensen
Compare Dahl-Jensen 1318
14cms
*
$50-125 MSRP $90

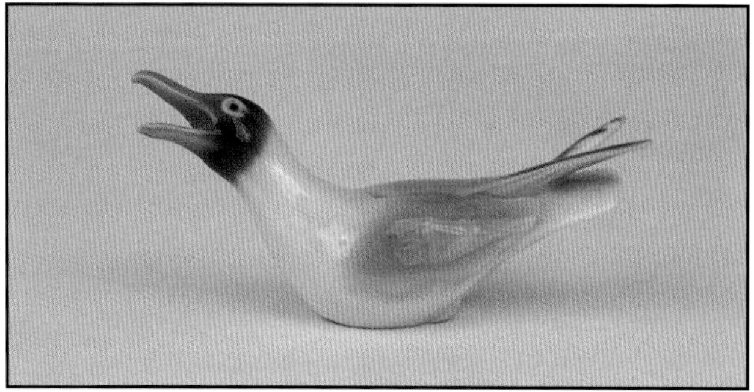

1809 RC number 429
Gull crying
Dahl-Jensen
Compare Dahl-Jensen 1318
9cms
*
$50-125 MSRP $75

1810 RC number 430
Gull
Dahl-Jensen
Compare Dahl-Jensen 1361
9cms
*
$50-125 MSRP $75

1811
Borzoi lying
Laurits Jensen
29cms
****
$400-600

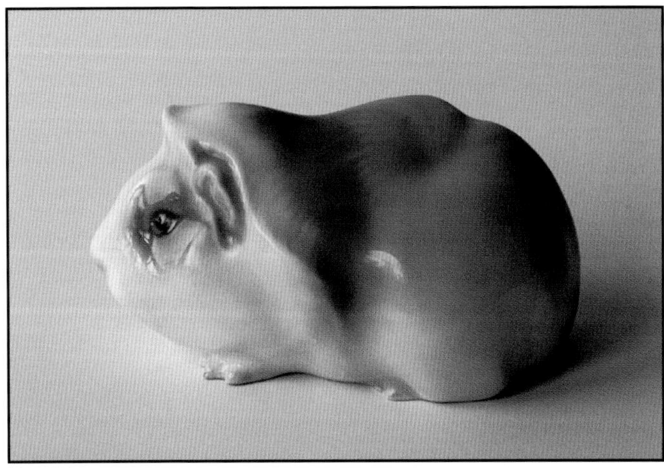

1812
Guinea-pig
17cms
*****
$225-325

1813
Elephant
18cms
***
$200-300

1814
Borzoi sitting
Laurits Jensen
22cms
****
$400-600

1815
Pointer puppies playing - three?
20cms
*****
$500-750

1816
Bears playing
14cms
*****
$150-350

1817
Swan
16cms
*****
$100-200

1818
Swan
15cms
*****
$100-200

1821 RC number 431
Penguin
Sveistrup Madsen
Compare Dahl-Jensen 1073
8cms
*
$40-60 MSRP $85

1822
Penguin - Blackfoot
Sveistrup Madsen
23cms
**
In production 1984
$125-200

1823
Lion with lioness
Knud Kyhn
37cms
*****
$650-900

1824
Bear brown
15cms
*****
$150-300

1825
Bears playing
19cms
**
In production 1984
$150-300

1828
Brother and sister
15cms
****
$150-250

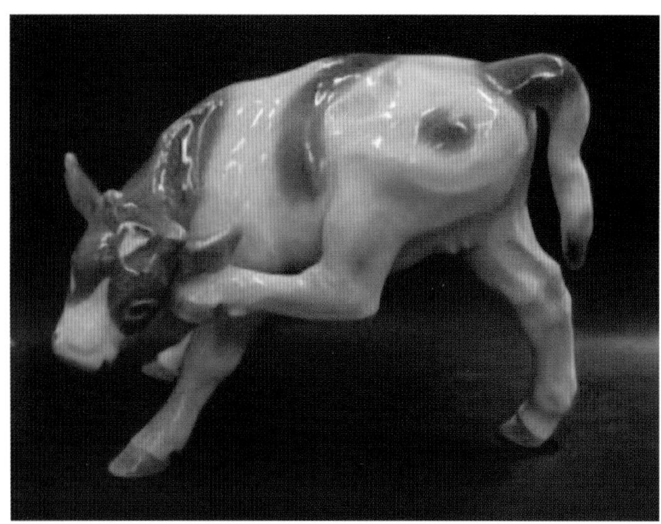

1826 RC number 432
Calf scratching ear
Knud Kyhn
18cms
*
$100-200 MSRP $370

1827
Boy standing
22cms
****
$75-150

1829
Mother with baby
31cms
****
$400-550

1830
Rabbits - lying
16cms
*****
$150-250

1831
Rabbit - lying
20cms
*****
$125-250

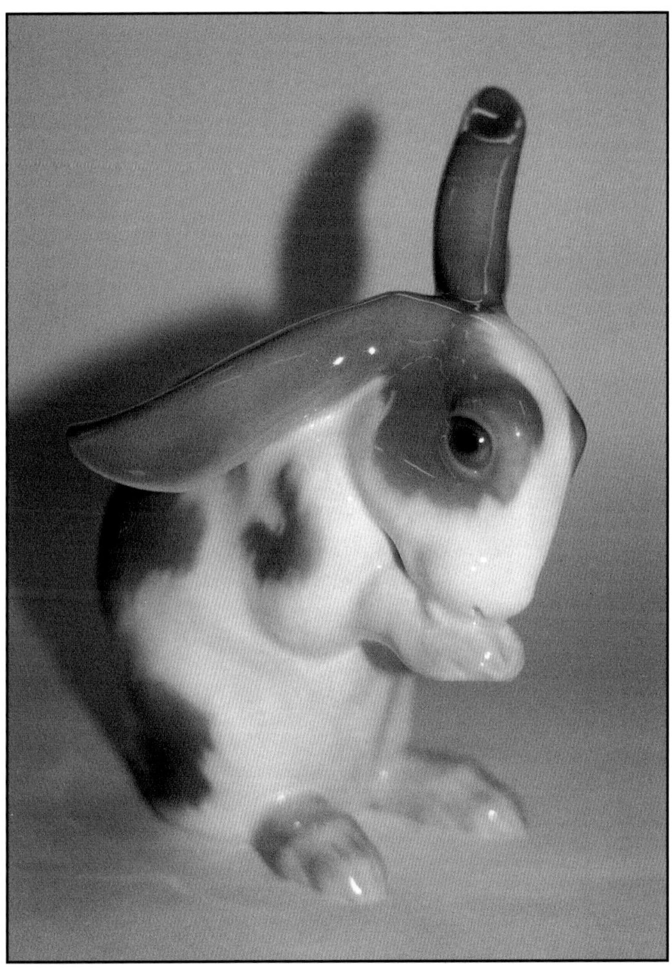

1832
Rabbit
15cms
****
$100-200

1833
Rabbit
Dahl-Jensen
11cms
***
$75-125

1834
Cat curled
20cms
*****
$250-350

1835
Elephants - pair
22cms
*****
$600-900

1836
Boy lying
19cms
****
$100-200

1837
Cat with ball
20cms
*****
$200-300

1838
Ballet dancer
15cms
****
$125-225

1839
Girl with toy
17cms
****
$100-200

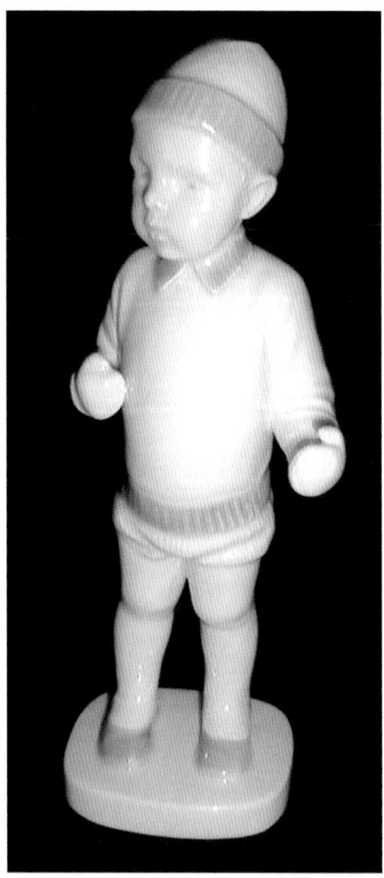

1843
Boy standing
23cms
****
$100-175

1841
Girl sitting
Ingeborg Plockross Irminger
21cms
****
$150-250

1842
Pigs pair
21cms
*****
$200-300

1844
Cat
Dahl-Jensen
30cms
*****
$200-300

1845
'Dancing School'
Ingeborg Plockross Irminger
21cms
**
In production 1984
$100-200

1846
Owl on base
Dahl-Jensen
Compare Dahl-Jensen 1104
51cms
***
$2000-3000

1847
Girl sitting
12cms
****
$100-175

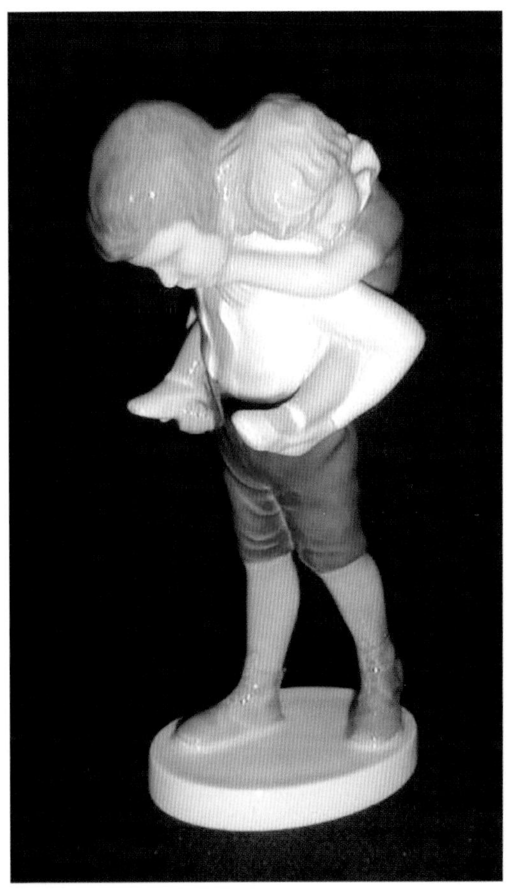

1848
Playfellows
Michaela Ahlmann
19cms
***
$100-200

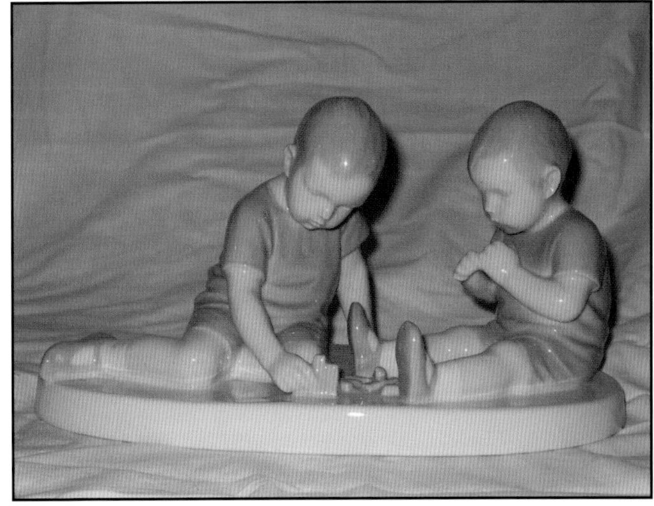

1849
Boys playing with bricks
24cms
****
$125-225

1850
Goldfinch
Dahl-Jensen
Compare Dahl-Jensen 1232
8cms
**
In production 1984
$75-125

1851
Lovebird
16cms
****
$100-175

1853
Wren
Knud Kyhn
7cms
**
In production 1984
$40-100

1852
Sparrow - fledgling
Knud Kyhn
7cms
**
Also available in stoneware. In production 1988
$40-80

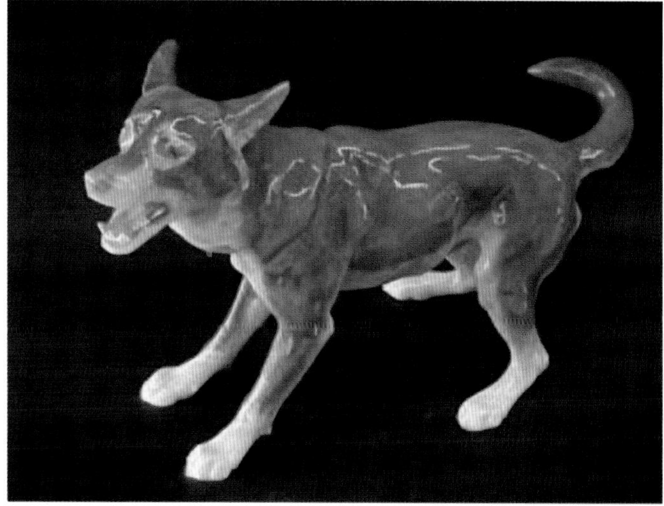

1854
German Shepherd
32cms
***
$300-450

1855
Tufted duck
Dahl-Jensen
Compare Dahl-Jensen 1281
10cms
**
Also available in stoneware. In production 1988
$50-100

1856
Bird
10cms
****
$75-150

1857 RC number 433
Polar bear
Knud Khyn
37cms
*
$400-650 MSRP $975

1858
Elephant and Mahout
37cms
*****
$600-1000

1859
Bird
20cms
****
$150-250

1860
Turkey chick
10cms
****
$75-150

1861
Dachshunds - pair
19cms
*****
$250-450

1862
Crab?
9cms
*****
$100-200

1863
Mice?
6cms
*****
$100-200

1864
Sparrow fledglings
13cms
****
$75-150

1865
Mice - pair
8cms
*****
$150-250

1866
Red Cross Nurse
17cms
****
$350-450

1867
Red Cross Nurse
20cms
****
$300-450

1868
Lemur
12cms
*****
$300-450

1869
Sparrow with young
Dahl-Jensen
15cms
**
In production 1988
$100-200

1870
Boy with crab
Ingeborg Plockross Irminger
20cms
**
In production 1984
$100-200

1871
Sisters
Ingeborg Plockross Irminger
18cms
****
$350-450

1872
Polar bear cub
6cms
***
$40-60

1875 RC number 434
Rabbits sitting
Niels Nielsen
6cms
*
Also available in stoneware.
$30-60 MSRP $55

1873
Polar bear cub
6cms
***
$40-60

1874
Rabbit
Niels Nielsen
6cms
**
Also available in stoneware. In production 1988
$30-60

1876 RC number 435
Cat sitting
Ingeborg Plockross Irminger
12cms
*
Also available in stoneware. See 2453 color variation
$75-125 MSRP $125

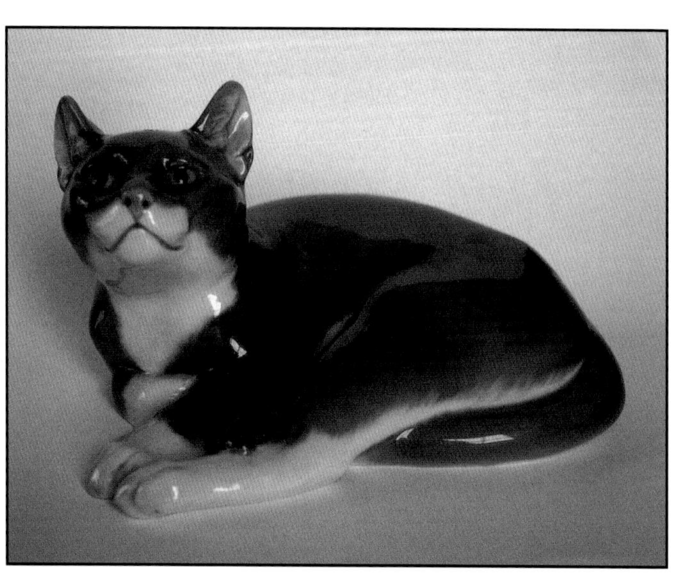

1878
Cat
Niels Nielsen
20cms
*****
$75-125

1879
Girl sitting
Ingeborg Plockross Irminger
18cms
****
$175-275

1880
Starling
Niels Nielsen
18cms
**
In production 1984
$75-150

1881
Pig
6cms
***
$20-60

1882
Pig
6cms
***
$20-60

1885 RC number 436
Kingfisher
Niels Nielsen
11cms
*
$75-150 MSRP $175

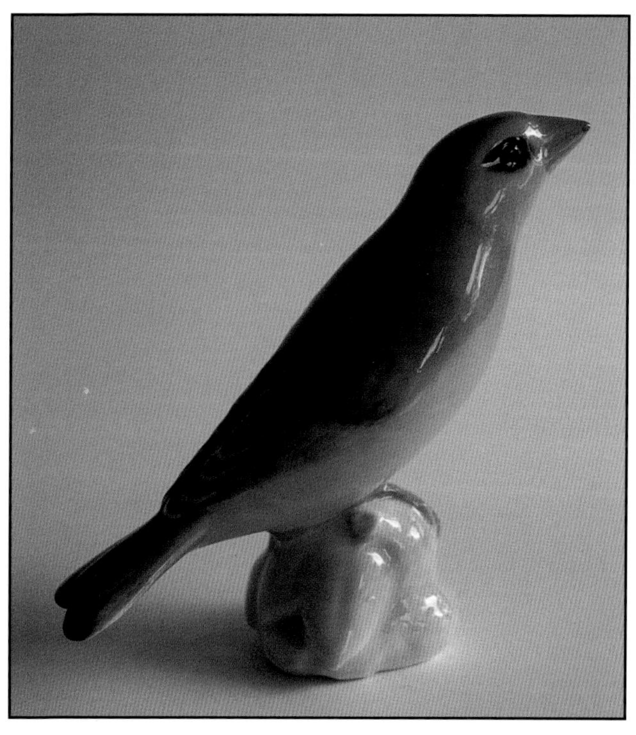

1887
Linnet
Niels Nielsen
11cms
***
$75-125

1888
Sparrow on base
Niels Nielsen
13cms
**
In production 1988
$75-125

1889
Cat curled
****
$200-300

1890
Dog standing
30cms
*****
$450-650

1891
Cat drinking from bowl
17cms
*****
$300-450

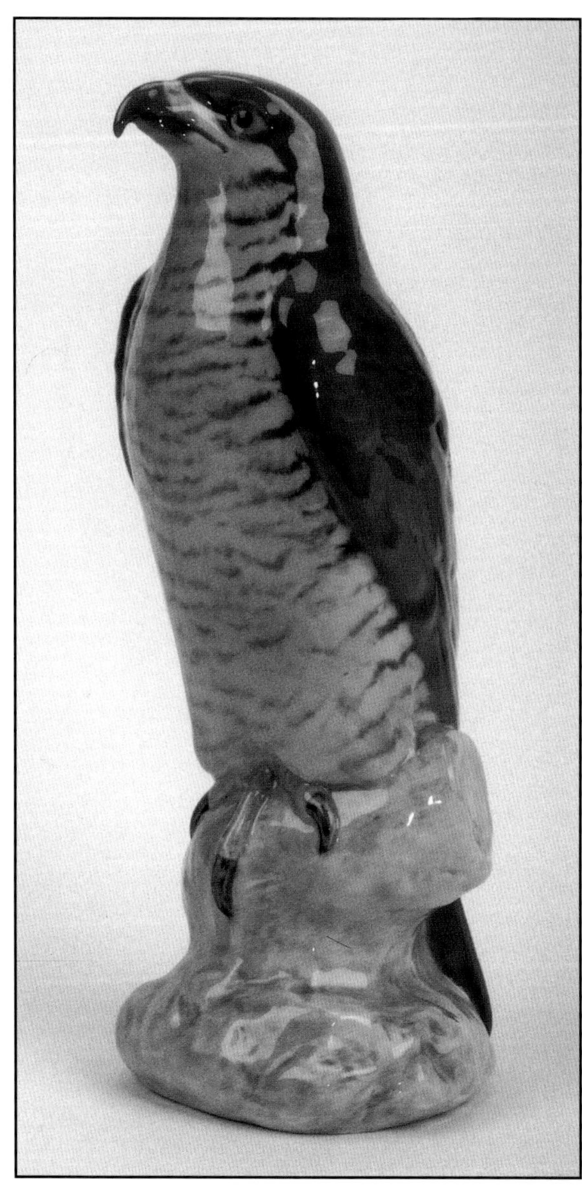

1892
Sparrow Hawk
Niels Nielsen
28cms
**
Also available in stoneware. In production 1988
$450-600

1893
French Bulldog
13cms
****
$100-200

1894
Kangaroo
28cms
*****
$400-700

1895
Pug sitting
8cms
****
$75-150

1897
Flute player
Ingeborg Plockross Irminger
29cms
**
In production 1984
$150-250

1898
Skunk
22cms
*****
$300-500

1899a and 1899b
Boy standing
25cms
****
Available in 2 versions
$350-450

1900
Rabbit
17cms
*****
$300-400

1901
Boy in raincoat
25cms
****
$300-400

1902 RC number 437
Goose
Niels Nielsen
9cms
*
$30-60 MSRP $75

1903
Pug sitting
13cms
****
$100-200

1905
Fox sitting
16cms
****
$150-250

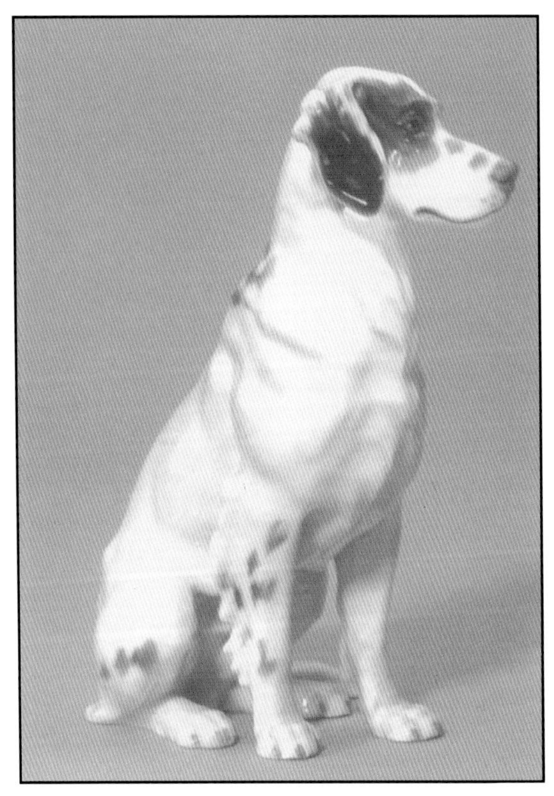

1904
Gordon Setter
Laurits Jensen
21cms
****
$200-350

1906
Foxes - pair
Niels Nielsen
16cms
*****
$450-550

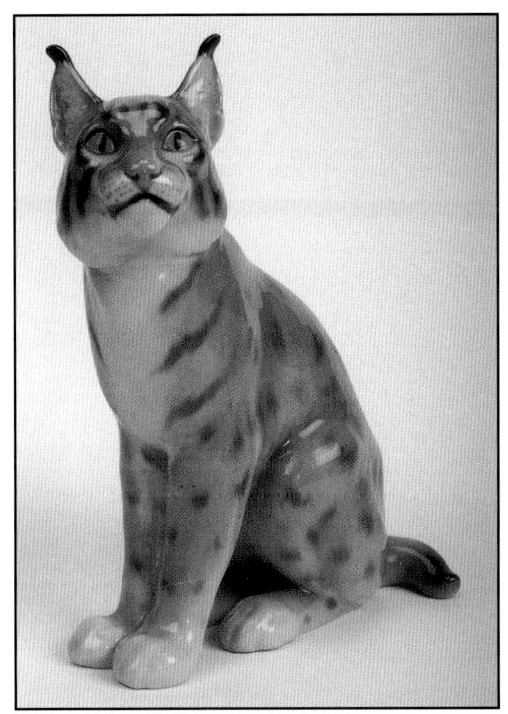

1907
Lynx
20cms
*****
$500-800

1909 RC number 438
Bullfinch
Niels Nielsen
12cms
*
$75-125 MSRP $180

1908
Schoolgirl
28cms
****
$350-450

1910
Mother with two girls
25cms
***
$250-450

1911
Pigeon
Niels Nielsen
22cms
**
In production 1984
$100-200

1913
Schoolboy
29cms
****
$350-450

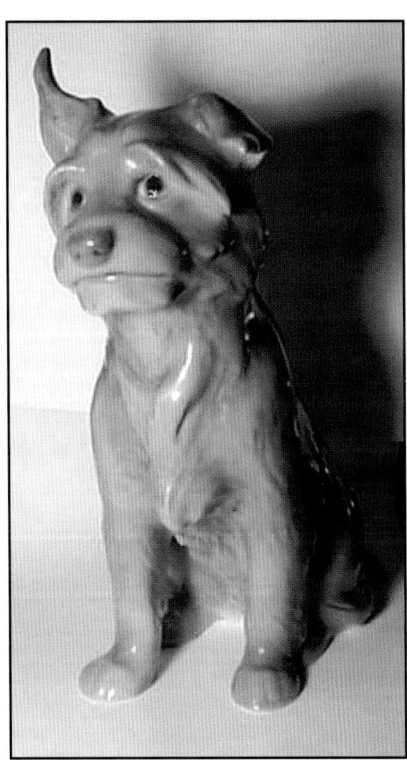

1914
Cairn terrier sitting
20cms
****
$225-350

1915
Bear
18cms
*****
$300-400

1916
St Bernard
26cms
****
$450-650

1917
Dog standing
29cms
*****
$450-650

1918
Poodle sitting
21cms
*****
$400-550

1919
Fox cub?
17cms
*****
$200-350

1920
Boy with kitten and cat
30cms
****
$350-450

1921
Terrier standing
15cms
****
$200-300

1922
Dog standing
15cms
*****
$300-450

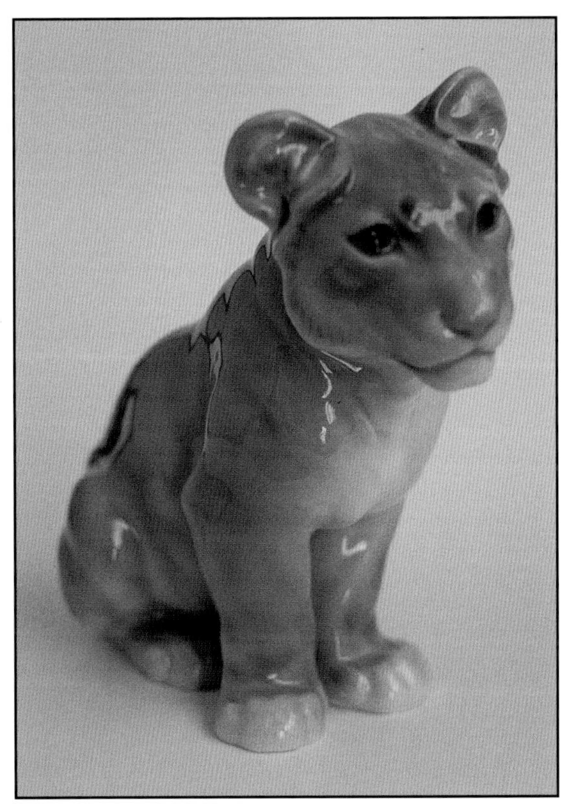

1923
Lion Cub
14cms
**
$100-200

1924
Bird?
16cms
*****
$200-300

1925
Eagle
Knud Moller
23cms
**
Also available in stoneware. In production 1988
$450-600

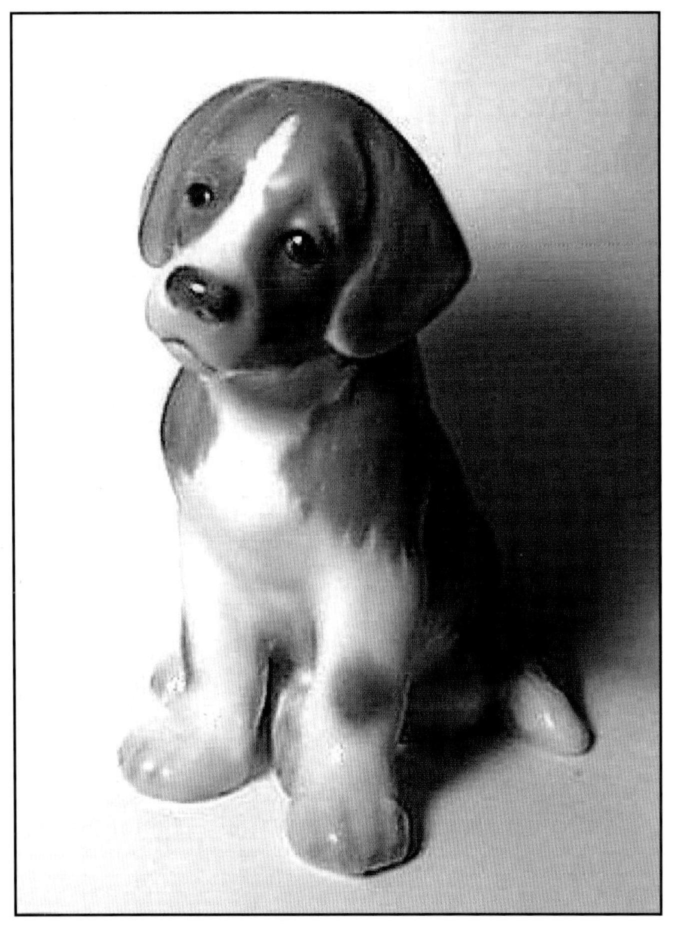

1926 RC number 439
St Bernard puppy
Niels Nielsen
12cms
*
Also available in stoneware
$50-100 MSRP $130

1928
Goat
23cms
****
$350-450

1927
Seal pup
21cms
****
$100-200

1930
Deer
23cms
**
$125-225

1931
Bird on base
24cms
*****
$500-600

1932
Eider duck
23cms
*****
$500-600

1934
Ostrich
27cms
*****
$750-900

1936
Stoat
19cms
****
$250-350

1929
Deer on base
Niels Nielsen
17cms
**
Also available in stoneware. In production 1984
$100-200

1938
Graduate
30cms
****
$250-350

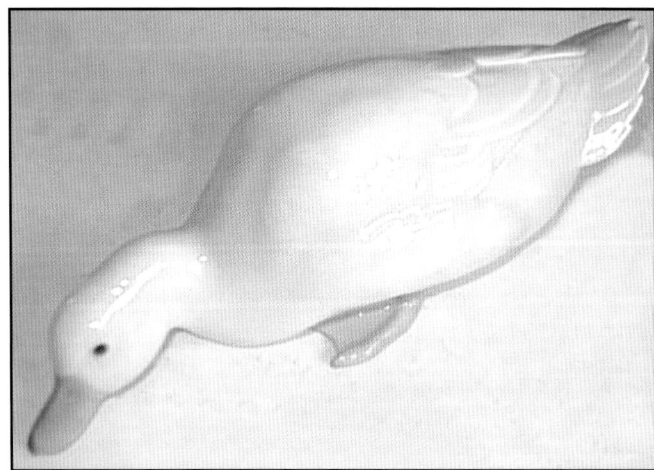

1939
Duck
16cms
***
$150-250

1940
Puffin
16cms
***
$150-275

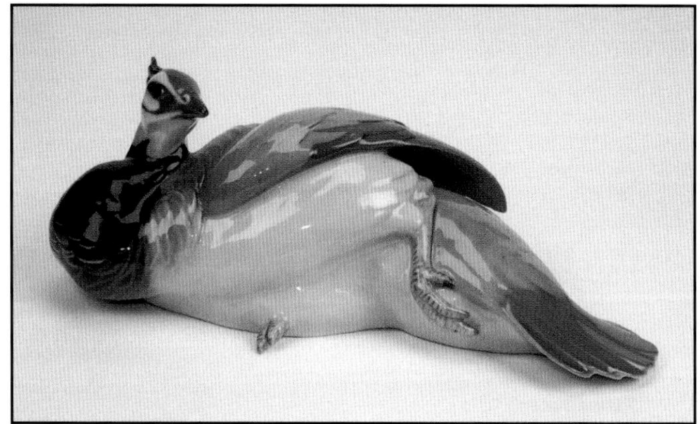

1941
Peahen
25cms
***
$350-500

1946
Bear with cub - lying
20cms
***
$200-300

1948
Tiger with cub
17cms
****
$700-850

1949
Chaffinch
10cms
***
$125-225

1951 RC number 440
Boy with dog
Ingeborg Plockross Irminger
13cms
*
$100-200 MSRP $300

1952
Pheasants - pair
Knud Moller
30cms
***
$500-750

1950
Girl with accordion
12cms
****
$150-275

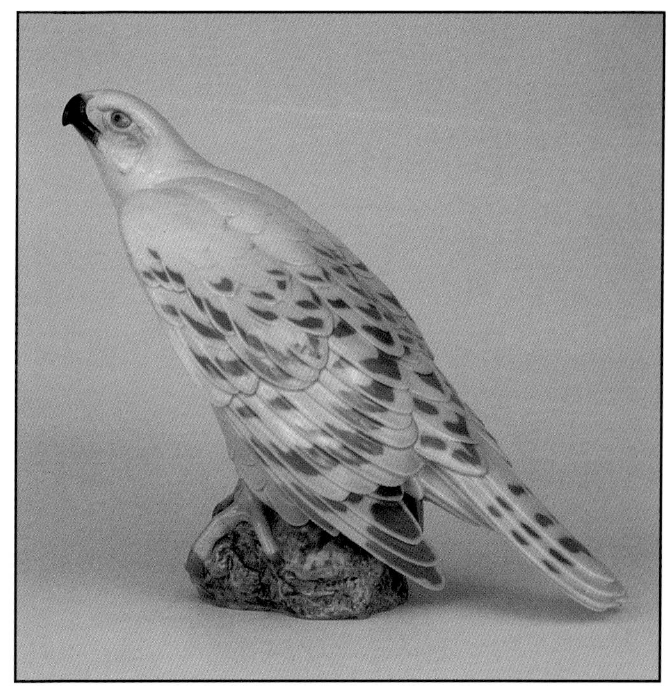

1953 RC number 441
Gerfalcon
Knud Moller
54cms
*
$1750-3500

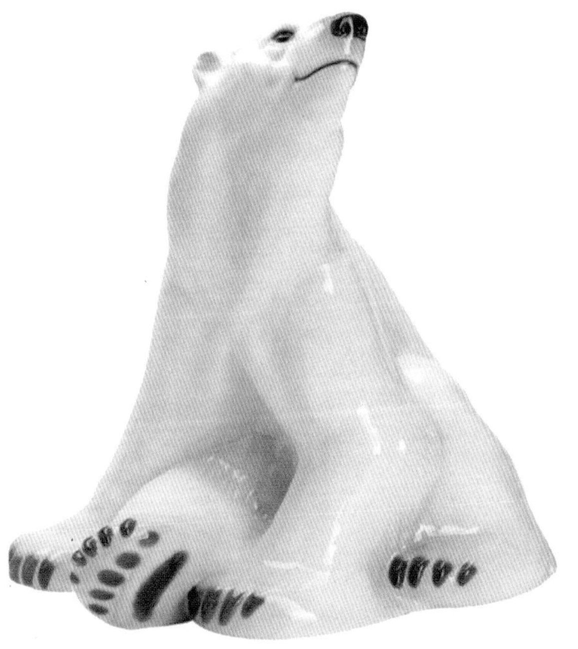

1954 RC number 442
Polar bear
Niels Nielsen
43cms
*
$1500-3150 MSRP $4,500

1958
Fox sitting
21.5cms
***
$250-500

1962
Dachshund
14cms
***
$200-300

1969
Otter with fish
19cms
***
$200-350

1973
Girl with dog
14cms
**
In production 1984
$100-200

1980
Peewit
Knud Moller
16cms
***
$75-175

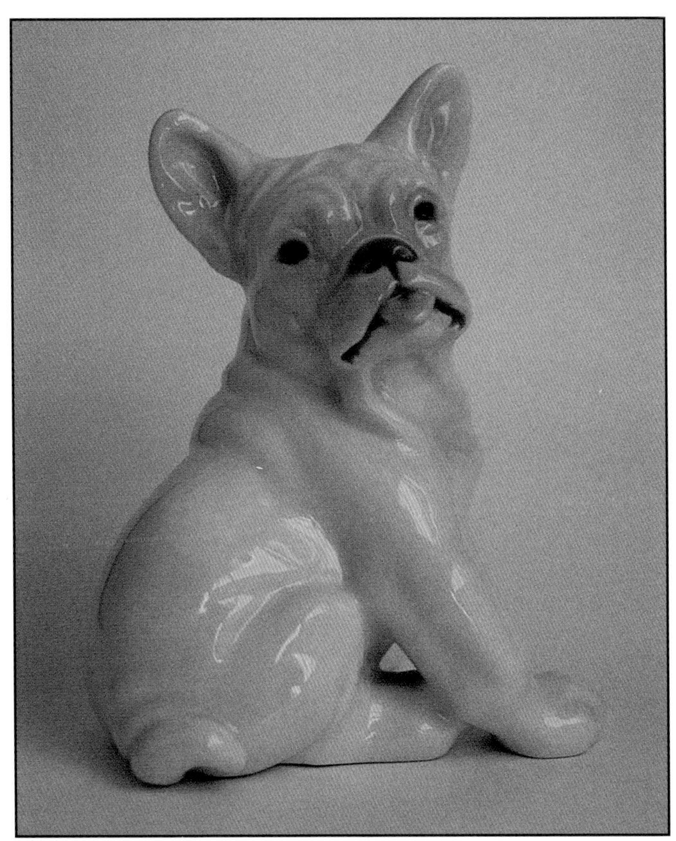

1983
Bulldog puppy
12.5cms
***
$125-250

1986
Pekinese sitting
Dahl-Jensen
Compare Dahl-Jensen 1003
5.5cms
***
$75-125

1987
Pekinese
Dahl-Jensen
Compare Dahl-Jensen 1003
5.5cms
***
$75-125

1990
Pekinese puppies
7cms
****
$150-300

1992
Bulldog
14cms
***
$200-300

1995
Girl touching hem of skirt
Adda Bonfils
13cms
**
In production 1984
$75-175

1993
Mountain Lion
Dahl-Jensen
Compare Dahl-Jensen 1019
13cms
****
$450-650

1997
Actors - Poulsen & Mantzius
Axel Locher
23cms
*****
$450-700

1998
Terrier
Dahl-Jensen
Compare Dahl-Jensen 1001 and 1118
17cms
**
In production 1984
$150-300

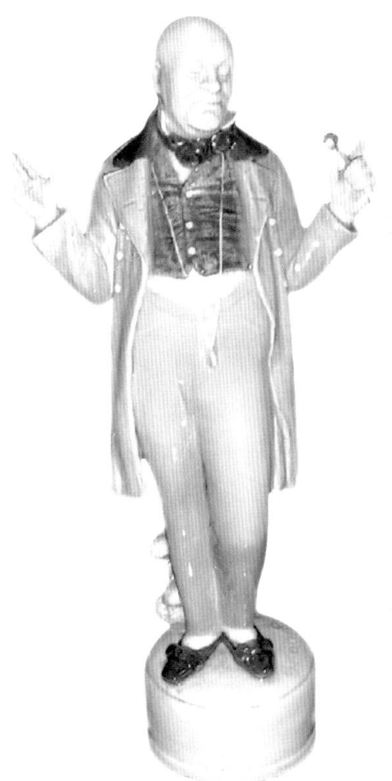

2004
Actor
Axel Locher
23cms
*****
$400-550

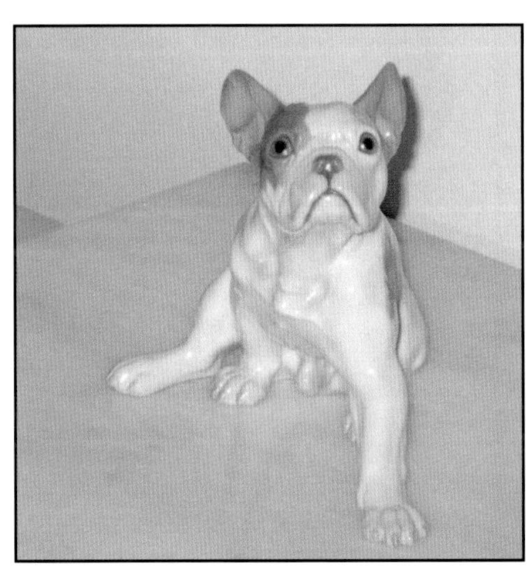

2000
French Bull Terrier
12.5cms
***
$200-300

2002
Mother, toddler & baby
***
$275-500

2006
Pointer
34cms
**
In production 1984
$350-600

2007
Deer - buck
Jean Gauguin
19cms
*****
$400-800

2008
Deer - doe
Jean Gauguin
17cms
*****
$400-800

2009
Stag
Jean Gauguin
25cms
*****
$400-800

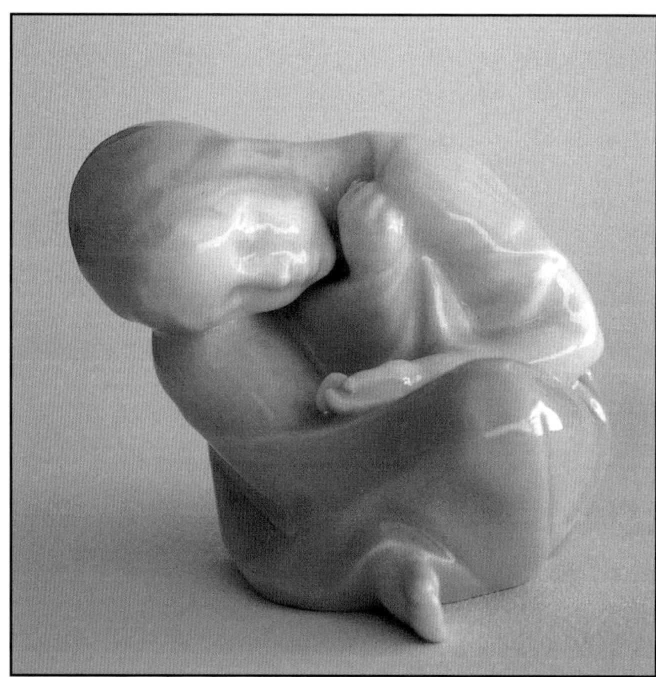

2012
'Little Match Girl'
10cms
$150-$275

2010
Shepherdess
Axel Locher
26cms
**
In production 1988
$200-300

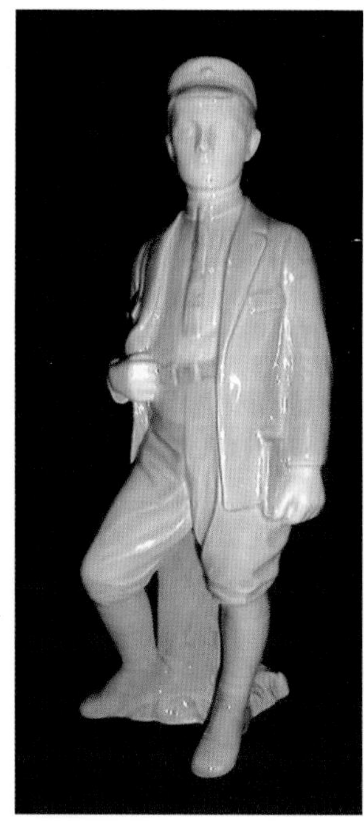

2013
Graduate
Ingeborg Plockross Irminger
30cms
****
$250-400

2011
Scottish Terrier
11cms
**
$125-200

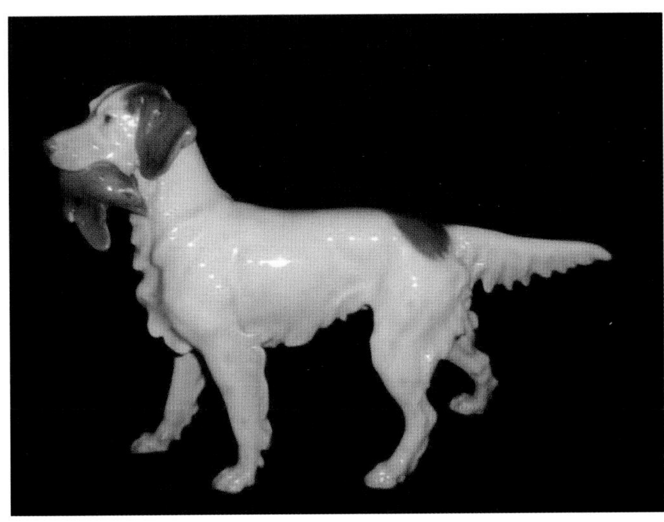

2015
Setter with bird
Laurits Jensen
30cms
**
In production 1988
$200-300

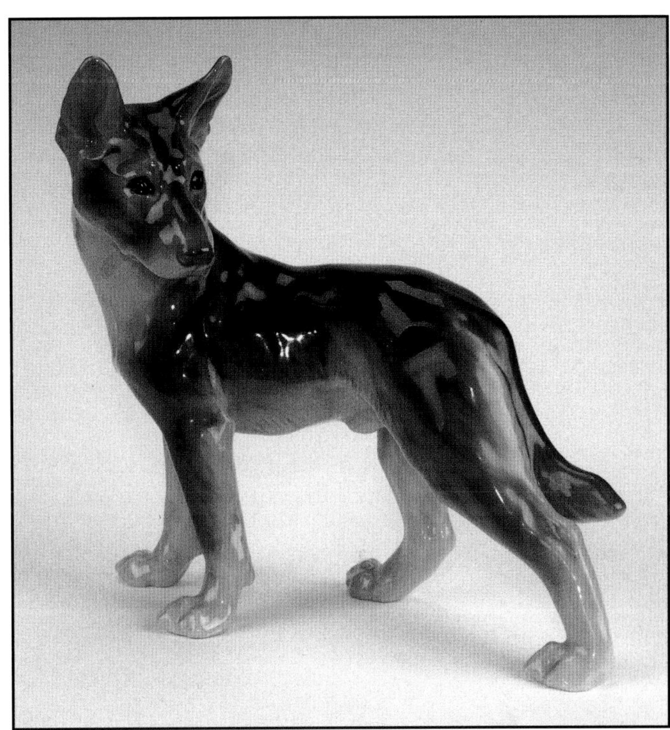

2018
German Shepherd standing
21cms
***
$300-450

2017 RC number 443
Dairy maid
Axel Locher
19cms
*
$500-700 MSRP $1,400

2019
Parrot
Dahl-Jensen
14cms
**
Also available in stoneware. In production 1988
$125-250

2020
Linnet
Platen Hallermund
11cms
**
In production 1984
$75-125

2022
Mother & two children
31cms
***
$300-450

2025
Fisher family
Axel Locher
31cms
**
In production 1984
$450-600

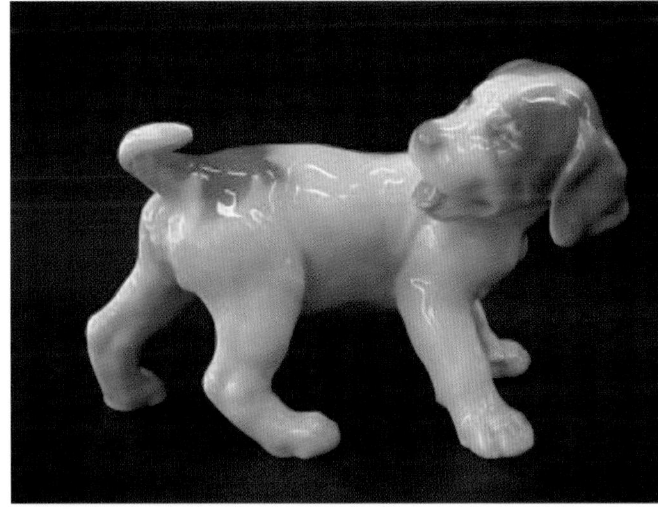

2026 RC number 444
Pointer
Laurits Jensen
16cms
*
$100-250 MSRP $240

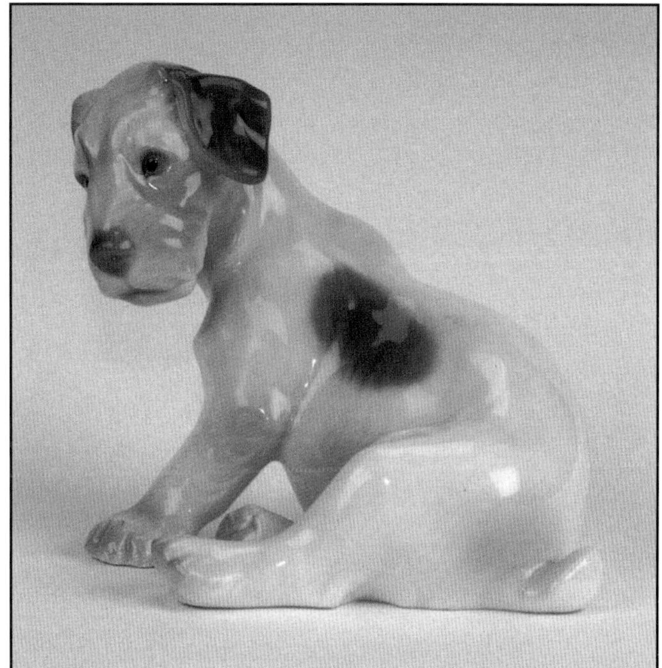

2027
Sealyham puppy
Dahl-Jensen
Compare Dahl-Jensen 1008
10cms
**
In production 1984
$75-175

2028
Sealyham puppy
Dahl-Jensen
Compare Dahl-Jensen 1008
10cms
**
In production 1984
$75-150

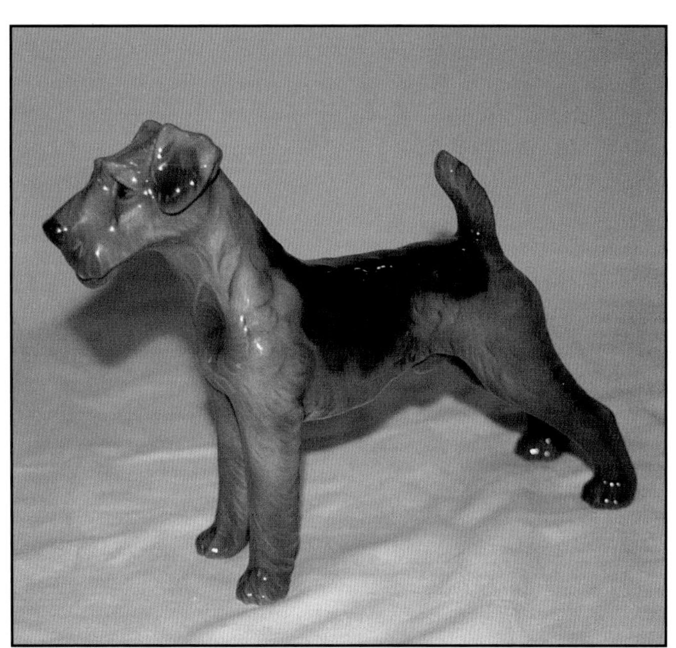

2030
Terrier
17cms
***
$175-275

2035
Cavalier King Charles Spaniel
15cms
***
$150-250

2036
Woman with fishing net
Axel Locher
22.5cms
***
$200-300

2032
Cellist
17cms
***
$200-300

2037 RC number 445
Hans Christian Andersen
Henning Seidelin
23cns
*
$250-450 MSRP $900

2038
Great Dane sitting
Laurits Jensen
24cms
***
$250-450

2039
Leopard
****
$500-850

2041
Dachshund standing
19cms
***
$250-350

2043
Shepherd Boy
Axel Locher
25cms
***
$150-300

2044
Pointer lying
Laurits Jensen
Compare Dahl-Jensen 1235 and Royal Copenhagen 1634 and 1635
25cms
**
In production 1984
$200-350

2049
Harvest Man
25cms
***
$150-300

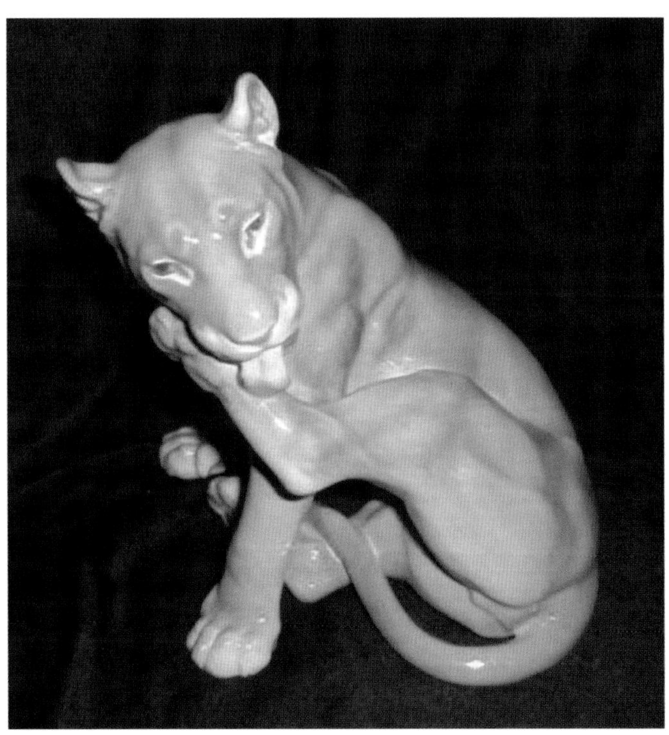

2051
Lioness grooming
22.5cms
***
$400-600

2050
Girl with rake
25cms
***
$150-300

2052
Lion standing
25cms
***
$400-650

2053
Ape
45cms
$2500-4000

2056
Tiger
Laurits Jensen
Compare Dahl-Jensen 1285 and Royal Copenhagen 714
36cms
***
In production 1984
$650-850

2055
'The Sandman'
Henning Seidelin
18cms
**
In production 1984
$100-200

2057
Lion on rock
20 x 25cms
***
$450-650

2059
Penguin on rock
Axel Locher
52cms
**
In production 1984
$850-1200

2060
Pointer pup scratching side
Laurits Jensen
12.5 x 20cms
**
$275-375

2071
Sealyham
8cms
**
$50-100

2072
Terrier
Laurits Jensen
11cms
**
In production 1984
$50-100

2061
Spaniel
Laurits Jensen
25cms
**
In production 1988
$200-300

2062
English Setter
19cms
****
$200-350

2069
Scottish Terrier standing
19cms
***
$150-225

2073
Scottish Terrier
12.5cms
***
$150-250

2075
Pointer standing
18cms
***
$200-350

2076
Greyhound standing
20cms
****
$200-375

2077
Scottish Terrier lying
13cms
***
$150-225

2078
Greyhound
****
$250-450

2079
Greyhound, lying
27.5cms
****
$300-450

2080
Hare sitting up
20.5cms
***
$75-125

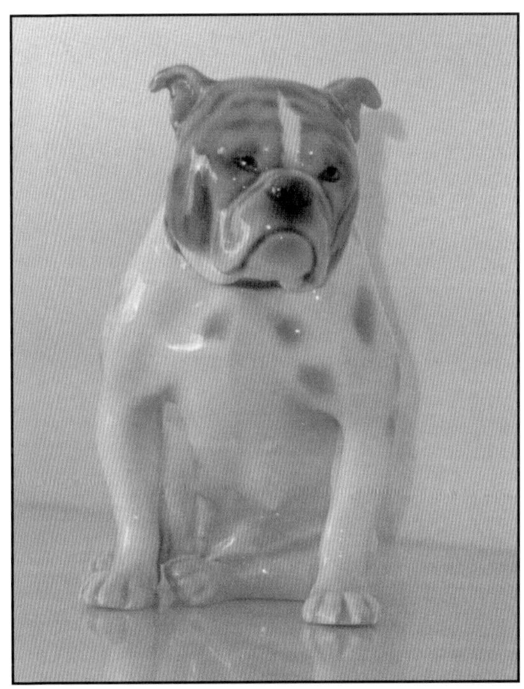

2083
Bulldog sitting
13cms
***
$250-400

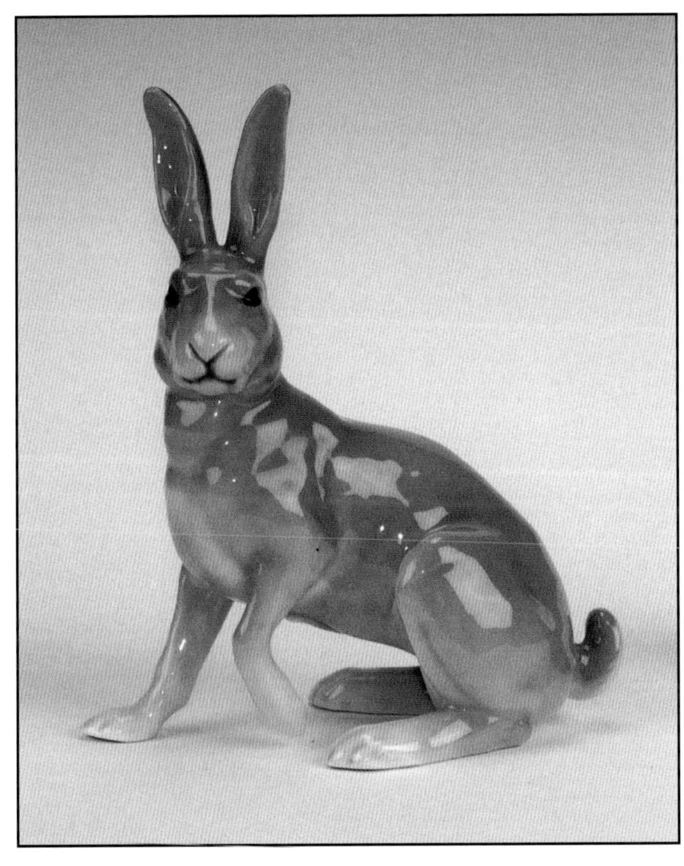

2081
Hare sitting
15cms
***
$75-125

2082
Bulldog
14cms
***
$300-400

2084
Bloodhound sniffing
20.5cms
***
Compare with Royal Copenhagen 1341 sculpted by Laurits Jensen
$400-650

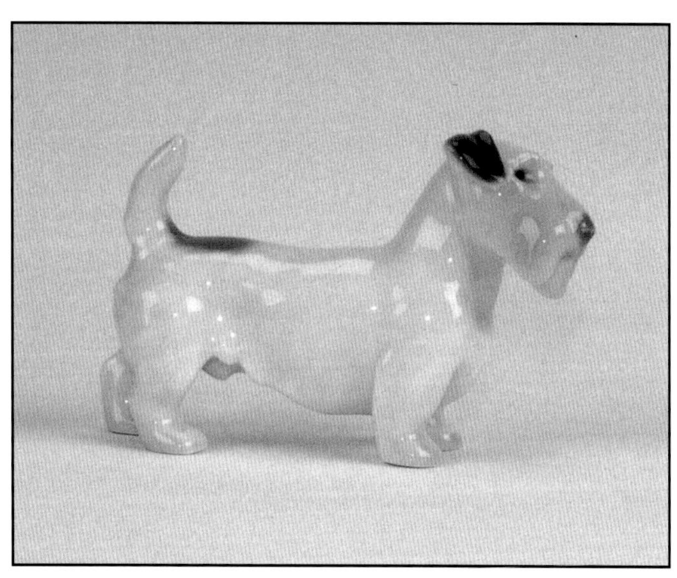

2085
Scottish Terrier standing
6cms
**
$50-100

2086
Terrier standing
6cms
***
$50-100

2089
Schnauzer
13cms
***
$250-350

2090
Chow Chow
13cns
***
$300-450

2091
Schnauzer
18cms
***
$200-400

2092
Pomeranian
9cms
****
$250-350

2095
Cocker Spaniel
Laurits Jensen
15cms
**
In production 1984
$200-300

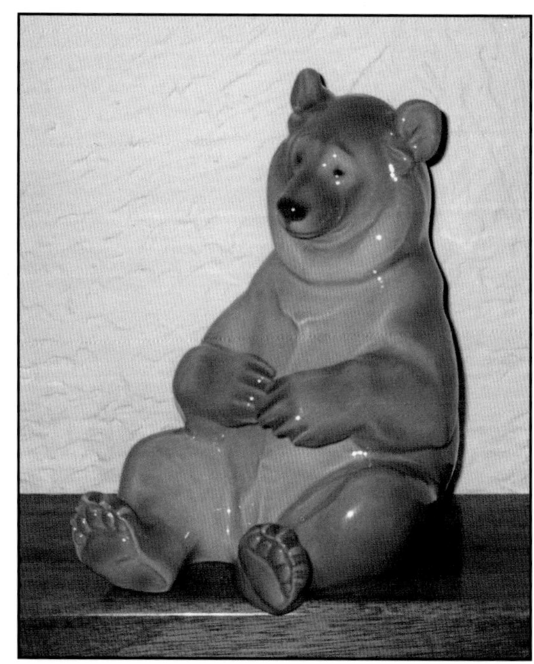

2098
Bear sitting – bookend
22cms
$500-600

2099
Airedale Terrier
20cms
***
$200-350

2101
Pekinese
20cms
****
$350-550

2103
German Shepherd standing
Laurits Jensen
22cms
***
$350-500

2104
Sisyphus
20cms
****
$250-500

2108
Mastiff
22cms
****
$400-600

2110
English Bulldog
16cms
***
$300-500

2105
Tinderbox dog
20cms
***
$200-400

2107
Tinderbox dog

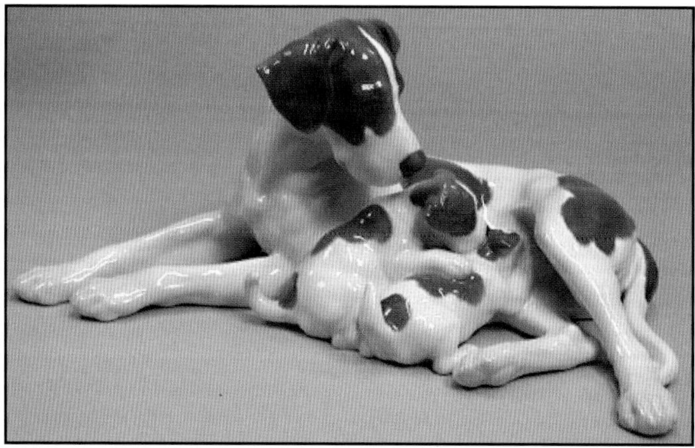

2111
Pointer bitch & pups
28cms
***
In production 1984
$500-750

2113
Japanese Chin
23cms
$450-650

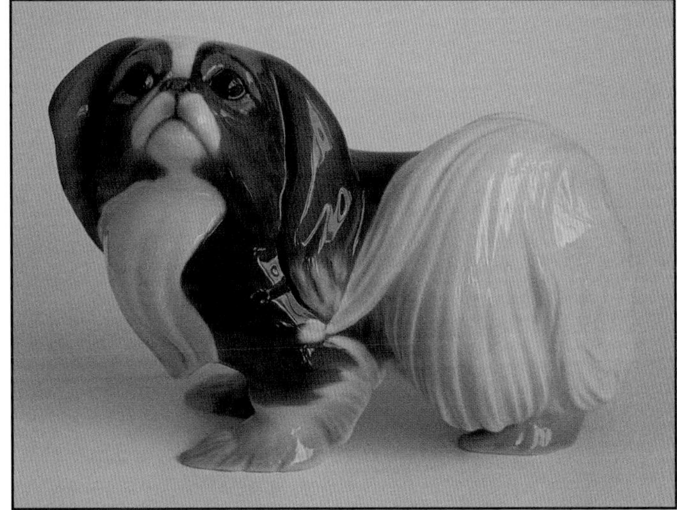

2114
Japanese Chin standing
Sveistrup Madsen
12.5cms
***
$225-325

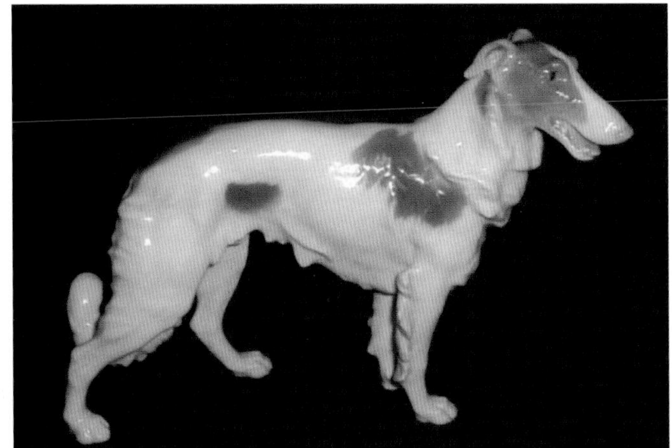

2115
Borzoi
21cms
****
$375-550

2116
Old English Sheepdog
13cms
***
$275-4005

2117
Scottish Terrier
13.5cms
***
$125-250

2118
Scottish Terrier
***
$125-200

2119
Farmer with two horses
24cms
****
$650-850

2120
Irish Wolfhound
20cms
****
$375-500

2121
Bull
Sveistrup Madsen
35cms
**
In production 1988
$300-450

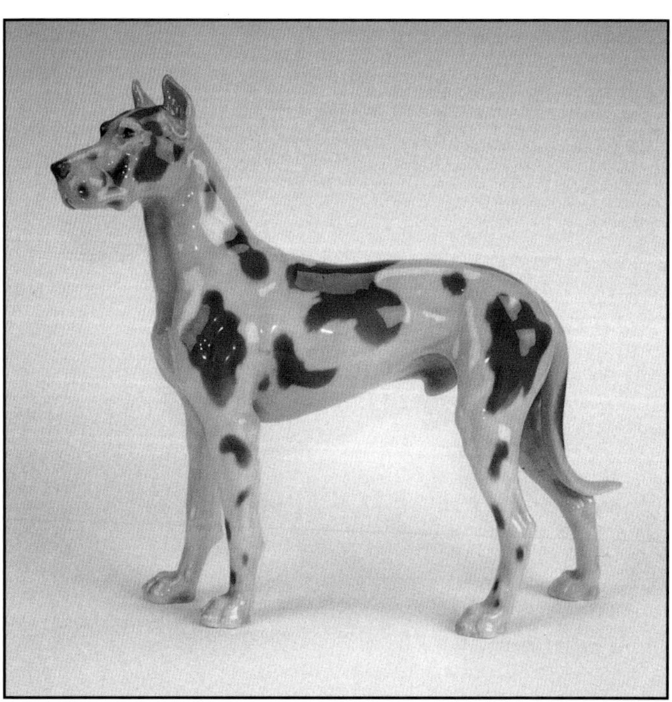

2124
Great Dane standing
24cms
***
$250-450

2125
Girl with butterfly
19cms
***
$150-250

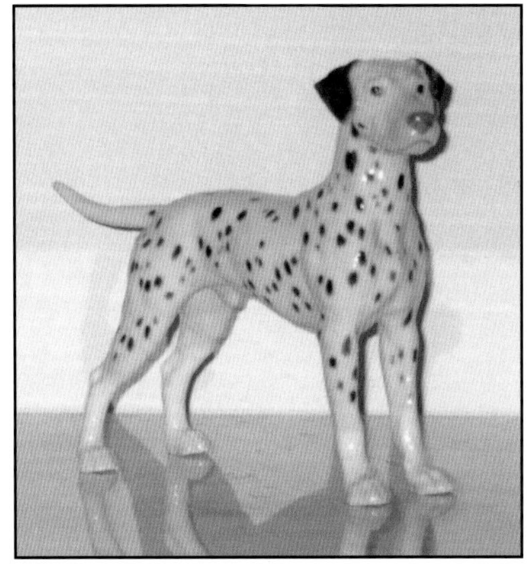

2122
Dalmatian
19cms
***
$175-275

2126
Woman with eggs
Svend Lindhart
22cms
**
In production 1984
$150-250

2128
Green Elephant with Howdah
***
$75-150

2127
Boy with bucket
Svend Lindhart
14cms
**
In production 1984
$75-150

2130
Skye Terrier
Laurits Jensen
25.5cms
***
$250-450

2132
Swimmer - female
27.5cms
***
See 2134
$200-300

2133
Skye Terrier
15.5cms
***
$150-250

2136
Wild Boar
8cms
****
$100-200

2134
Swimmer - male
28cms
****
See 2132
$250-450

2137
Skye Terrier
11cms
***
$75-150

2138
Eel
18.5cms
****
$100-200

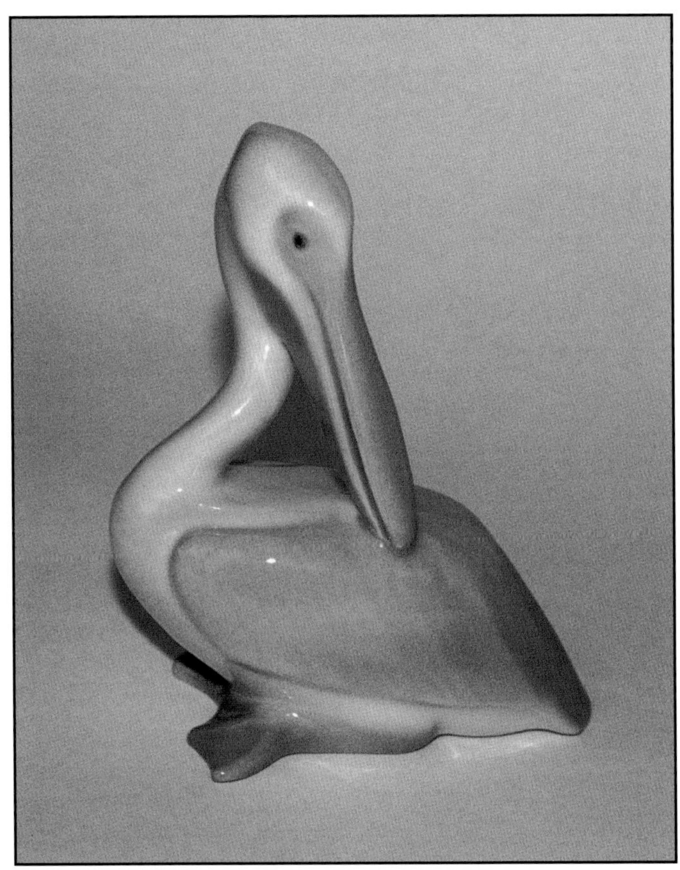

2139
Pelican
10cms
***
$75-150

2141
Hare
Svend Jespersen
9cms
**
In production 1984
$30-60

2142
Kitten
7.5cms
**
$30-60

2143
Kitten
7.5cms
**
$30-60

2140
Elephant calf
8.5cms
**
$40-80

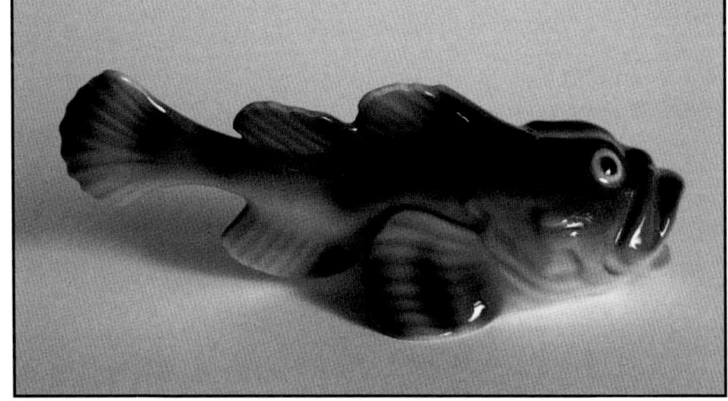

2144
Sea Scorpion
Svend Jespersen
9cms
**
In production 1984
$50-125

2145
Roach
Svend Jespersen
9cms
**
In production 1984
$50-125

2146
Horse
25cms
***
$350-450

2161 RC number 446
Cow licking side
Laurits Jensen
25cms
*
$250-350

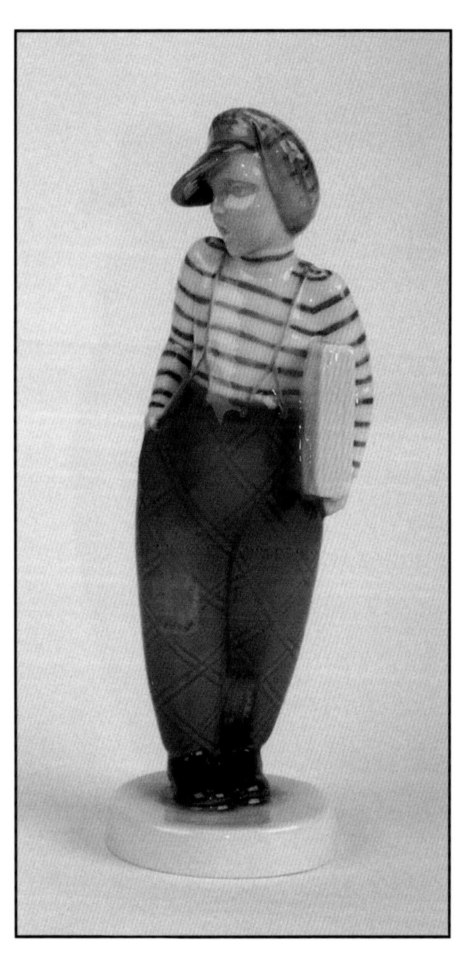

2148
Boy with papers
20cms
**
In production 1984
$125-225

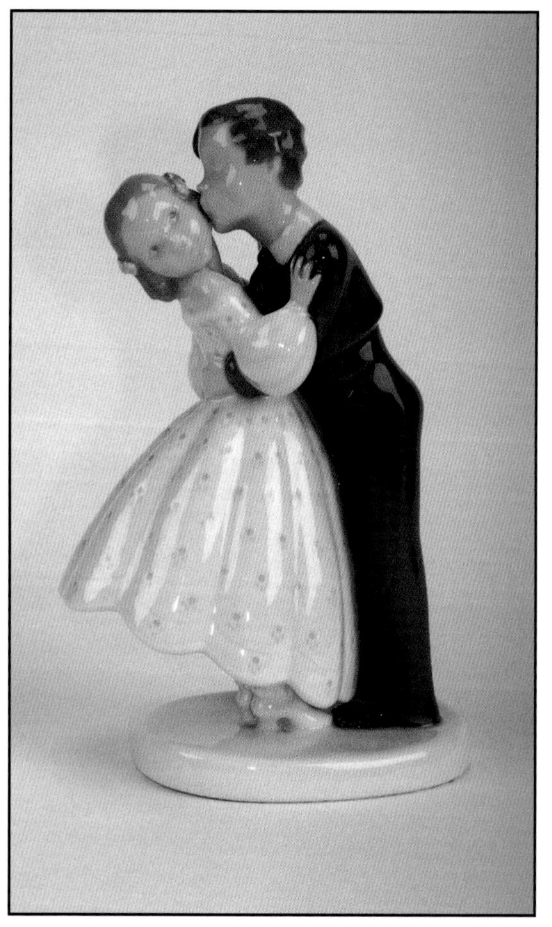

2162 RC number 447
'Youthful boldness'
Claire Weiss
20cms
*
$100-200 MSRP $450

2163
Girl with dog
Claire Weiss
11cms
**
In production 1984
$100-150

2168 RC number 448
Calf
Svend Jespersen
8cms
*
$50-100 MSRP $90

2166
Penguin
27cms
**
In production 1984
$125-225

2167
Scottish Terrier standing
7.5cms
***
$60-125

2169 RC number 449
Trout
Svend Jespersen
15cms
*
$50-100 MSRP $110

2170
Scottish Terrier sitting
7.5cms
***
$60-125

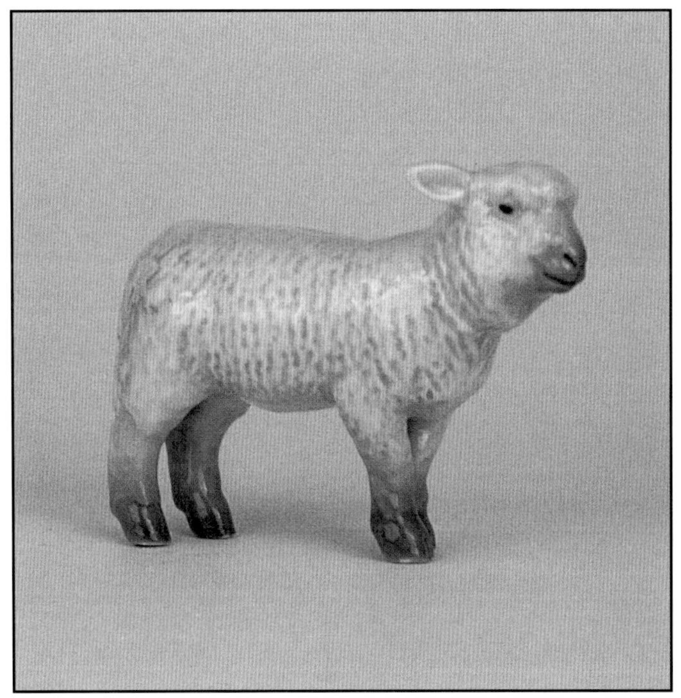

2171
Lamb
Svend Jespersen
9cms
**
In production 1988
$30-60

2173
Herring
Svend Jespersen
9cms
**
In production 1988
$50-125

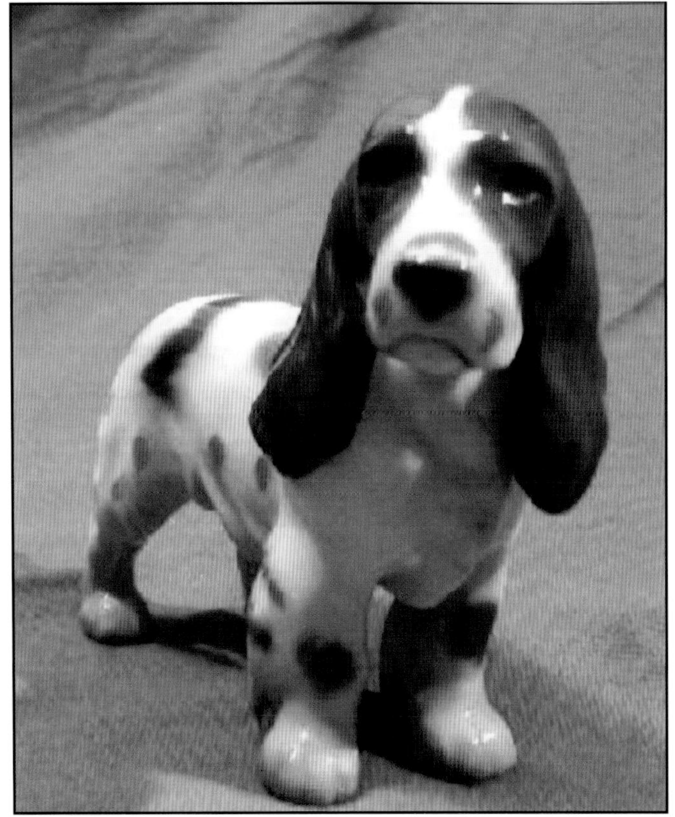

2172 RC number 450
Cocker Spaniel
Svend Jespersen
11cms
*
$75-125 MSRP $110

2174
Perch
Svend Jespersen
9cms
**
In production 1984
$50-125

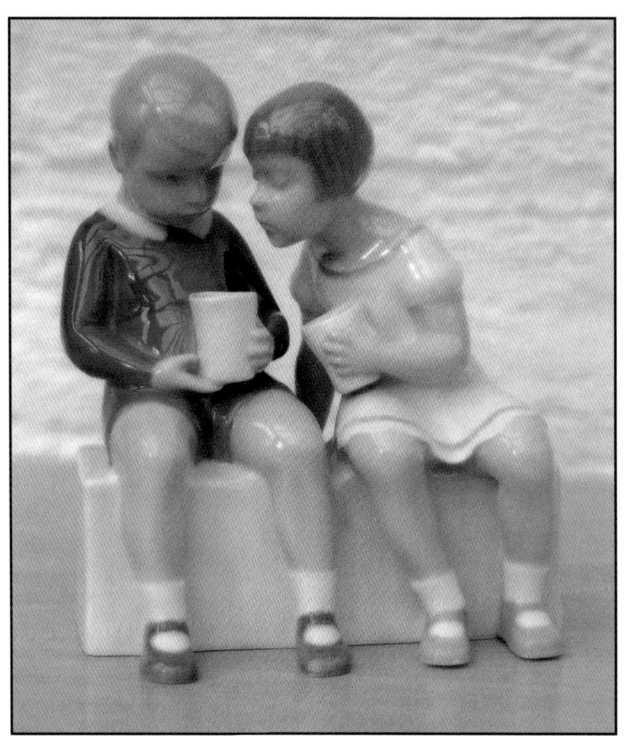

2175
'Unfair Treatment'
Claire Weiss
14cms
**
In production 1988
$125-200

2178
Cockatoo
Svend Jespersen
10cms
**
In production 1988
$50-100

2177
Squirrel
Svend Jespersen
8cms
**
Also available in stoneware. In production 1984
$40-60

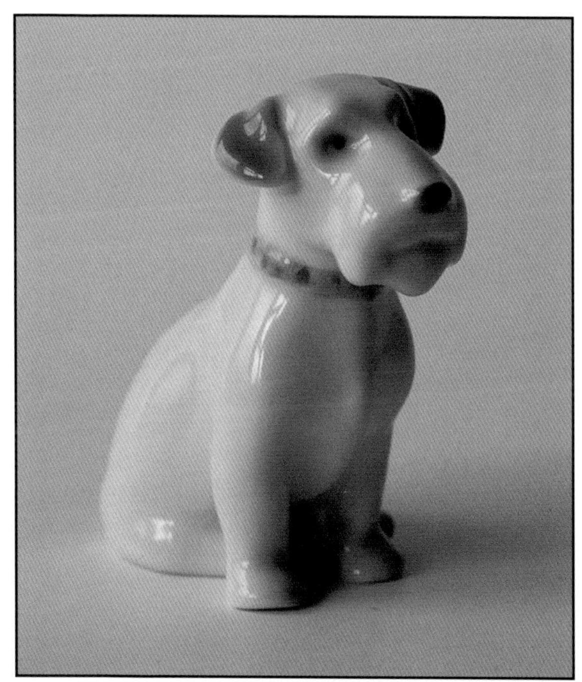

2179 RC number 451
Sealyham
Laurits Jensen
6cms
*
$50-100 MSRP $70

2180
Girl with goat
Axel Locher
20cms
**
In production 1984
$250-350

2182
Girl comforting boy
18.5cms
**
$100-200

2183
Boy & girl
18.5cms
**
$100-200

2181 RC number 452
Girl with milkcan
Axel Locher
21cms
*
$200-300

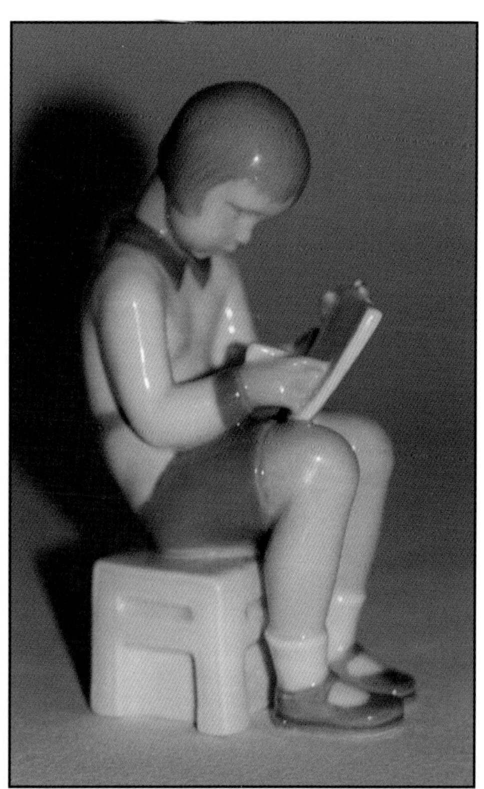

2184
'Little Artist'
17.5cms
**
$50-125

2185
Girl with doll
18.5cms
**
$75-175

2187
Puma
23cms
****
Matte finish
$450-700

2188
Boy & girl singing
18.5cms
**
$100-200

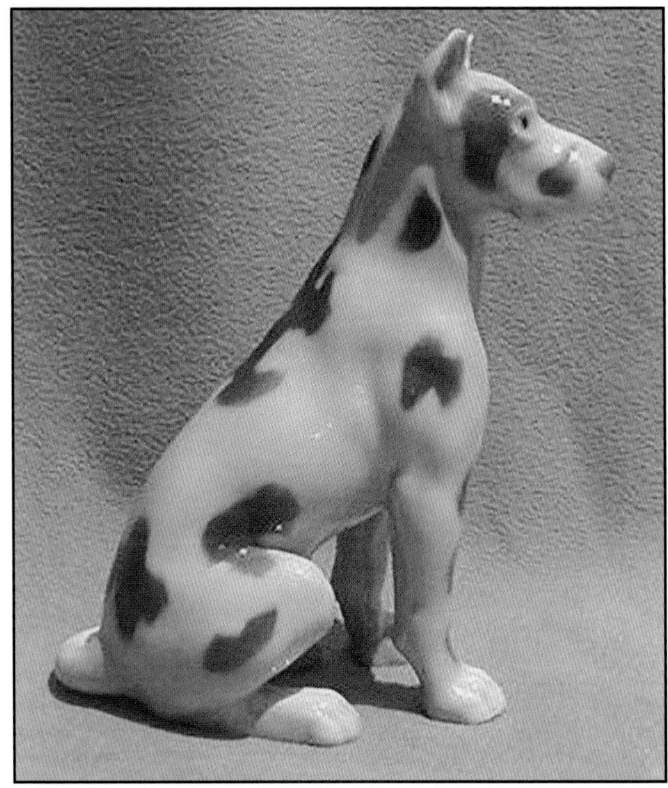

2189
Great Dane sitting
Svend Jespersen
11cms
**
In production 1984
$75-125

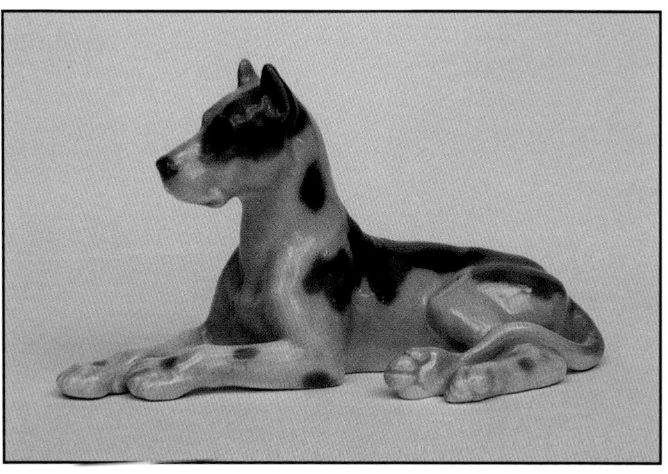

2190
Great Dane lying
Svend Jespersen
13cms
**
In production 1984
$75-125

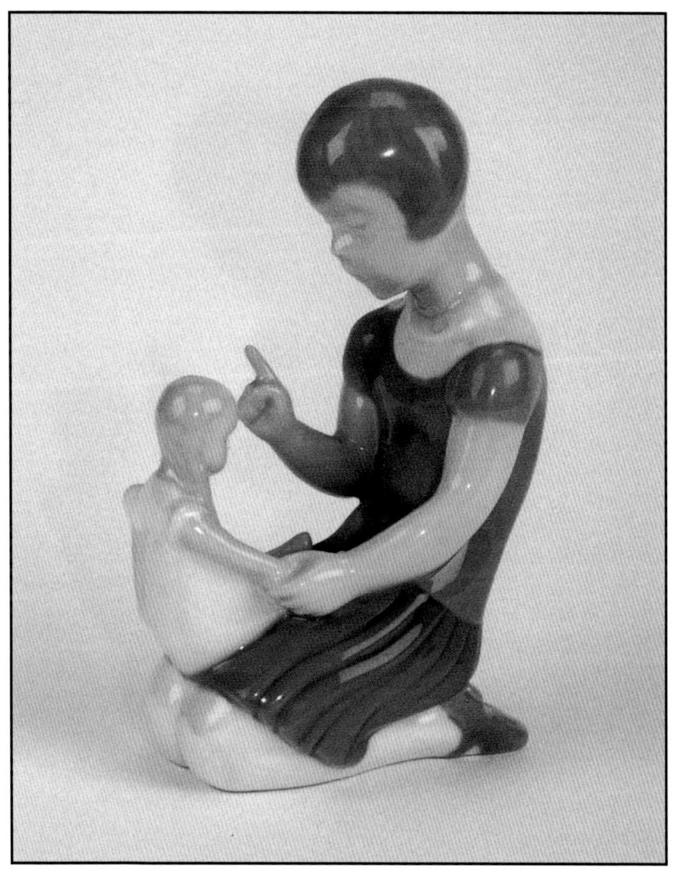

2191
Girl with doll
15cms
**
$75-150

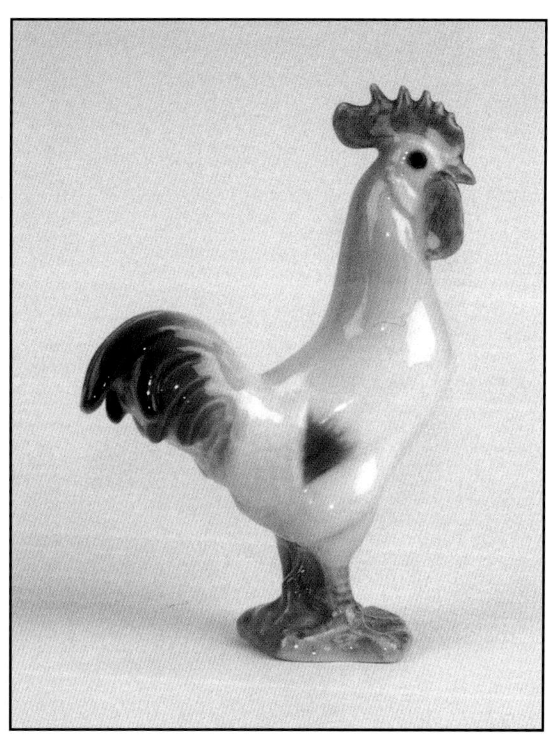

2192
Cock
Svend Jespersen
12cms
**
In production 1988
$40-80

2194
Chick
Svend Jespersen
7cms
**
In production 1988
$30-70

2193
Hen
Svend Jespersen
12cms
**
In production 1988
$40-80

2195
Boy with foal
18.5cms
***
$250-400

2196
Mother with children
22.5cms
***
$250-450

2197
German Shepherd
Svend Jespersen
9cms
**
In production 1984
$75-125

2198
German Shepherd lying
9cms
**
$75-125

2199
Boy taking off sock
15cms
**
$50-125

2200
Mother with baby
26cms
***
$250-350

2201
Boy with scottie
Claire Weiss
17.5cms
**
$75-150

2202
Girl with puppy
18.75cms
**
$125-225

2204
Bear
****
Also available in stoneware
$250-450

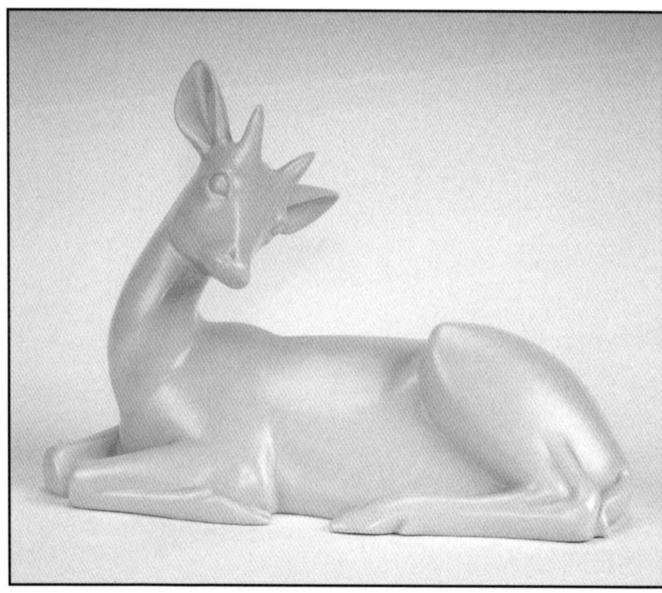

2205
Deer
20cms
****
Matte finish
$250-375

2207 RC number 454
Toothache
Svend Lindhart
11.5cms
*
Blanc de chine
$25-60 MSRP $60

2206 RC number 453
Headache
Svend Lindhart
11.5cms
*
Blanc de chine
$25-60 MSRP $60

2208 RC number 455
Tummyache
Svend Lindhart
11.5cms
*
Blanc de chine
$25-60 MSRP $60

2209 RC number 456
Earache
Svend Lindhart
11.5cms
*
Blanc de chine
$25-60 MSRP $60

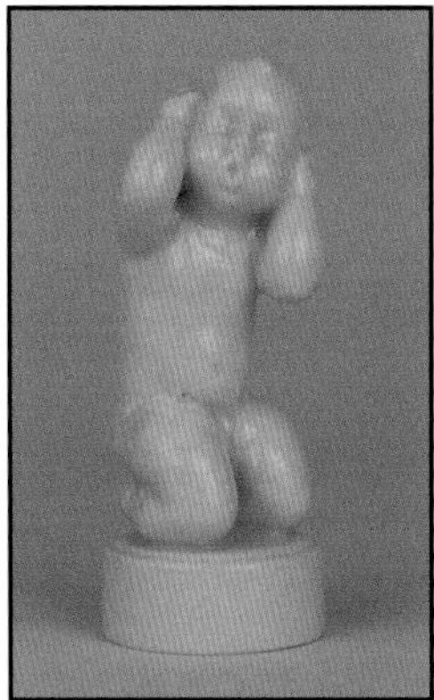

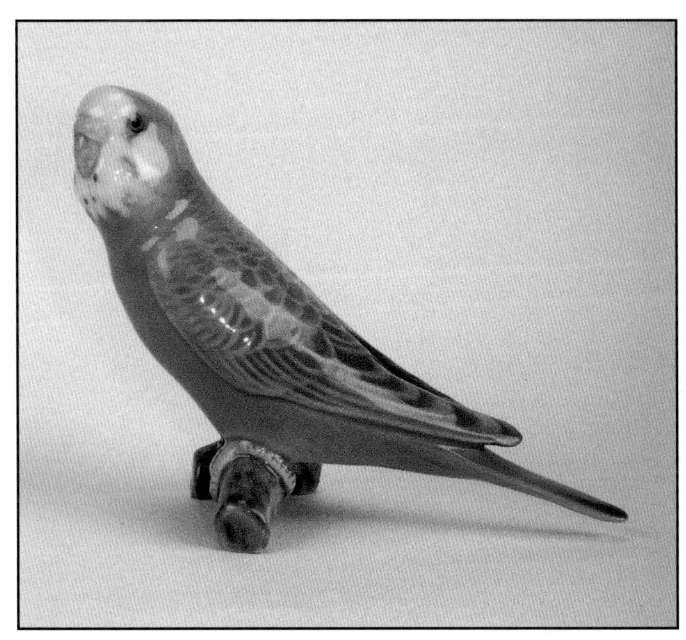

2210 RC number 457
Budgerigar - blue
Svend Jespersen
15cms
*

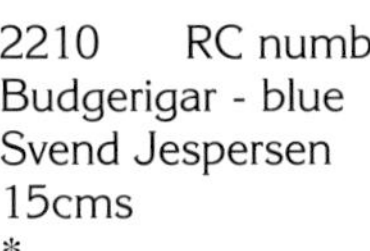

Also available in stoneware
$50-105 MSRP $170

2211
Deer standing
13cms
***
$100-200

2212
Boxer
Svend Jespersen
16cms
**
In production 1984
$150-300

2213
Bear, walking
10cms
***
$125-225

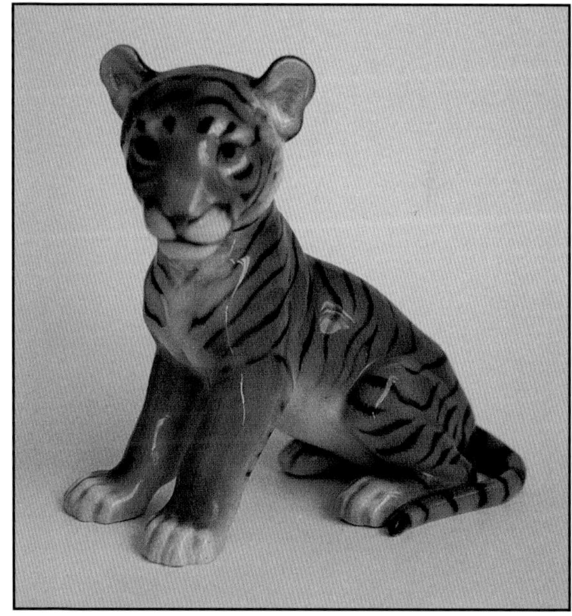

2214
Tiger cub
13cms
***
$150-250

2215
Camel lying
25cms
*****
$350-600

2217 RC number 458
Polar bear sitting
Svend Jespersen
11cms
*
$50-125 MSRP $95

2218 RC number 459
Polar bear
Svend Jespersen
12cms
*
See 1785
$50-125 MSRP $95

2219
Washer woman
17cms
***
$250-350

2220
Poultry girl
Axel Locher
23cms
**
In production 1988
$200-300

2221
Monkey
15cms
****
$150-250

2222
Soccer player
24cms
**
$100-200

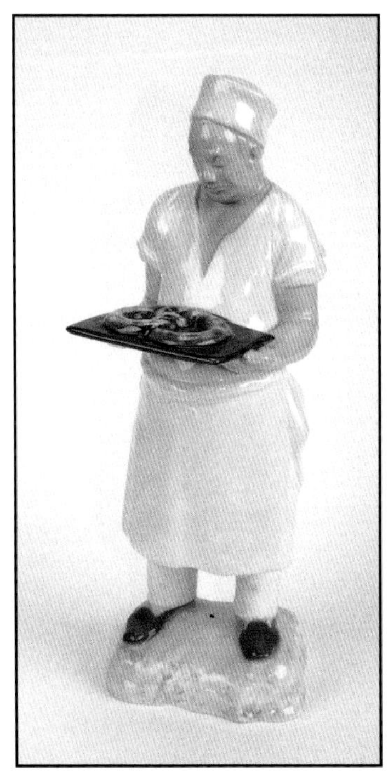

2223
Baker
Axel Locher
28cms
**
In production 1984
$250-350

2224
Girl in swimsuit
22.5cms
**
$125-225

2225 RC number 460
Smith
Axel Locher
29cms
*
Also available in stoneware
$250-400 MSRP $875

2229
'So big'
Svend Lindhart
17cms
**
Blanc de chine
$50-150

2230
'Eve'
Svend Lindhart
17cms
**
Blanc de chine. In production 1988
$50-150

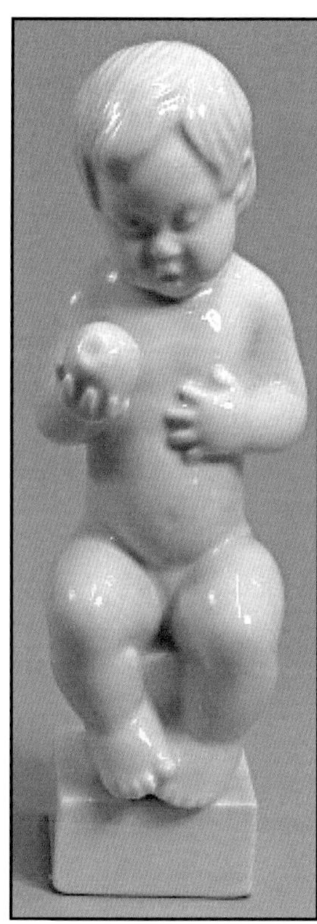

2226
Nurse
22.5cms
***
$200-300

2227
Boxer
20cms
**
$150-300

2228
Cobbler
Axel Locher
22cms
**
In production 1984
$250-350

2231
'Adam'
Svend Lindhart
17cms
**
Blanc de chine. In production 1988
$50-150

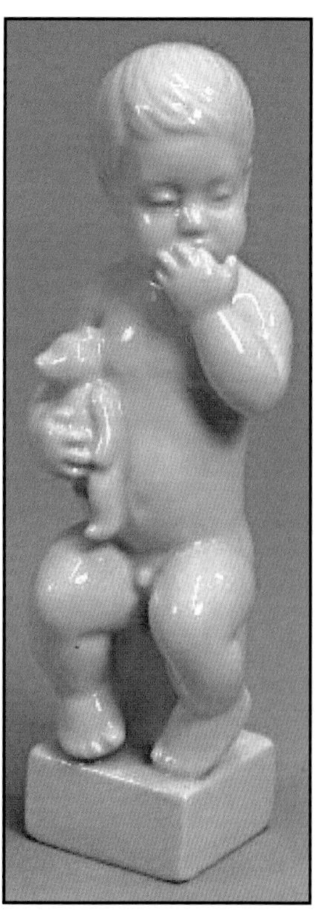

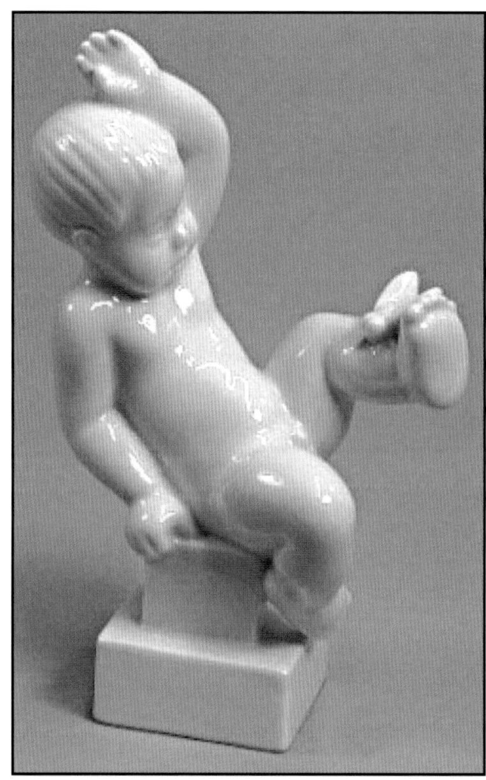

2232
'Fright'
Svend Lindhart
15cms
**
Blanc de chine. In production 1988
$40-140

2233 RC number 465
'Fish Market'
Axel Locher
20cms
*
$250-450 MSRP $1,300

2234
Belgian Stallion
Svend Jespersen
30cms
***
Also available in stoneware. In production 1984
$350-450

2235 RC number 503
Blue Ara
Armand Petersen
41cms
*
$450-700

2236
Cat lying
18.5cms
****
$150-250

2237
Woman with pig
Axel Locher
22.5cms
***
$300-400

2238
Bowling
15cms
**
$100-200

2239
Polar bear with cub
15cms
****
$175-350

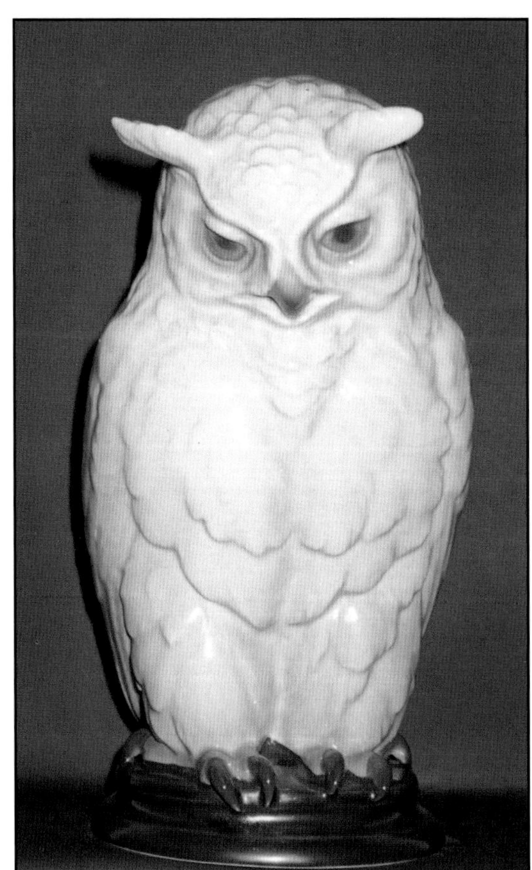

2240
Owl
23cms
****
$400-700

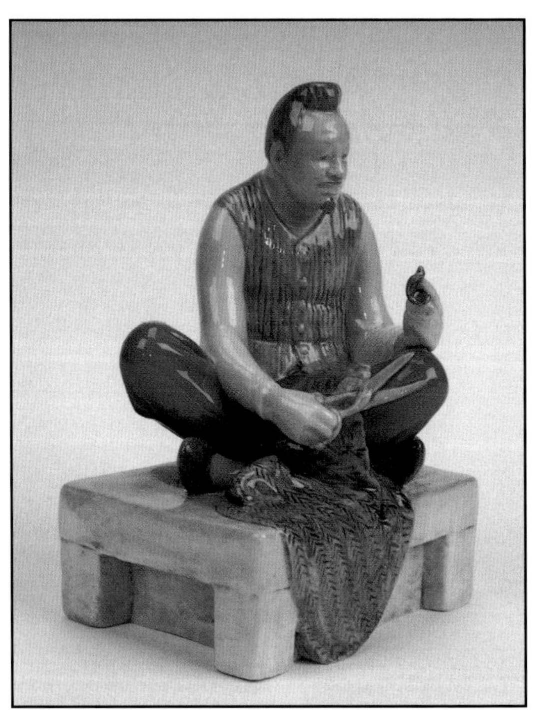

2241
Tailor
18.5cms
***
$275-375

2242
Finch
Svend Jespersen
7.5cms
**
$50-100

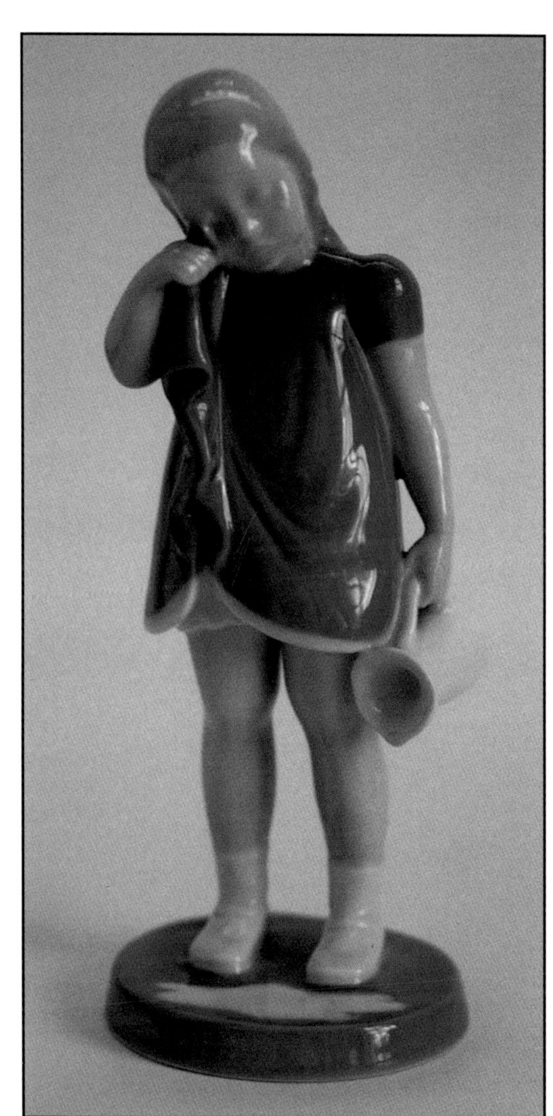

2244
Chihuahua
13.5cms
****
$300-450

2246 RC number 466
'Spilt milk'
Claire Weiss
18cms
*
$100-200 MSRP $275

2247 RC number 467
'First Book'
Claire Weiss
11cms
*
$75-150 MSRP $250

2250
Girl & baby
11cms
**
$150-250

2249
'Friends'
Claire Weiss
10cms
**
In production 1984
$75-150

2251
'Who is Calling?'
Michaela Ahlmann
15cms
**
In production 1984
$50-125

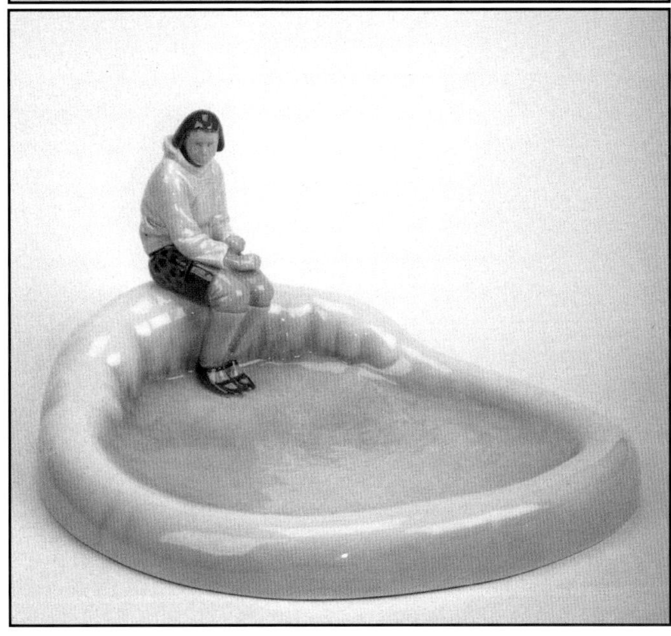

2253
Greenlander
**
2 sizes
$150-250

2254
Goose girl
Axel Locher
24cms
**
In production 1988
$175-300

2255
Mother & child
12.5cms
***

$200-300

2256
Cat sitting
Svend Jespersen
18cms
**
In production 1972. See also 2452 and 2465 size variations
$75-125

2257
Girl braiding hair
12.5cms
***
$50-125

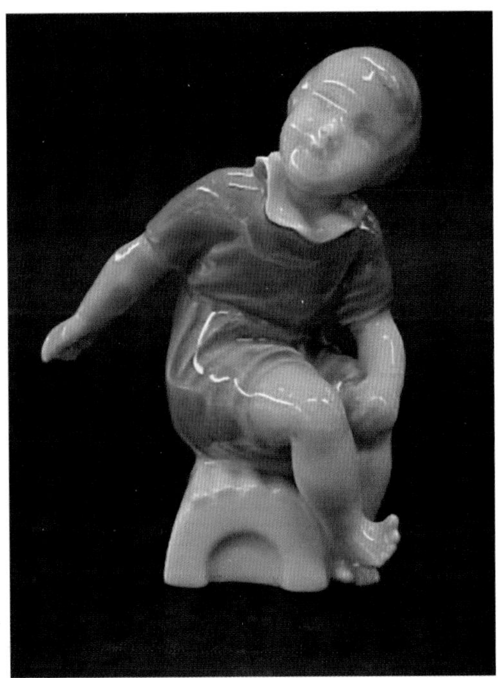

2258
Girl on footstool
11cms
**
$50-125

2259
Horse
15cms
***
$125-225

2262 RC number 468
'Happy family'
Michaela Ahlmann
20cms
*
$200-650 MSRP $950

2261
'Offended'
12.5cms
***
$100-200

2263
Farmer with pig
Axel Locher
18.5cms
***
$300-400

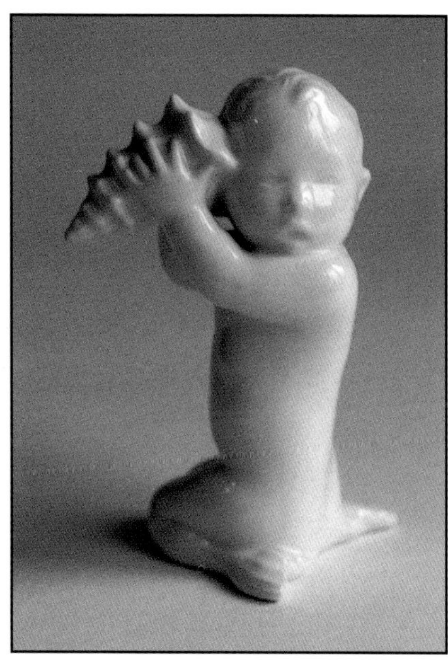

2264
Sea boy with shell
Ebbe Sadolin/Svend Jespersen
11cms
**
Blanc de chine, also available with gold edging. In production 1972.
$40-100

2265
Sea boy with starfish
Ebbe Sadolin/Svend Jespersen
11cms
**
Blanc de chine, also available with gold edging. In production 1972.
$40-100

2266
Sea boy with sea-weed
Ebbe Sadolin/Svend Jespersen
10cms
**
Blanc de chine, also available with gold edging. In production 1972.
$40-100

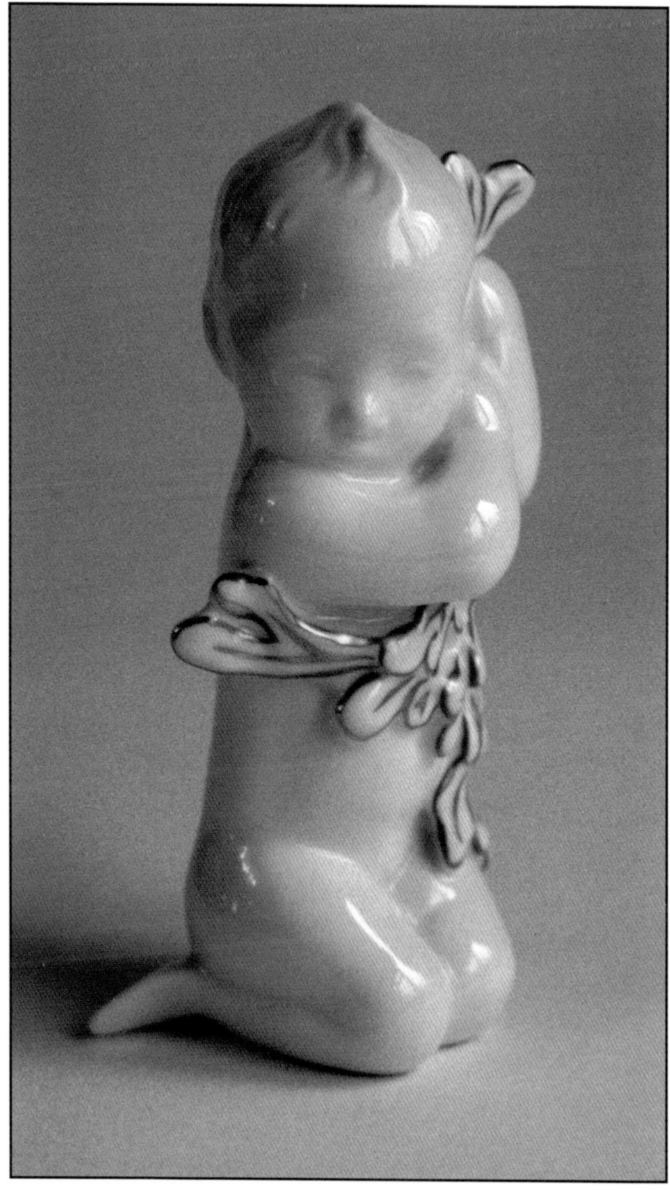

2267
Sea girl
Ebbe Sadolin/Svend Jespersen
11cms
**
Blanc de chine, also available with gold edging. In production 1972.
$40-100

2268
Lioness & cub
Laurits Jensen
Compare Royal Copenhagen 804
31cms
***
1984
$650-850

2270
Girl with calves
Axel Locher
21cms
**
In production 1984
$300-400

2269
Fish (pair) & crab
Svend Jespersen
23cms
**
$150-250

2271
Arabian horse
27cms
****
In production 1984
$400-550

2272
Girl with cow & goose
Axel Locher
20cms
***
$300-400

2273
'My Balloon'
Michaela Ahlmann
23cms
**
In production 1984
$50-125

2274
Boy
10cms
***
$50-125

2275
'Help Me, Mum'
Michaela Ahlmann
14cms
**
In production 1988
$75-150

2276
Girl with kittens
16.5cms
**
Blanc de chine
$100-200

2277
Mother, child on knee looking at tortoise
11cms
***
$125-225

2278
Throw down the ball
Michaela Ahlmann
18.5cms
**
$75-150

2279
Lion & lioness
Laurits Jensen
Compare Dahl-Jensen 1259
30 x 17.5cms
*****
$750-1200

2280
Greenland girl sitting
22.5cms
***
Blanc de chine
$250-350

2281
Greenland girl sitting
22.5cms
***
Blanc de chine
$250-350

2282
Greenland girl standing
45cms
***
Blanc de chine
$275-375

2283
Nude kneeling
22.5cms
***
Blanc de chine
$250-350

2285
Girl with starfish
20.5cms
***
Blanc de chine
$300-500

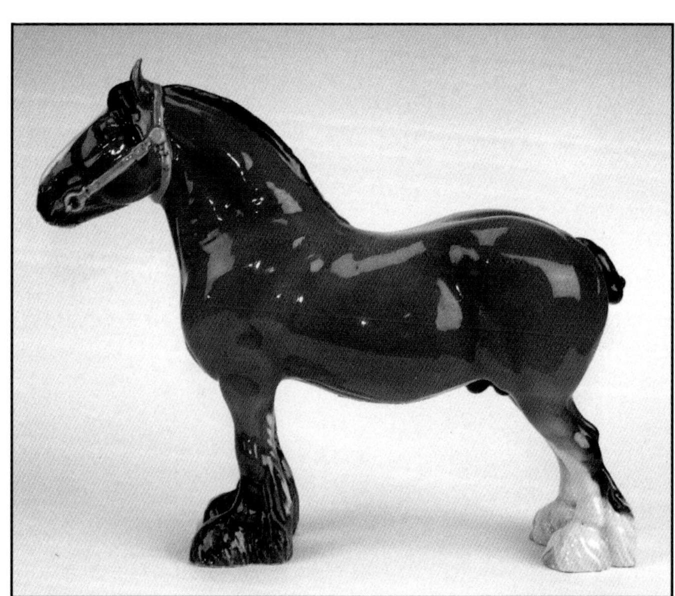

2293
Shire Horse
***
$300-450

2296
Girl potter
***
Blanc de chine
$75-150

2300
Ballet girl
35cms
***
$250-350

2298 RC number 473
Ida's flowers
Ebbe Sadolin/Svend Jespersen
15cms
*
$75-150 MSRP $250

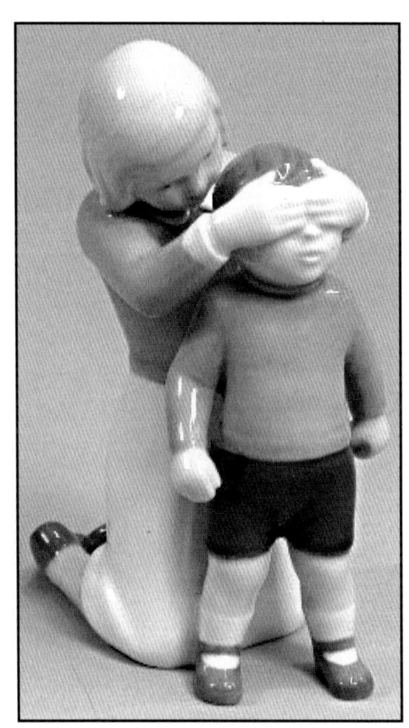

2301
'Guess who?'
20cms
**
$100-200

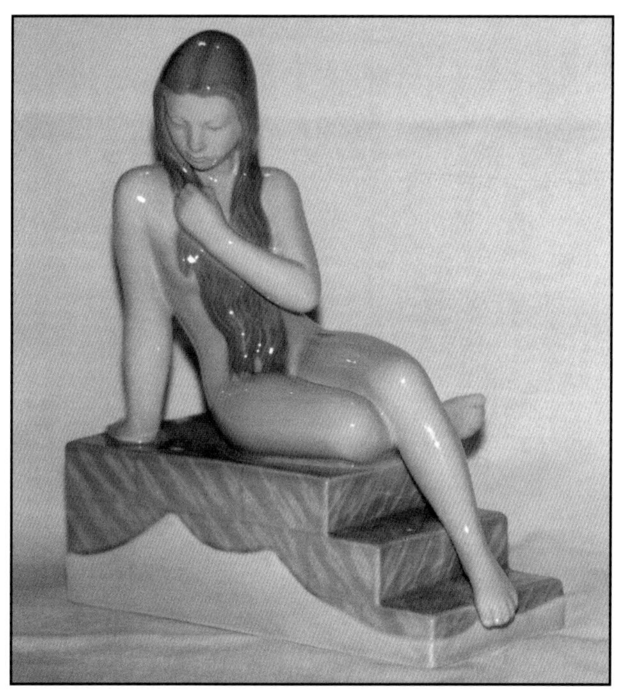

2302
Nude on steps
20cms
***
$200-300

2304
'Merete'
Svend Jespersen
20cms
**
In production 1988
$75-125

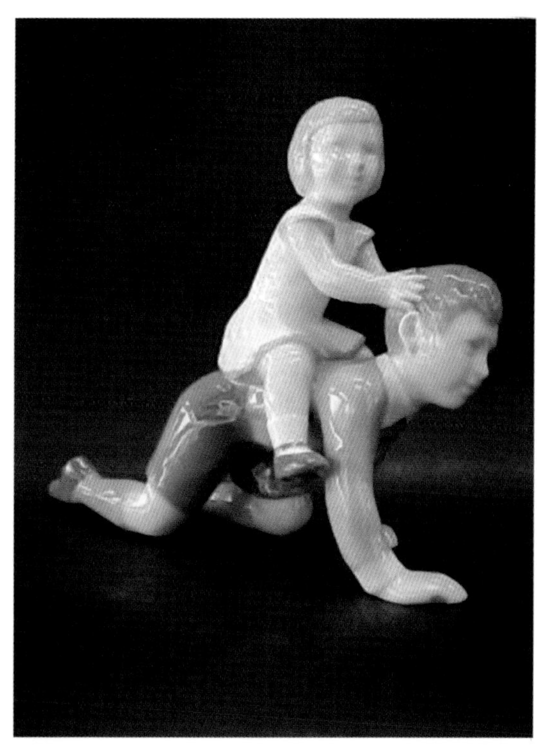

2303
My horse
18cms
**
$100-200

2305
'Christmas Meal'
13cms
***
$75-150

2306
'The Little Builder'
Svend Jespersen
10cms
**
In production 1984
$75-150

2307
Motherly care
12.5cms
**
$75-150

2309
Cat sleeping
15cms
***
$75-125

2308
Siamese cat
Svend Jespersen
14cms
**
In production 1972
$50-100

2310 RC number 474
Robin
Svend Jespersen
10cms
*
$50-100 MSRP $115

2311
Robin on twig
Svend Jespersen
9cms
**
In production 1988
$50-100

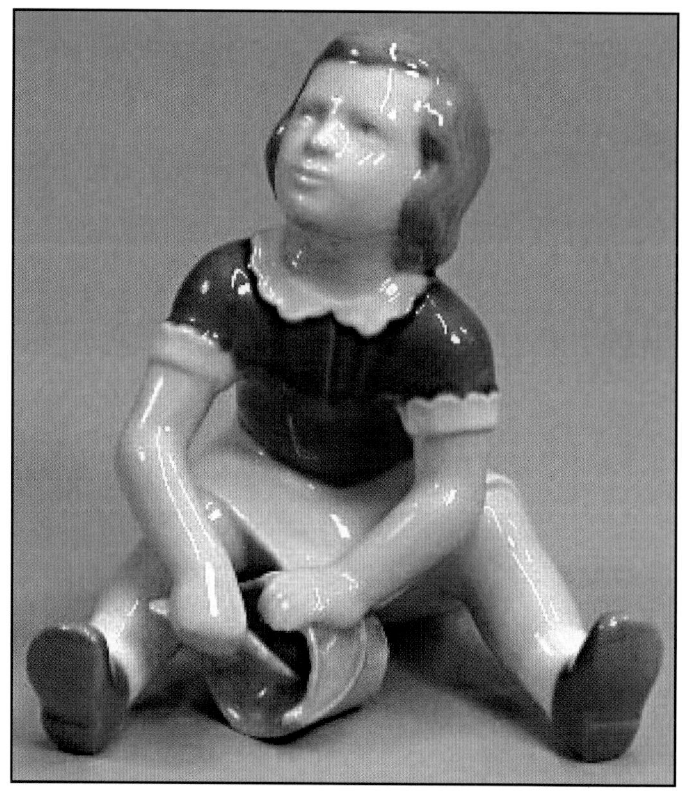

2313
'Ruth'
Svend Jespersen
11cms
**
In production 1984
$75-150

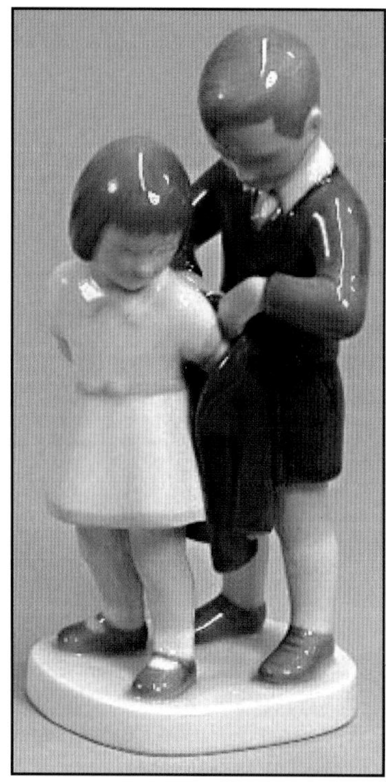

2312
'Gentleman'
Svend Jespersen
18cms
**
In production 1988
$75-150

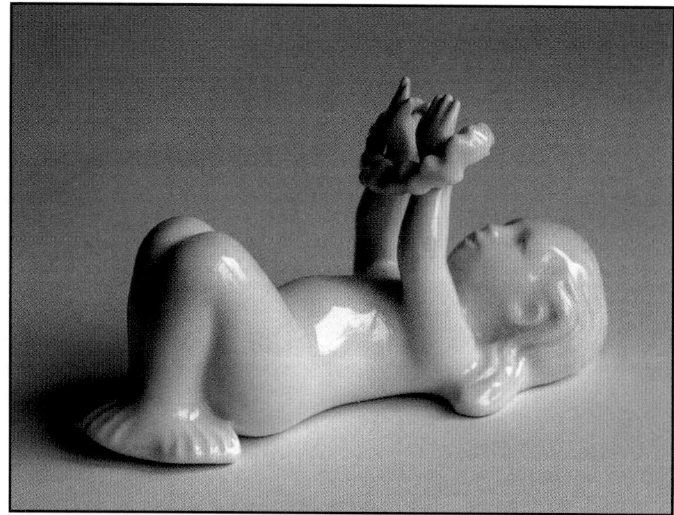

2314
Sea girl- lying
Ebbe Sadolin/Svend Jespersen
12cms
**
Blanc de chine, also available with gold edging. In production 1972
$40-100

2315
Sea boy- resting
Ebbe Sadolin/Svend Jespersen
10cms
**
Blanc de chine, also available with gold edging. In production 1972
$40-100

2317
Girl buttoning shoe
Svend Jespersen
10cms
**
In production 1988
$75-150

2316 RC number 477
Girl with puppy
Vita Thymann
13cms
*
$80-160 MSRP $225

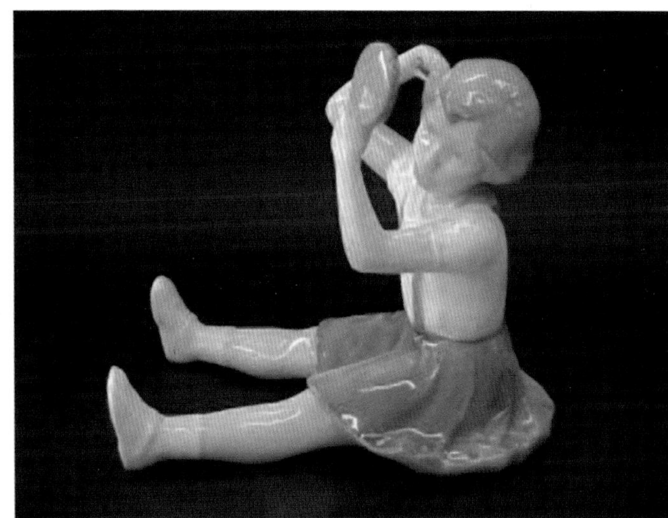

2318
'Vanity'
Svend Jespersen
14cms
**
In production 1984
$75-150

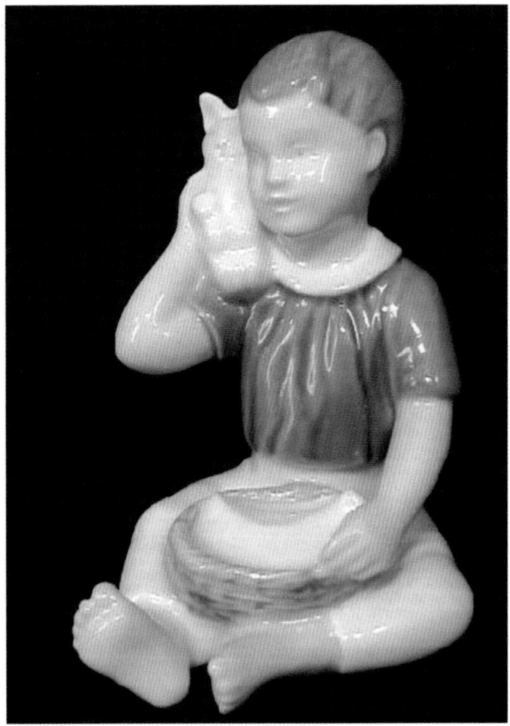

2319
Child with rabbit
15cms
**
$75-150

2321
'Little Sailor'
Vita Thymann
13.5cms
**
$75-150

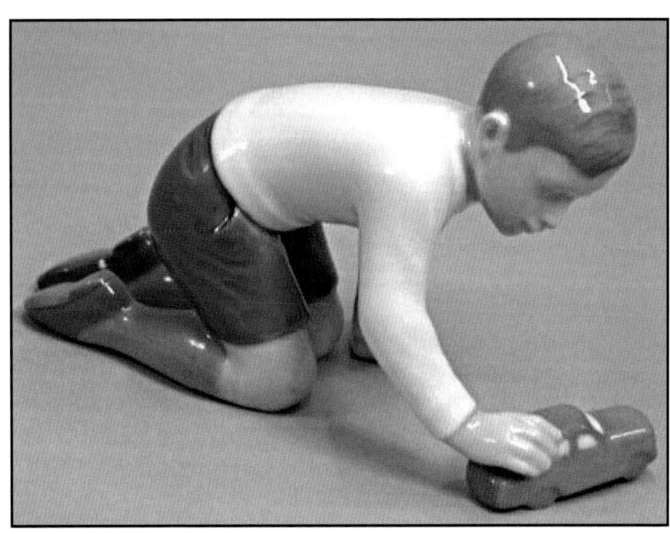

2320
Boy with toy car
12.5cms
**
$75-150

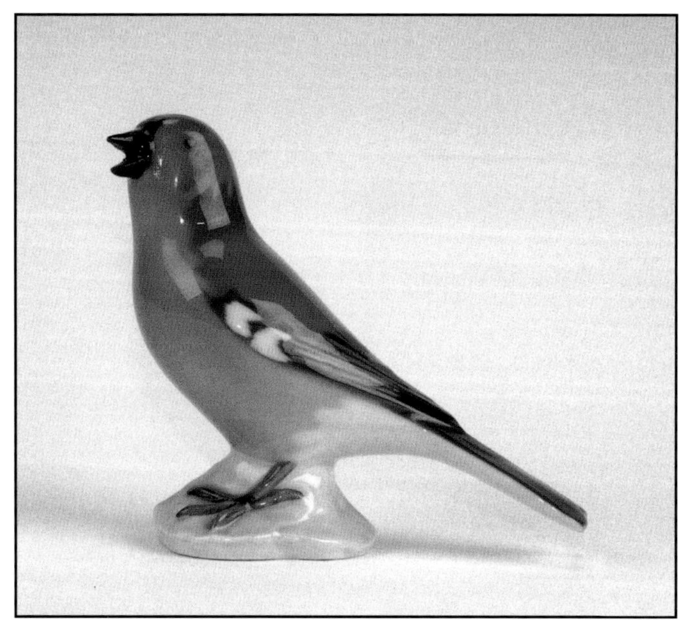

2322
Chaffinch
Svend Jespersen
14cms
**
In production 1984
$50-125

2323
Great Titmouse
Svend Jespersen
11cms
**
In production 1984
$50-100

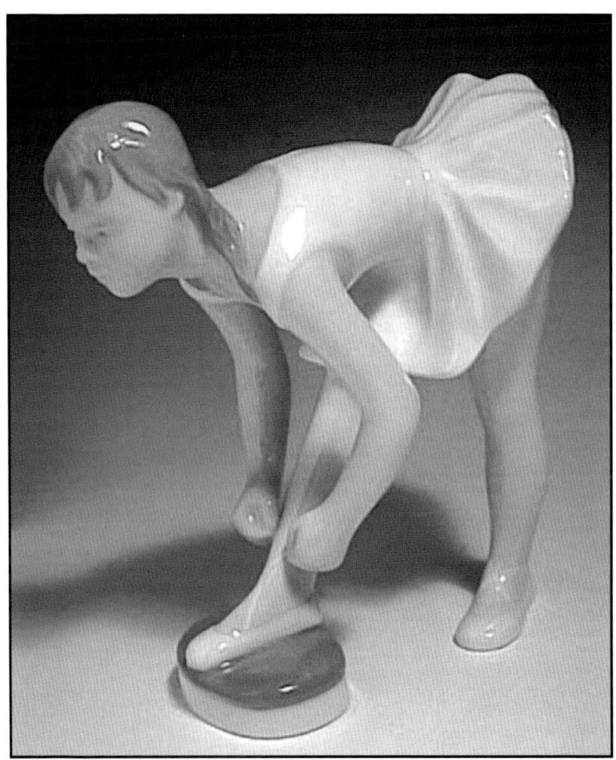

2325
Ballet dancer
Vita Thymann
13cms
**
In production 1984
$100-150

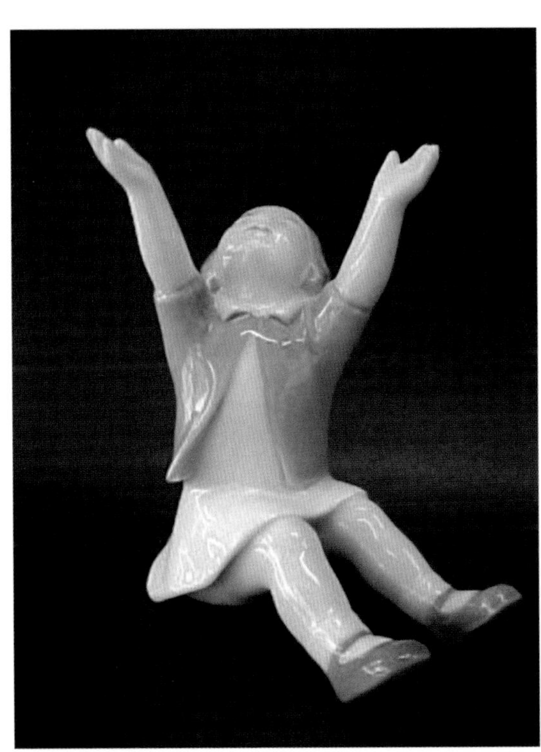

2324 RC number 478
'Up to Mom'
Svend Jespersen
11cms
*
$80-160 MSRP $230

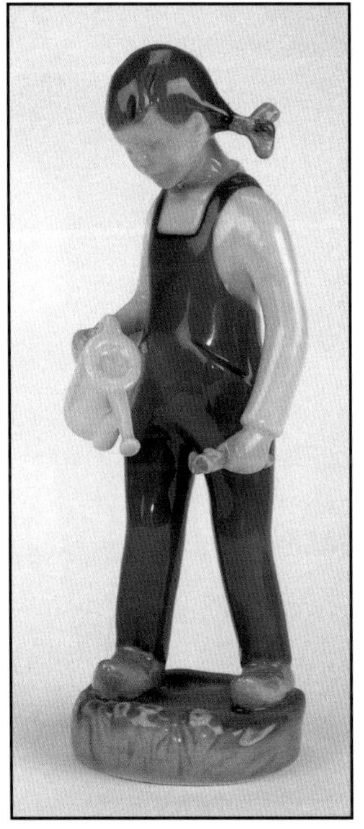

2326
'Little Gardener'
Vita Thymann
20cms
**
In production 1988
$75-150

2327
'Little Hunter'
Vita Thymann
13.5cms
**
$75-150

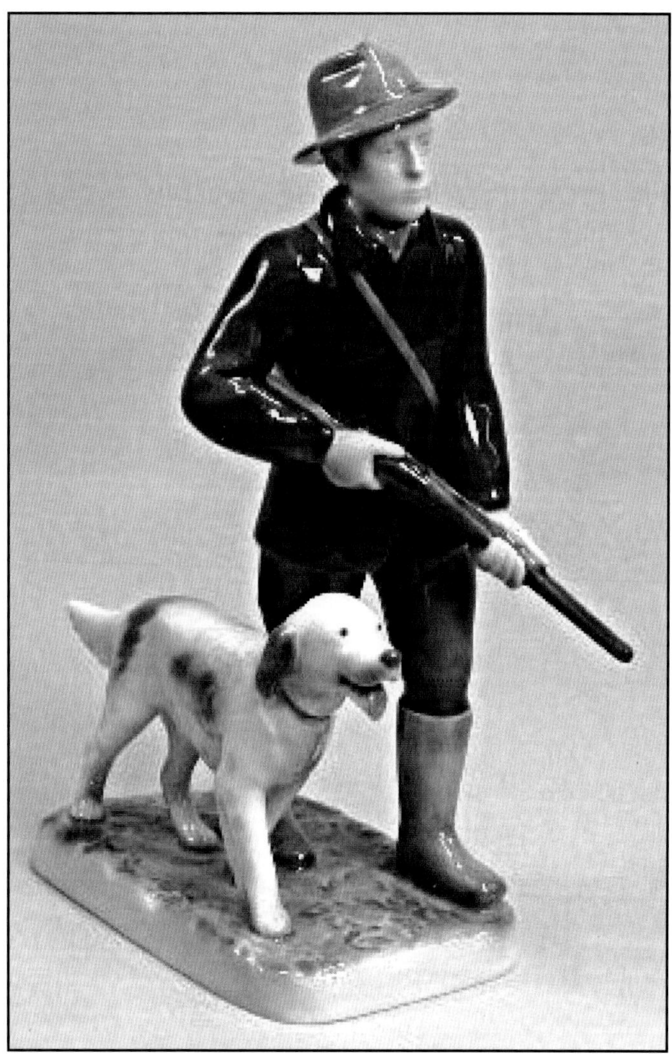

2328
Hunter with dog
Svend Jespersen
29cms
**
In production 1984
$250-350

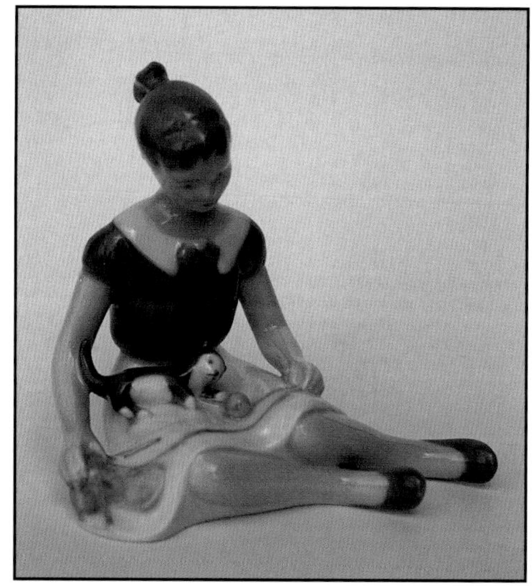

2329 RC number 479
'Birgite'
Vita Thymann
13cms
*
$75-150

2330
Boston Terrier
19cms
**
In production 1984
$125-200

2331
Boy with dog
22.5cms
**
$100-200

2332
Madonna
Ebbe Sadolin/Svend Jespersen
23cms
***
$100-200

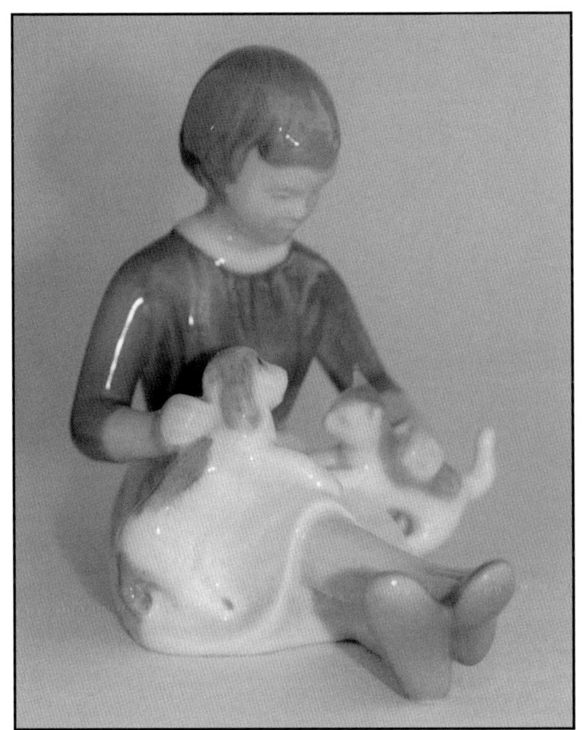

2333
'Make friends'
Vita Thymann
11cms
**
In production 1988
$75-150

2335
Foundry worker
Svend Jespersen
30cms
***
$250-350

2334
'Must I be washed?'
Vita Thymann
13cms
***
$75-150

2336
Girl with kid goat
Vita Thymann
13cms
***
$150-250

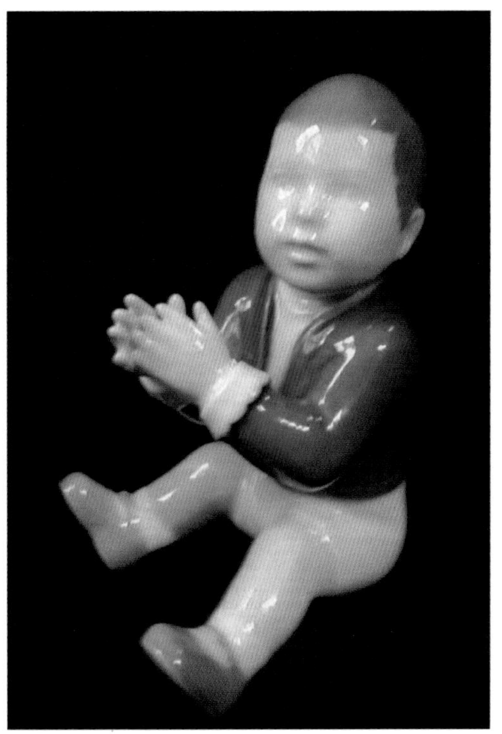

2337
Boy sitting
11cms
**
$50-125

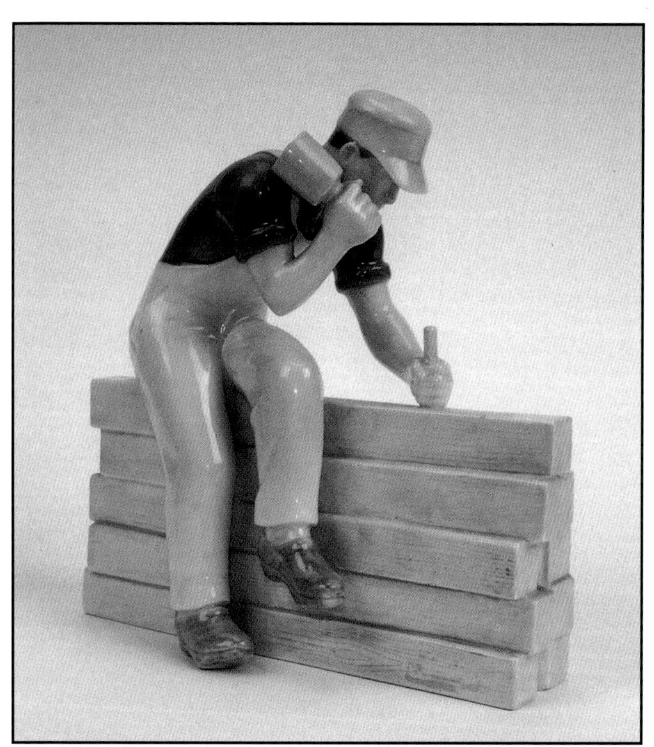

2339
Carpenter
Svend Jespersen
23cms
***
$300-400

2338
Boy with fish & net
Vita Thymann
20cms
***
$75-150

2340
Girl feeding dove
Vita Thymann
13cms
***
$75-150

2341
Budgerigar - green
Svend Jespersen
15cms
**
Also available in stoneware. In production 1988
$50-105

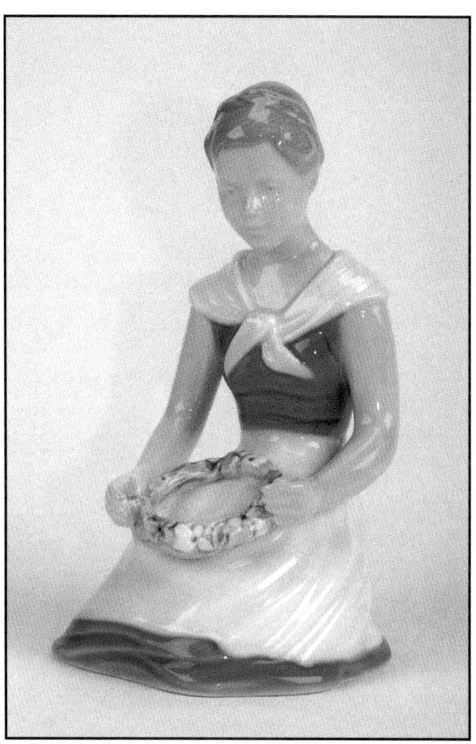

2345
Girl with garland
Vita Thymann
14cms
**
In production 1988
$75-150

2342
Guardsman
Svend Jespersen
27cms
***
In production 1972
$350-500

2344
Boy playing flute
Vita Thymann
15cms
***
$75-150

2346
Boy holding flowers
Vita Thymann
16cms
***
In production 1972
$75-125

2347
White eye -robin?
Svend Jespersen
5.5cms
**
$50-100

2348
Finch
7.5cms
**
$75-125

2351
'Skating Girl'
Vita Thymann
15cms
***
In production 1972
$100-175

2350
'The Little Painter'
Vita Thymann
22.5cms
***
$125-200

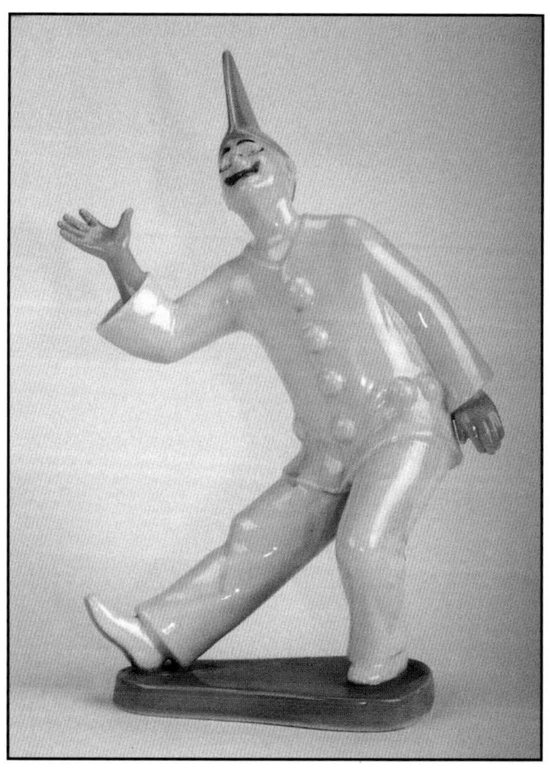

2353 RC number 486
Pierrot
Ebbe Sadolin/Svend Jespersen
23cms
*
$150-250

2354 RC number 487
Harlequin
Ebbe Sadolin/Svend Jespersen
28cms
*
$250-450

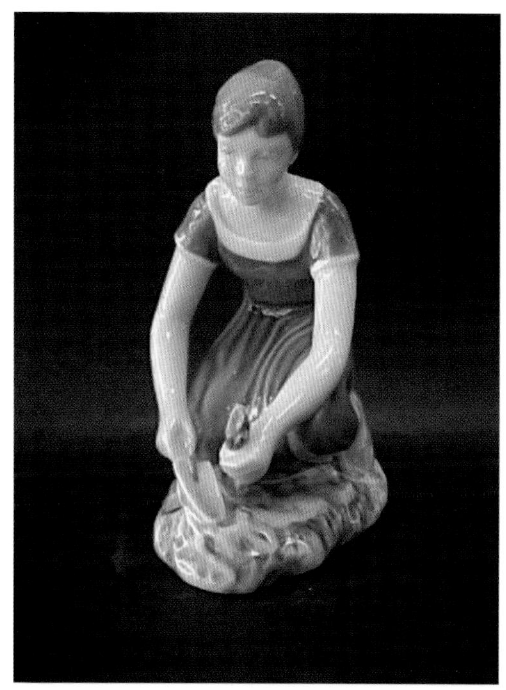

2356
Girl
Vita Thymann
14cms
***
$75-150

2355 RC number 488
Columbine
Ebbe Sadolin/Svend Jespersen
25cms
*
$150-250

2357
Youth with basket
20cms
**
$75-150

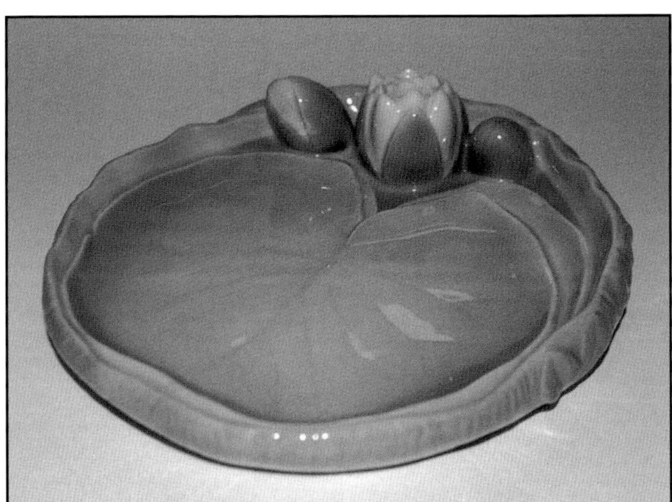

2360
Lily pad
Svend Jespersen
18cms

2358
Boy with skis
Vita Thymann
22cms
***
In production 1972
$100-175

2359
Lily pad
Svend Jespersen
26cms
600%
box BFI

2361
Bird preening tail -Chaffinch ?
8.5cms
***
$50-100

2362
Finch
8.5cms
**
$50-100

2364
Tennis player - female
Vita Thymann
20.5cms
**
$100-150

2367
'Hairdresser'
Vita Thymann
11cms
***
In production 1972
$100-175

2366 RC number 502
Salmon trout
Erling Vangedal
Compare Dahl-Jensen 1379 and 1387
22cms
*
$75-150 MSRP $195

2368
'Aalborg'
20.5cms
$150-250

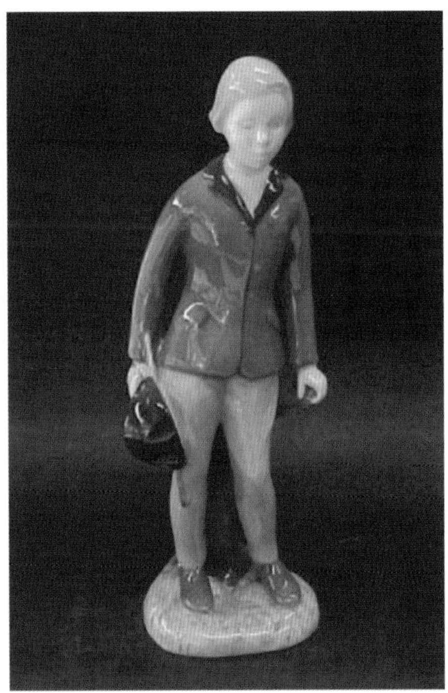

2369
Horsewoman
Vita Thymann
20.5cms
**
$100-175

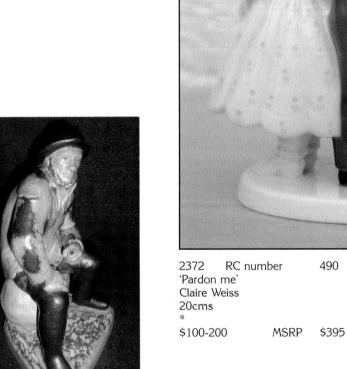

2372 RC number 490
'Pardon me'
Claire Weiss
20cms
*
$100-200 MSRP $395

2370 RC number 489
Old fisherman
Svend Jespersen
22cms
*
Also available in stoneware
$300-400 MSRP $950

2371
Dish with anchor
21cms

2373
'Marianne'
Claire Weiss
14cms
**
In production 1988
$75-150

2374
'Erik'
Claire Weiss
12cms
**
In production 1988
$75-150

2375
Footballer
Vita Thymann
22cms
***
In production 1972
$100-175

2377
Dish with anchor
Svend Jespersen
21cms

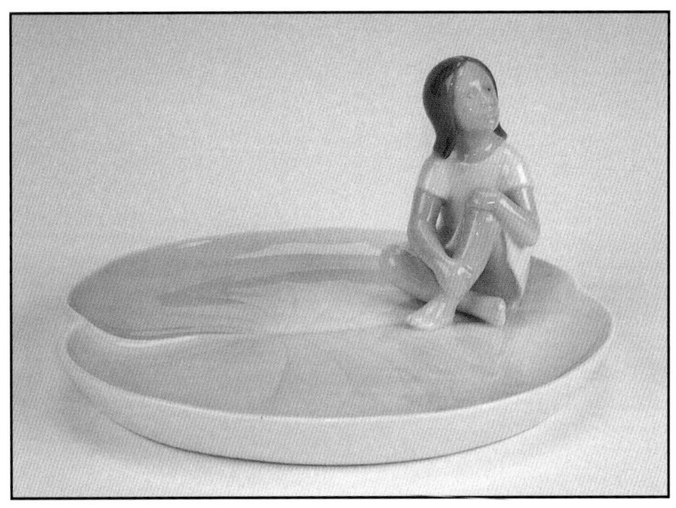

2378
'Thumbelina' on tray
Ebbe Sadolin/Svend Jespersen
***
In production 1972

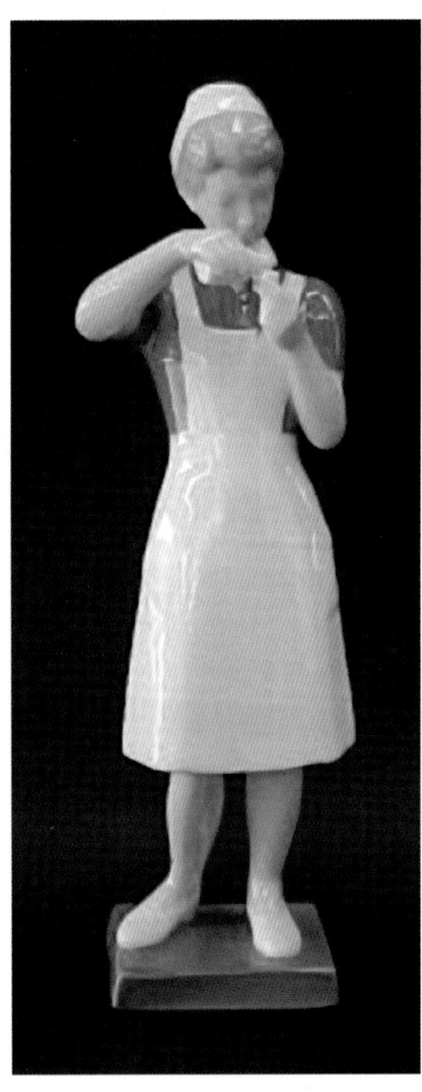

2379 RC number 491
Nurse
Svend Jespersen
23cms
*
$100-200

2380
Boy with sailing boat
Claire Weiss
18cms
***
In production 1972
$75-150

2384
Puffin
Svend Jespersen
16cms
**
In production 1988
$75-175

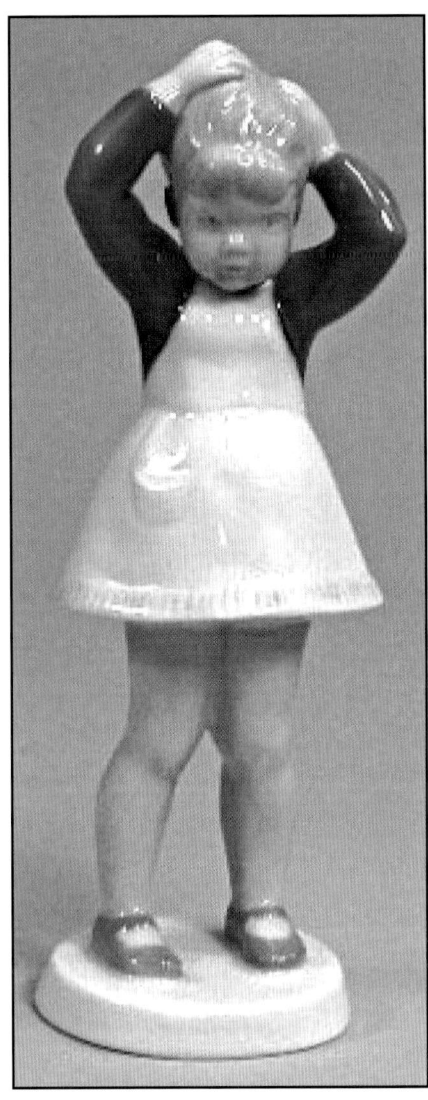

2381
'Anne'
Claire Weiss
19cms
***
In production 1972
$100-150

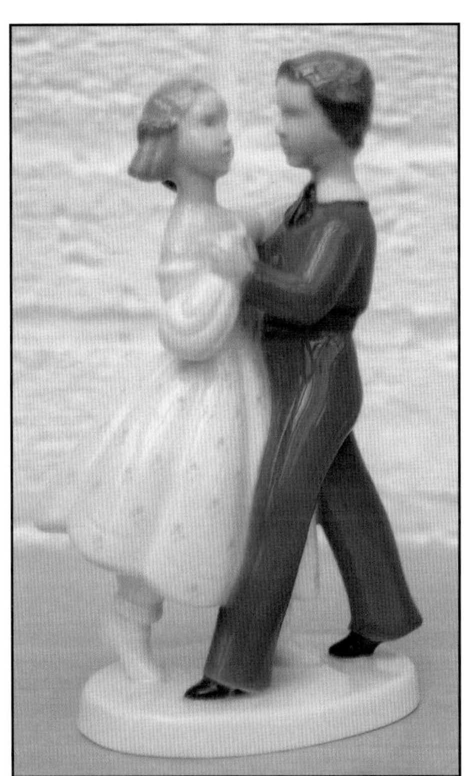

2385 RC number 492
Dancing couple
Claire Weiss
20cms
*
$100-200 MSRP $395

2386
Partridge
Svend Jespersen
18cms
**
In production 1988
$125-225

2388
Girl with bricks
Claire Weiss
9cms
***
In production 1972
$100-150

2389
Cock pheasant
Svend Jespersen
27cms
**
In production 1988
$200-300

2387
'Miss Charming'
Claire Weiss
18cms
**
In production 1988
$75-125

2390
Boy with flowers
Claire Weiss
18.5cms
**
$75-125

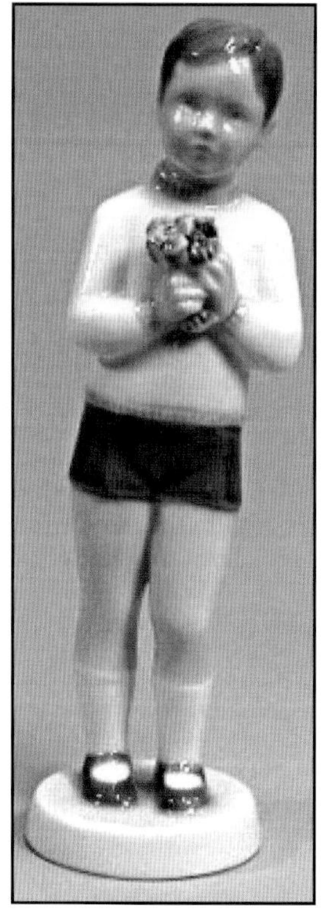

2391
Girl with ball
Claire Weiss
18.5cms
**
$75-125

2392
'Cathrine'
Claire Weiss
14cms
**
$75-125

2393
'Jacob'
Claire Weiss
12.5cms
**
$75-125

2394
Child with sea horse
Ebbe Sadolin/Svend Jespersen
13cms
**
Blanc de chine
$50-120

2395
Child with sea horse
Ebbe Sadolin/Svend Jespersen
10.5cms
**
Blanc de chine
$50-120

2396
Child with sea horse
Ebbe Sadolin/Svend Jespersen
13cms
**
Blanc de chine
$50-120

2397
Child with sea horse
Ebbe Sadolin/Svend Jespersen
13cms
**
Blanc de chine
$50-120

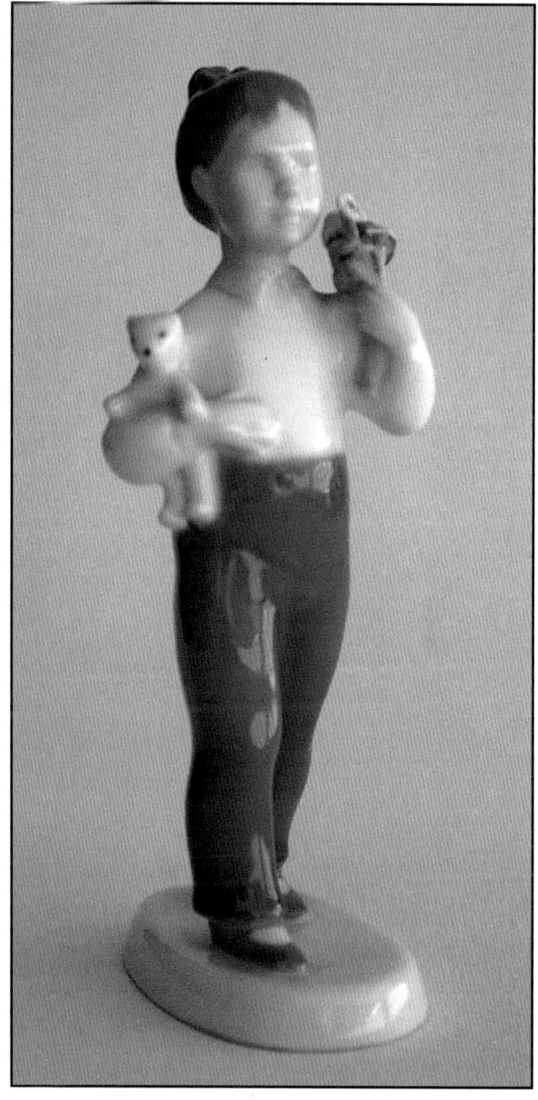

2398
'Congratulations Mama'
Claire Weiss
16.5cms
**
$75-150

2399
'I am coming now'
Claire Weiss
11cms
**
$75-150

2401
'Jorgen'
Claire Weiss
16.5cms
**
$75-150

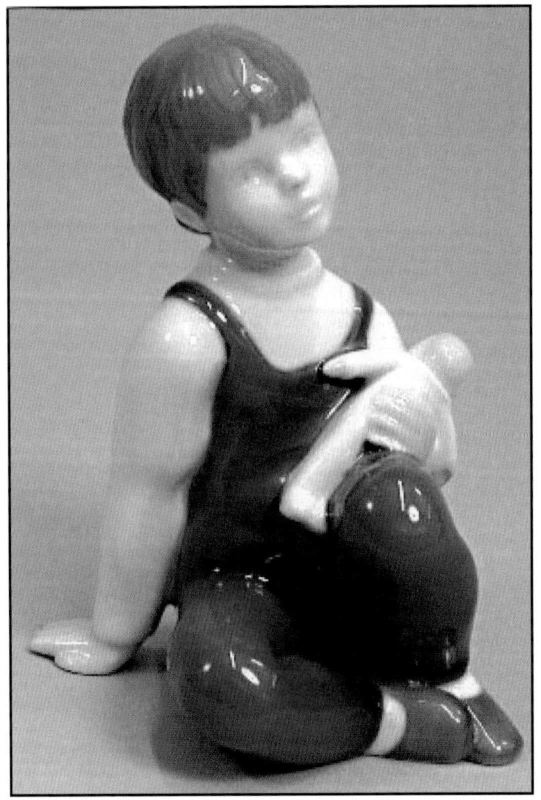

2400
'Children's Hour'
Claire Weiss
12.5cms
**
$75-150

2402
'The Little Player'
Claire Weiss
16.5cms
**
$75-150

2403
Boy with ball
Claire Weiss
17cms
**
$75-150

2404
Girl singing
Claire Weiss
18cms
**
$75-150

2406
Nuthatch
Emil Petersen
13cms
**
In production 1988
$75-125

2405
Blackbird
Emil Petersen
21cms
**
Also available in stoneware. In production 1984
100-150

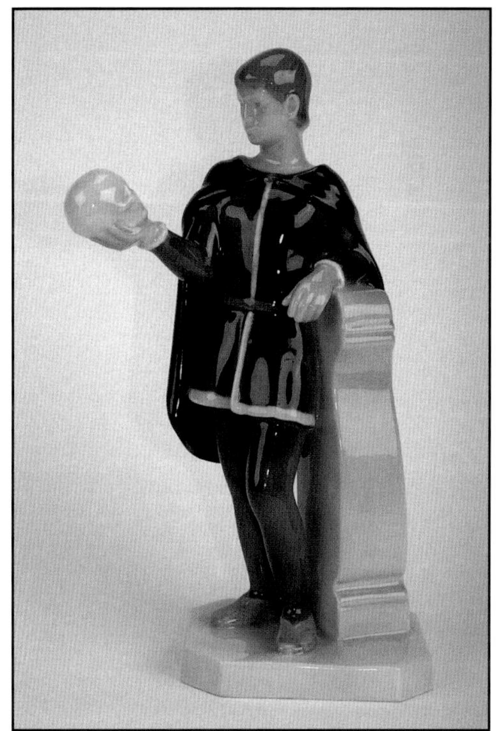

2408
Hamlet
Ebbe Sadolin/Svend Jespersen
22cms
***
$150-250

2409
Ophelia
Ebbe Sadolin/Svend Jespersen
22cms
***
$150-250

2410
Greenlander lifting stone
Karl Kristoffersen
***
$100-200

2411
Greenlander standing
Mathias Lavstrom
***
$100-175

2412
Greenlander with child
Simon Kristoffersen
18cms
***
$150-250

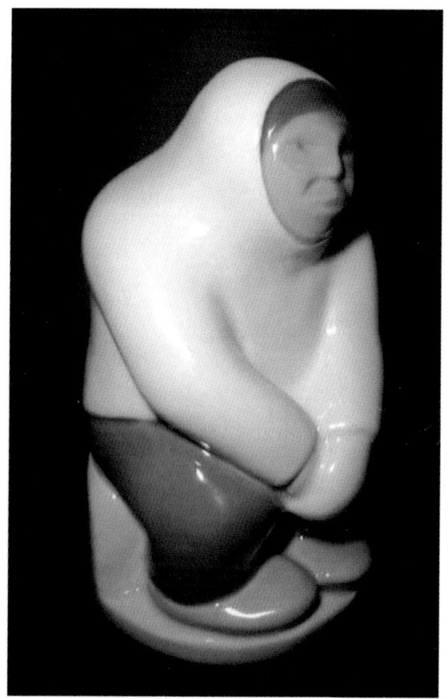

2413
Greenlander sitting
Karl Kristoffersen
***
$100-175

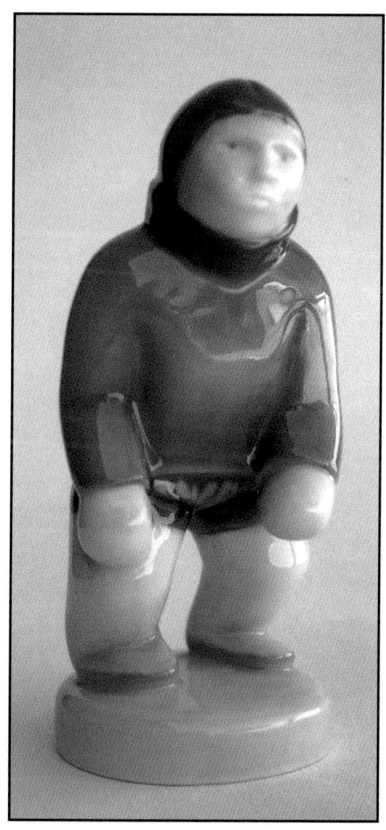

2414
Greenland woman
Karl Kristoffersen
16cms
***
$75-150

2415
Greenlander standing
Karl Kristoffersen
18.5cms
***
$75-150

2416
Greenland woman with bucket
Karl Kristoffersen
22cms
***
$150-250

2419
Potter
***
$250-350

2417
Greenlander - angry
Karl Kristoffersen
***
$100-175

2421
Rabbit - lying
12.5cms
**
In production 1984
$40-70

2422
Rabbit - sitting
12.5cms
**
In production 1988
$40-70

2424
Little owl
25cms
**
In production 1988
$300-500

2423
Rabbit - standing
12.5cms
**
In production 1988
$40-70

2425 RC number 493
Turkey cock
32.5cms
*
Limited edition - 750
$2,000-4,000

2426 RC number 494
Turkey hen
30cms
*
Limited edition - 750
$1,500-3,000

2428
Electrician
28.5cms
***
$250-350

2431
House painter
28.5cms
***
$250-350

2429
Baker
29cms
***
$250-350

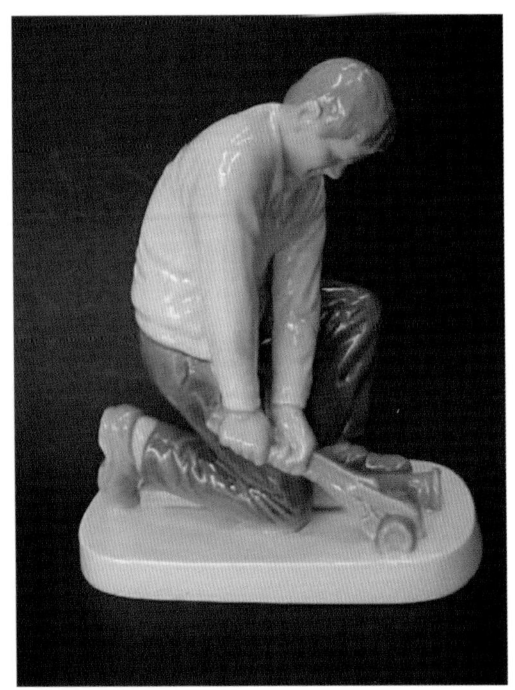

2432
Pipe fitter
21cms
***
$250-350

2433
Butcher
25.5cms
***
$250-350

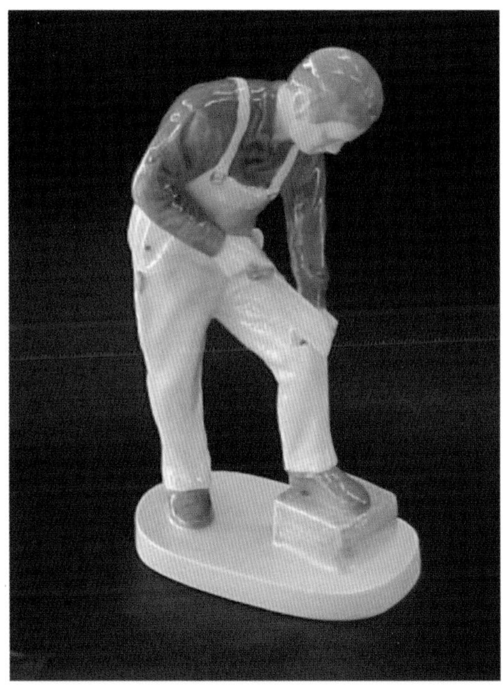

2434
Carpenter
26cms
***
$250-350

2435 RC number 495
'Thirst'
20.5cms
*
$250-350 MSRP $725

2436
Policeman
30cms
***
$250-350

2439
Grebe & chicks
28cms
****
In production 1984
$250-400

2441
Rabbit lying - white
11cms
**
In production 1984
$30-60

2442
Rabbit, sitting - white
12.5cms
**
In production 1988
$30-60

2443
Rabbit, standing - white
12.5cms
**
In production 1988
$30-60

2444
Gunner - Army
29cms
***
$350-500

2445
Pilot
29cms
***
$350-500

2451
Postman
29cms
***
$350-500

2446
Sailor - Navy
29cms
***
$350-500

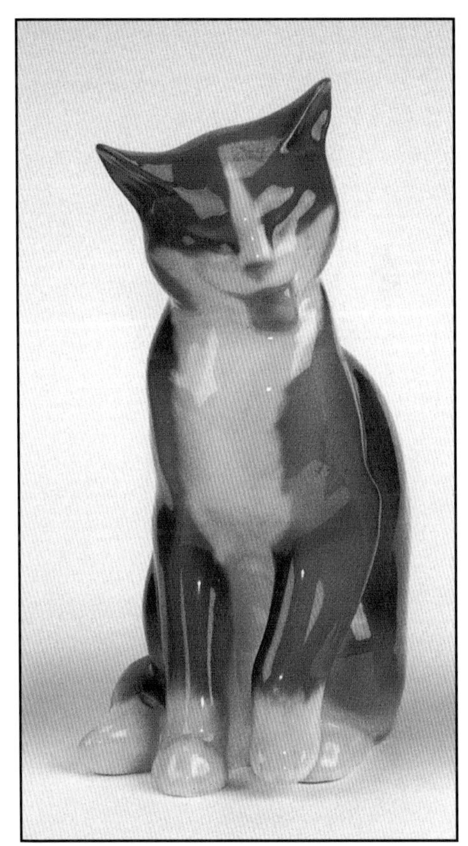

2452
Cat - gray
16cms
**
See also 2256 and 2465 size variations
$75-150

2453 RC number 499
Cat - white
11cms
*
See 1876 identical cat different color
$50-100 MSRP $90

2454 RC number 500
Cat - gray
11cms
*
$75-125 MSRP $110

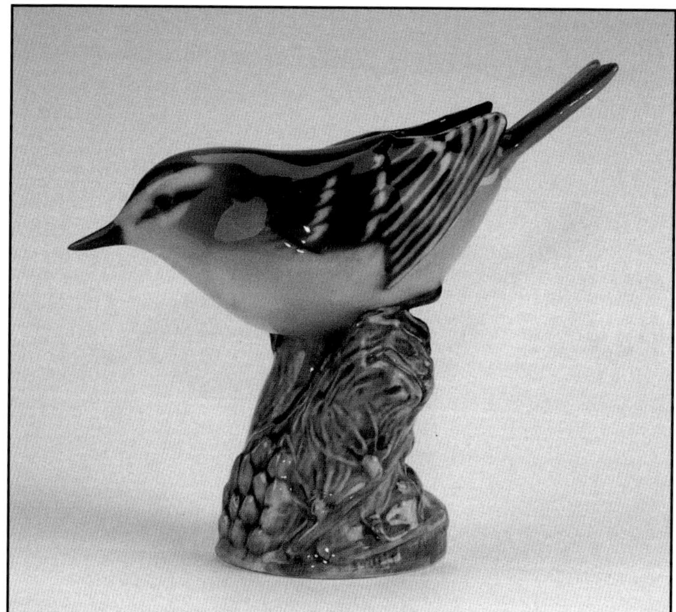

2455
Goldcrest
10cms
***
$75-150

2458
Kinglet
8.5cms
**
In production 1988
$75-125

2459
Bird preening
7.5cms
**
In production 1988
$50-100

2461
Bird preening
7.5cms
**
In production 1988
$50-100

2463
Blue Tit on base
10cms
**
In production 1984
$75-150

2465
Cat - gray
13.5cms
**
In production 1984. See also 2256 and 2452 size variations.
$75-125

2464
Siamese cat - white
14cms
**
In production 1988
$50-100

2466
Cat sitting
12cms
**
In production 1984
$50-100

2467
Frog
8.5cms
**
In production 1988
$50-125

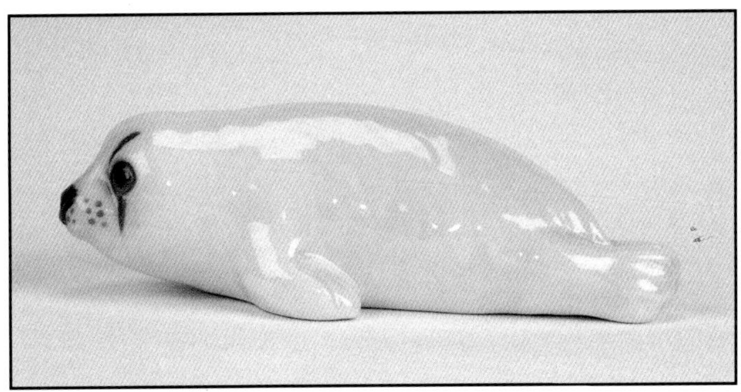

2468 RC number 541
Seal
15cms
*
$50-100

2470
Girl with ice lolly
**
$50-125

2469
Owl
17cms
**
In production 1984
$125-200

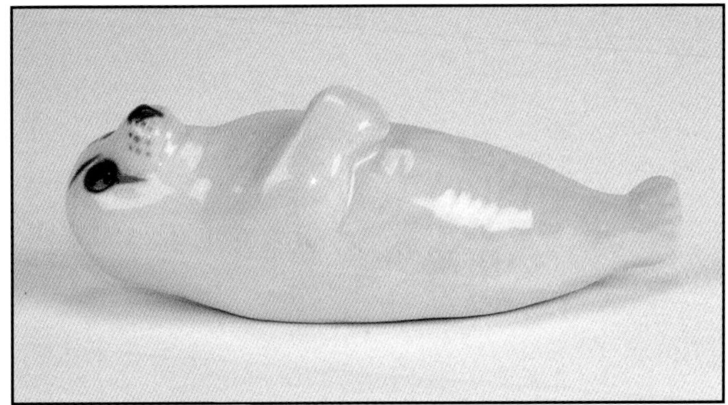

2471 RC number 542
Seal on back
15cms
*
$50-100

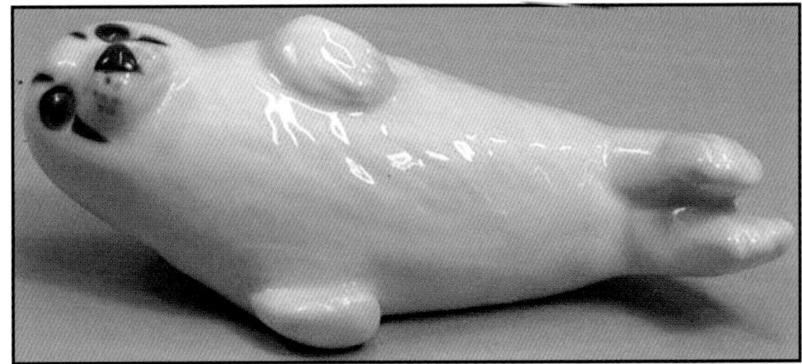

2472 RC number 543
Seal
14cms
*
$50-150

2473
Vagabond
21cms
***
$125-225

2475
Snowy Owl
21cms
**
In production 1988
$150-200

2476
Cat - white
12cms
**
In production 1988
$40-80

2478
Vagabond with bottle
21cms
***
$125-225

2474
Squirrel
14cms
**
In production 1984
$50-100

2479
Guinea-pig - sitting
8cms
**
In production 1984
$75-150

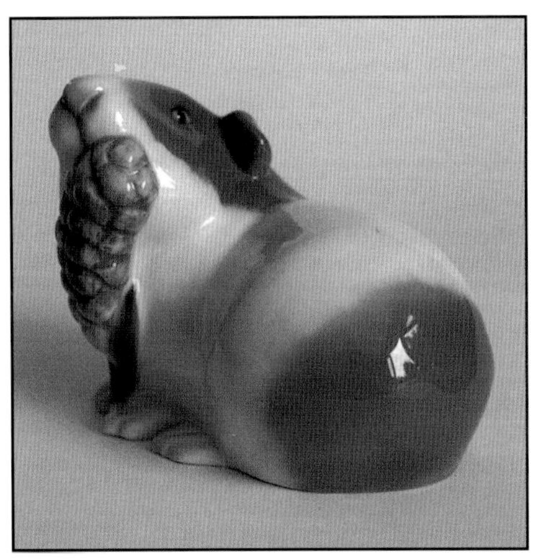

2480
Guinea-pig - lying
8cms
**
In production 1984
$75-150

2481 RC number 481
Titmouse spread wings
10cms
*
Also in bisque
$75-125 MSRP $75

2482 RC number 482
Titmouse
7cms
*
Also in bisque
$50-100 MSRP $75

2483 RC number 483
Titmouse
7cms
*
Also in bisque
$50-100 MSRP $75

2484 RC number 484
Titmouse
6cms
*
Also in bisque
$50-100 MSRP $75

2485 RC number 485
Titmouse
6cms
*
Also in bisque
$50-100

2486
Sailor
***
$350-500

2487
Girl bowling
***
$100-175

2489
Guinea-pig - sitting
8cms
**
In production 1984
$75-150

2490
Guinea-pig - lying
8cms
**
In production 1984
$75-150

2491
Sparrow wings spread
10cms
**
In production 1988
$75-125

2492
Sparrow - Swollen
7cms
**
In production 1988
$50-100

2493
Sparrow - head left
7cms
**
In production 1988
$50-100

2494
Sparrow - raised tail
6cms
**
In production 1988
$50-100

2495
Sparrow
6cms
**
In production 1988
$50-100

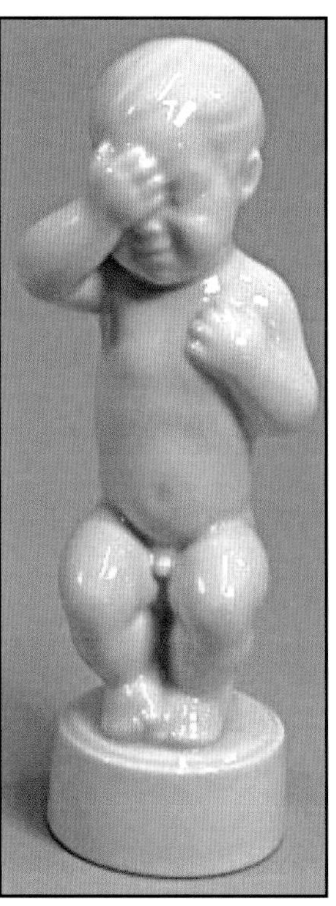

2497
Do not see
**
Blanc de chine. In production 1988
$50-100

2498
Do not speak
**
Blanc de chine. In production 1988
$50-100

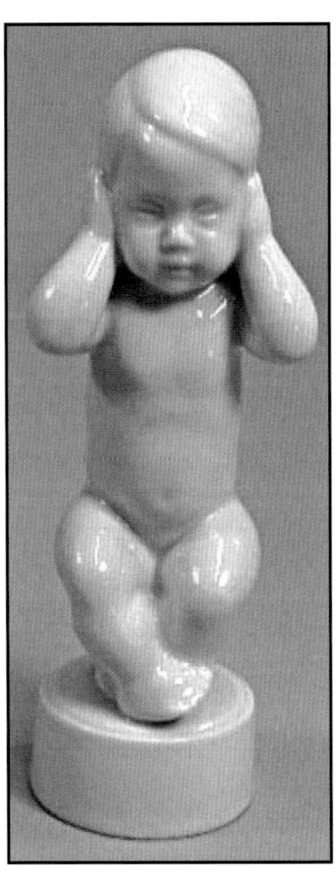

2496
Do not hear
**
Blanc de chine. In production 1988
$50-100

2499
Guinea-pig - sitting
8cms
**
In production 1984
$75-150

2500
Guinea-pig - lying
8cms
**
In production 1984
$75-150

2501
Titmouse with chain
**
In production 1988
$75-125

2502
Parliament attendant
28.5cms
***
$350-500

photo02/556>
2504 RC number 504
Kitten lying - white
8cms
*
$50-100 MSRP $95

2505 RC number 505
Kitten sitting - white
11.5cms
*
$50-100 MSRP $95

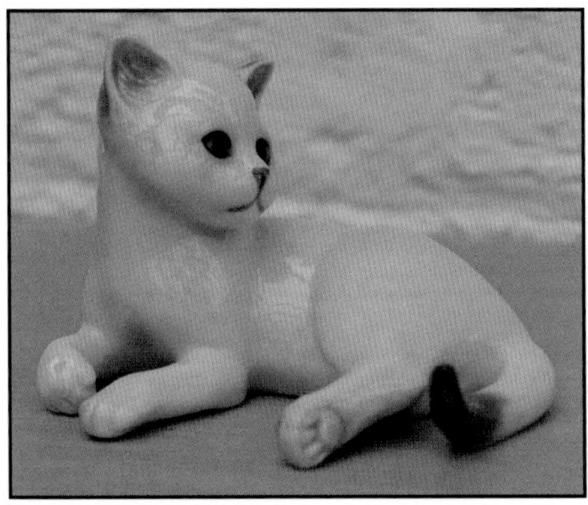

2506 RC number 506
Kitten standing - white
13cms
*
$50-100 MSRP $95

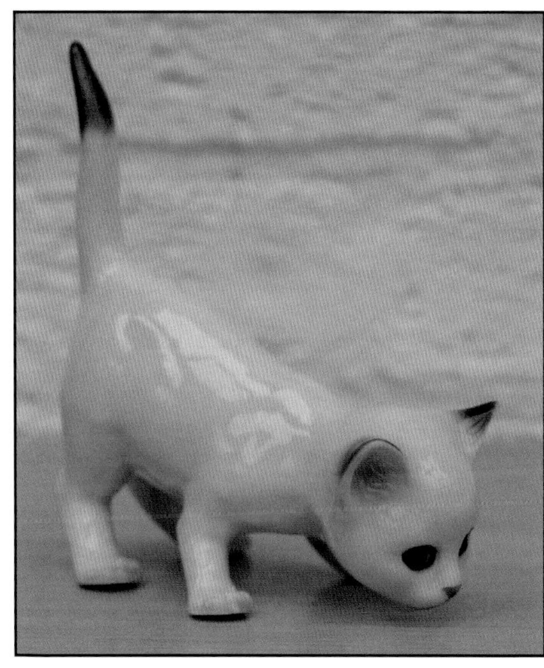

2507 RC number 507
Kitten tail up - white
14cms
*
$50-100 MSRP $95

2508 RC number 508
Clown
11cms
*
$75-125

2509 RC number 509
Clown hands at sides
11cms
*
$75-125

2511 RC number 511
Clown hands on braces
11cms
*
$75-125

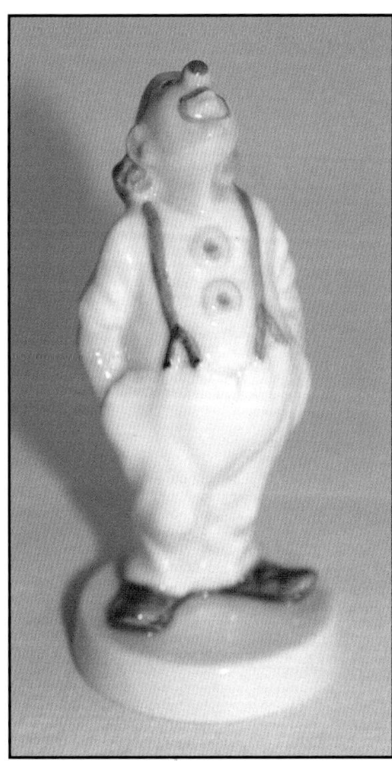

2510 RC number 510
Clown hands in pockets
11cms
*
$75-125

2512
Girl in long dress
**
$125-200

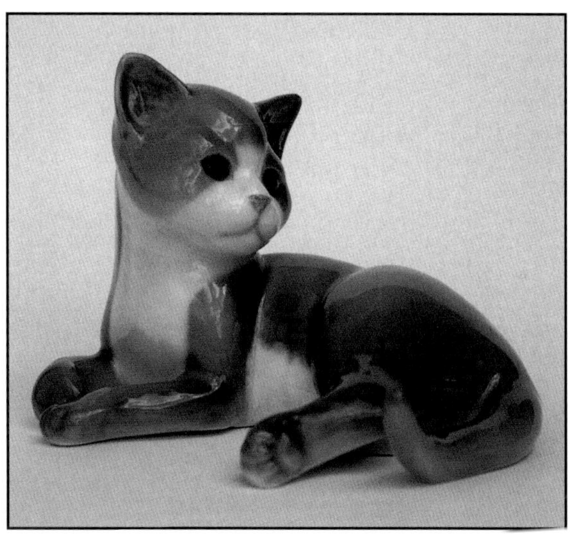

2514 RC number 514
Kitten lying - gray
8cms
*
$75-125 MSRP $125

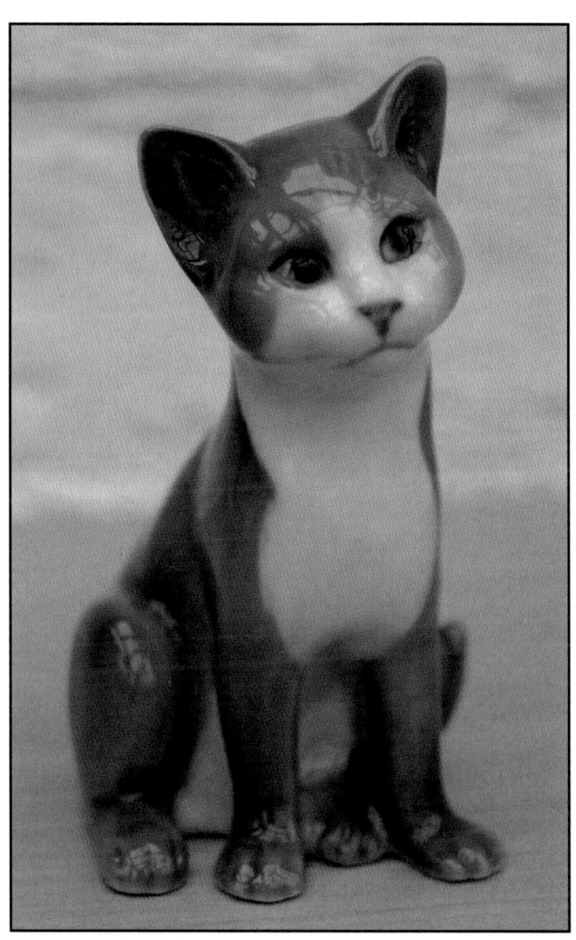

2515 RC number 515
Kitten sitting - gray
11.5cms
*
$75-125 MSRP $125

2516 RC number 516
Kitten standing - gray
13cms
*
$75-125 MSRP $125

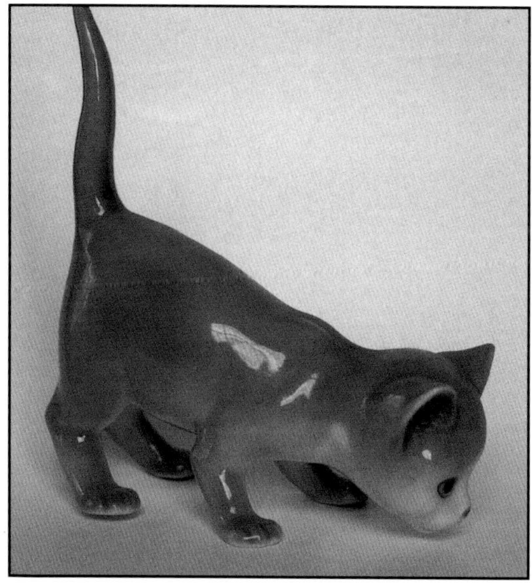

2517 RC number 517
Kitten tail up - gray
14cms
*
$75-125 MSRP $125

2525 RC number 525
'The Tea Party'
*
$75-125

2526
'The Magical Tea Party'
16cms
**
In production 1988
$75-150

2527 RC number 527
Cat
4cms
*
(belongs to 2526)
$20-40

2528
Lion cub
**
$50-75

2531
Lion cub
**
$50-75

2529
Lion cub
**
$50-75

2530 RC number 530
Lion cub
*
$50-75

2532 RC number 532
Boy with raincoat
Soren Brunoe
*
$75-125

2533 RC number 533
Girl - dressed up
20cms
*
$100-200

2535 RC number 535
Polar bear cub standing
Merete Agergaard
7.5cms
*
$50-75 MSRP $110

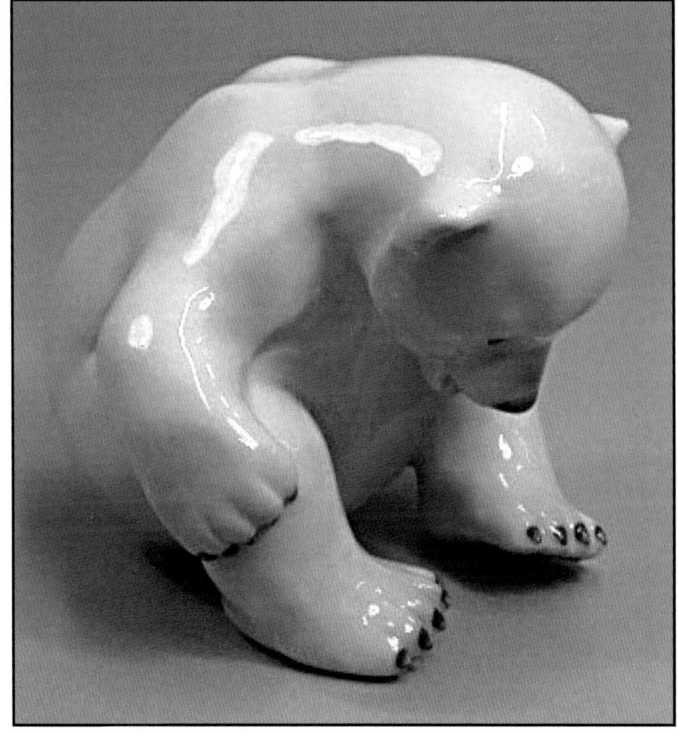

2536 RC number 536
Polar bear cub feet up
Merete Agergaard
10.5cms
*
$50-75 MSRP $110

2537 RC number 537
Polar bear cub on back
Merete Agergaard
10.5cms
*
$50-75 MSRP $110

2538 RC number 538
Polar bear cub lying on back
Merete Agergaard
9cms
*
$50-75 MSRP $110

2539 RC number 539
Pigeon
10.5cms
*
$50-125

2540 RC number 540
Pigeon
6cms
*

$50-125

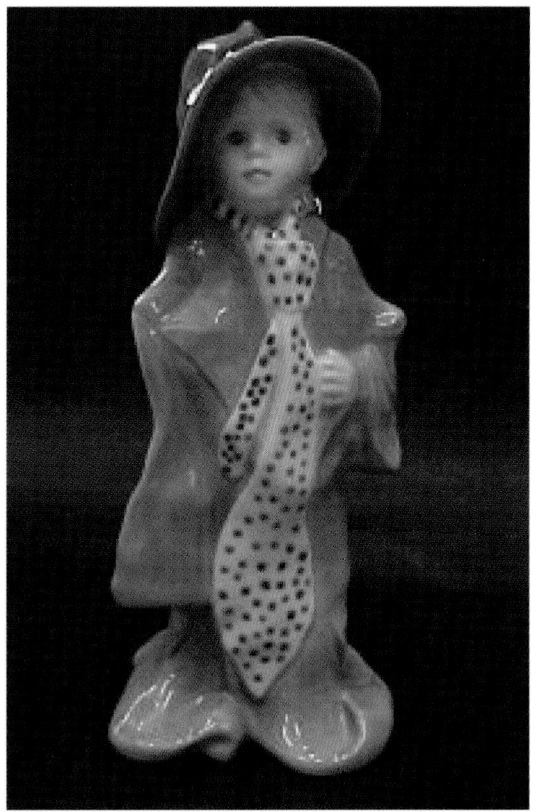

2544 RC number 544
Boy - dressed up
20cms
*
$100-200

2546 RC number 546
'The Little Gardner'
*
$75-125

2541
'A Joyful Flight'
16cms
**
In production 1988
$150-225

2547 RC number 547
Spaniel - white
5cms
*
$20-50

2548 RC number 548
Gipsy girl
17.5cms
*
$100-200

2549 RC number 549
Witch
20cms
*
$100-200

2551
Billy
**
$100-200

2556
Lapwing
6cms
**
$50-125

2558 RC number 558
Lamb sleeping
*
$25-50

2559
Lamb
*
$25-50

2560 RC number 560
Lamb
*
$25-50

2562 RC number 562
Lamb
*
$25-50

2563
Children's Day figurine 88
**
$75-125

2563
'Wash Day'
12.5cms
**
$75-125

2564 RC number 564
Beagle - standing
12.5cms
*
$75-150

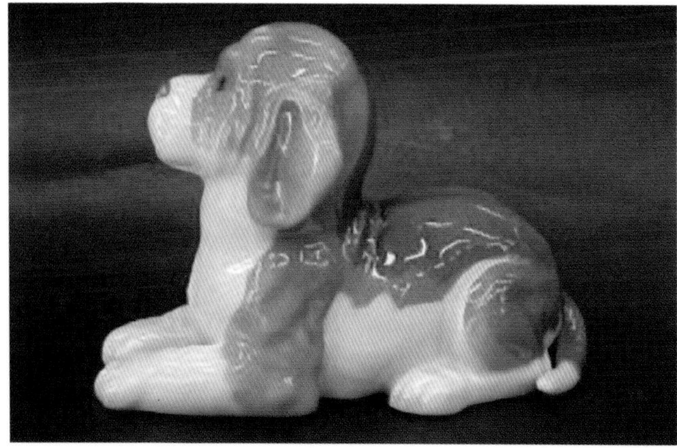

2565 RC number 565
Beagle - lying
*
$75-150

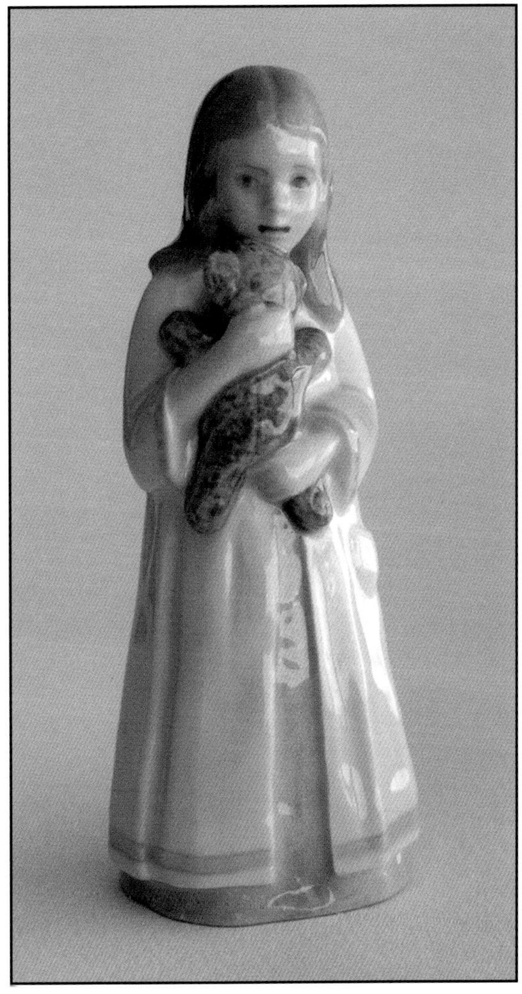

2571
Girl with teddy
15cms
***
$125-225

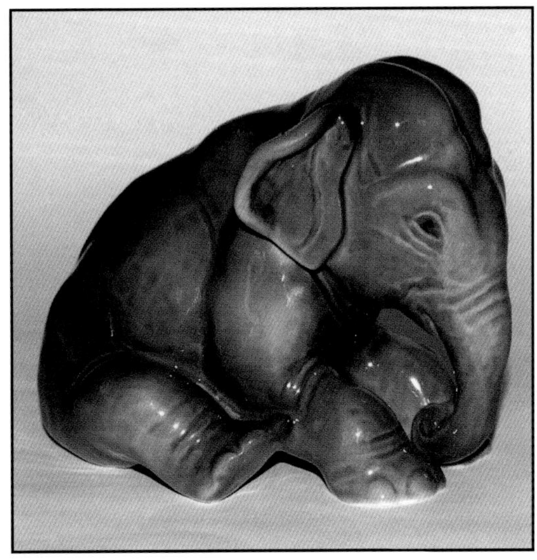

2573 RC number 573
Elephant
*
$50-100

2575 RC number 575
Elephant
*
$50-100

2576 RC number 576
Elephant
*
$50-100

2581
Kid on rock
**
$50-75

2586
See my dress
12.5cms
**
$150-225

2631
Bird head back
**
$50-125

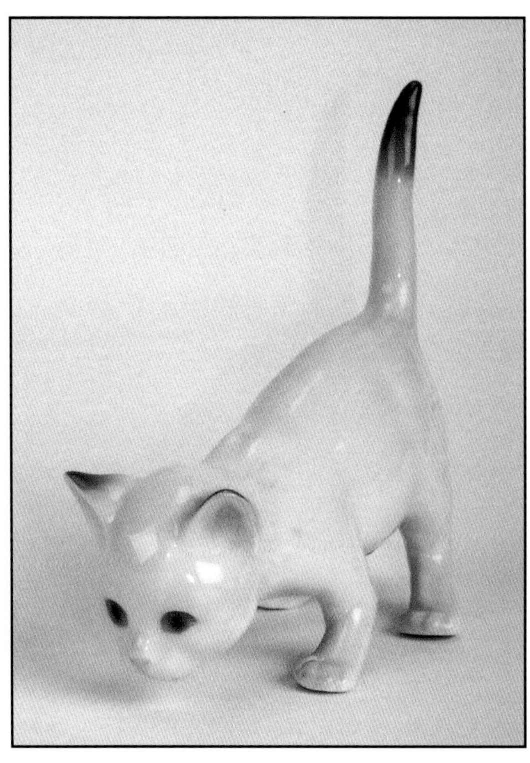

2807
Kitten
**
$50-125

2917
Cat
**
$50-125

2995
Mercury
Bertel Thorvaldsen
15.5cms
**
Biscuit. In production 1984
$150-250

2996
Venus
Bertel Thorvaldsen
15.5cms
**
Biscuit. In production 1984
$150-250

2997
Ballerina
Bertel Thorvaldsen
15.5cms
**
Biscuit. In production 1984
$150-250

3027
Girl carrying serving dish
**
$100-200

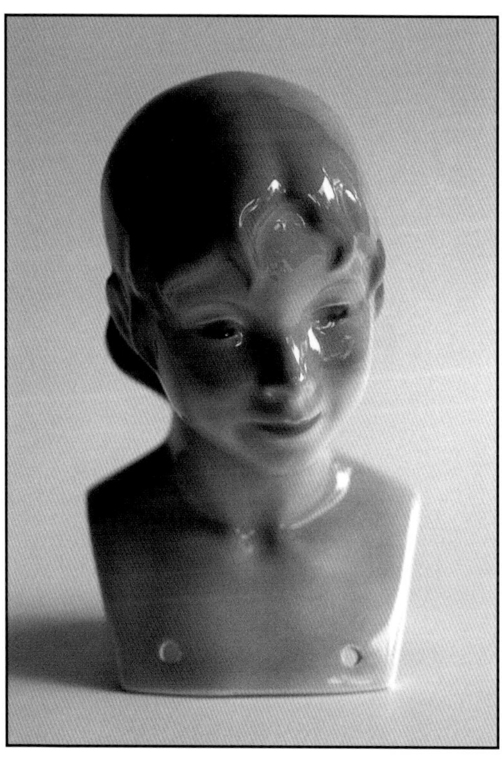

3028
Dolls head
***
$100-200

3188
Budgie stoneware
**
$75-150

4020
Woman with grapes
Kai Nielsen
20cms
***
Blanc de chine
$150-250

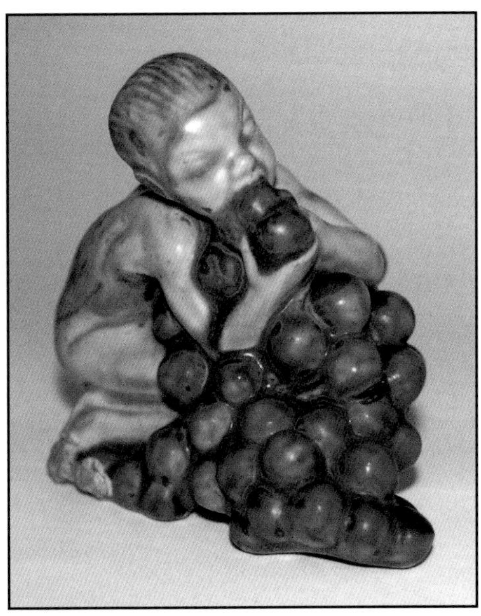

4021
Man with grapes
Kai Nielsen
11cms
***
Blanc de chine
$150-250

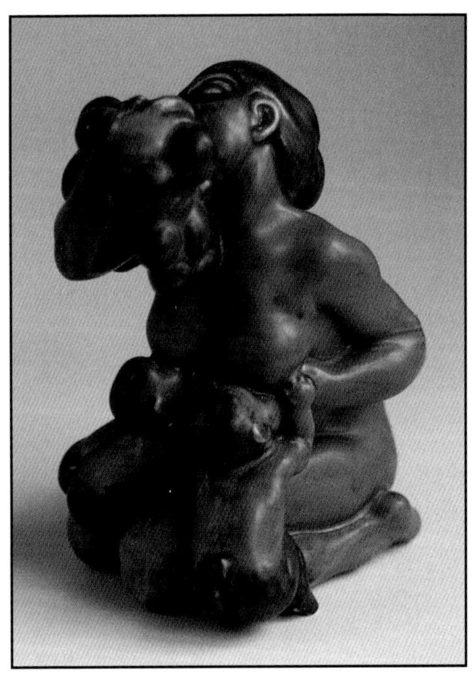

4022
Woman with grapes
Kai Nielsen
15cms
***
Blanc de chine
$200-300

4023
Man & woman
Kai Nielsen
32.5cms
***
Blanc de chine
$350-450

4024
Man with grapes sitting
Kai Nielsen
15cms
***
Blanc de chine
$200-300

4025
Man with grapes
Kai Nielsen
22.5cms
***
Blanc de chine
$200-300

4026
Man, horse & child
Kai Nielsen
22.5cms
****
Blanc de chine
$200-300

4027
Faun with grapes
Kai Nielsen
11cms
****
Blanc de chine
$150-250

4028
Nude, children, man
Kai Nielsen
27.5cms
****
Blanc de chine
$400-500

4029
Woman lying
Kai Nielsen
17.5cms
***
Blanc de chine
$200-300

4030
Neptune, woman
Kai Nielsen
13.5cms
***
Blanc de chine
$175-275

4031
Woman standing
Kai Nielsen
20cms
***
Blanc de chine
$200-300

4032
Woman bending
Kai Nielsen
20cms
***
Blanc de chine
$200-300

4033
Children
Kai Nielsen
11cms
***
Blanc de chine
$100-200

4034
Child with dolphin
Kai Nielsen
7.5cms
**
Blanc de chine
$75-150

4035
Child with dolphin
Kai Nielsen
7.5cms
**
Blanc de chine
$75-150

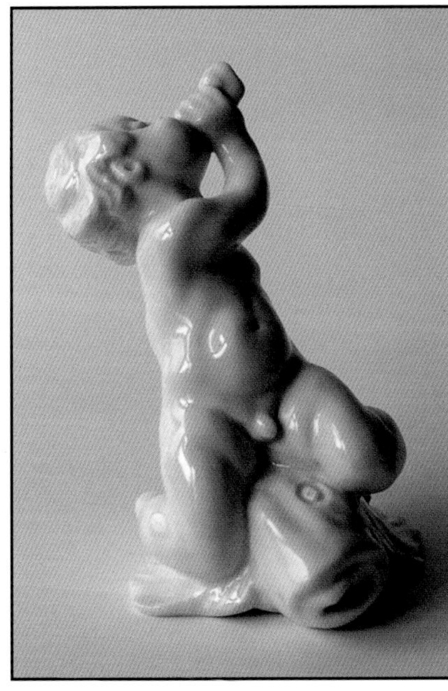

4036
Boy on fish
Kai Nielsen
11cms
**
Blanc de chine
$100-200

4037
Child with dolphin
Kai Nielsen
7.5cms
**
Blanc de chine
$75-150

4038
Girl with dolphin
Kai Nielsen
7.5cms
**
Blanc de chine
$75-150

4055
Mother Nile
Kai Nielsen
40cms
***
Blanc de chine
$700-1000

4056
Girl riding dolphin
Kai Nielsen
40cms
**
Blanc de chine
$700-1000

4057
Girl riding dolphin
Kai Nielsen
40cms
**
Blanc de chine
$700-1000

4058
Girl with dolphin
Kai Nielsen
13cms
**
Blanc de chine
$100-200

4059
Girl with dolphin
Kai Nielsen
13cms
**
Blanc de chine
$100-200

4060
Girl with dolphin
Kai Nielsen
13cms
**
Blanc de chine
$100-200

4061
Girl with dolphin
Kai Nielsen
13cms
**
Blanc de chine
$100-200

4108
Eve & Apple
Kai Nielsen
30cms
***
Blanc de chine
$250-400

4109
Mother & child
Kai Nielsen
30cms
***
Blanc de chine
$250-400

4110
Mother & child
Kai Nielsen
30cms
***
Blanc de chine
$250-400

4111
Mother & child
Kai Nielsen
30cms
***
Blanc de chine
$250-400

4201
Cats - pair
Agnethe Jorgensen
***
$150-250

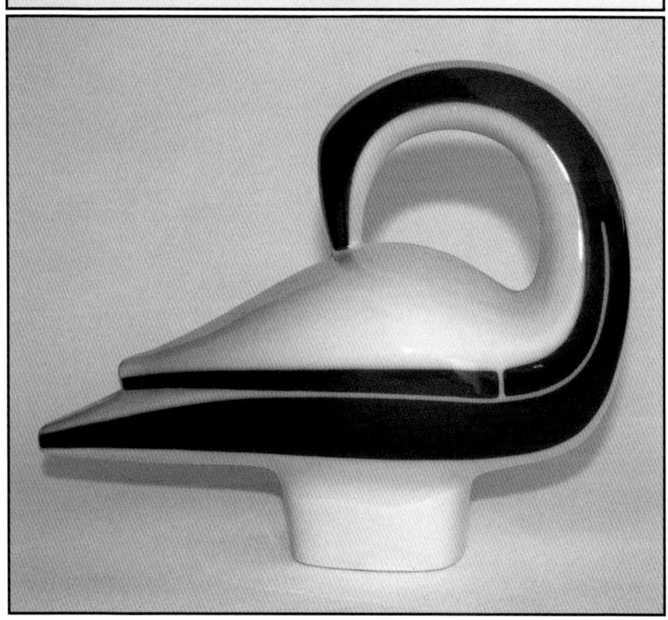

4202
Swan
Agnethe Jorgensen
***
$150-250

4200
Horses - large pair
Agnethe Jorgensen
***
$150-300

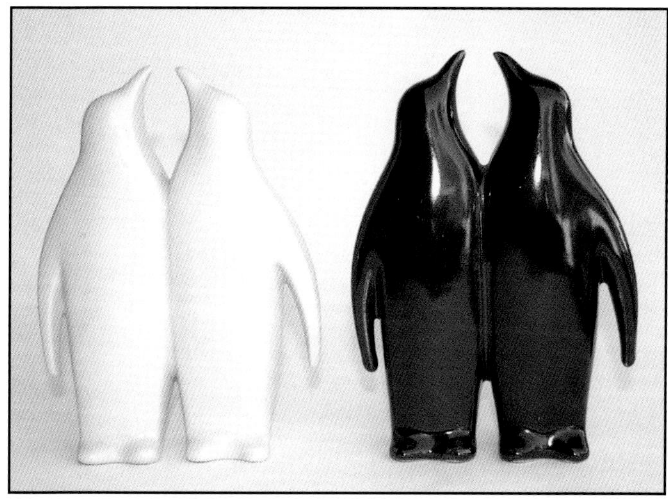

4205
Penguins - pair
Agnethe Jorgensen
***
$150-250

4203
Rams - pair
Agnethe Jorgensen
***
$150-250

4206
Cows - three
Agnethe Jorgensen
***
$150-250

4207
Horses - three
Agnethe Jorgensen
***
$150-250

4208
Horses small - pair
Agnethe Jorgensen
***
$150-250

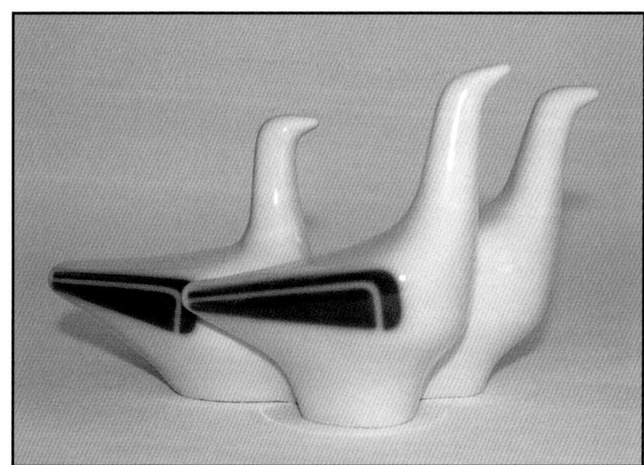

4204
Geese - three
Agnethe Jorgensen
***
$150-250

4209
Llamas – pair
Agnethe Jorgensen
***
$150-250

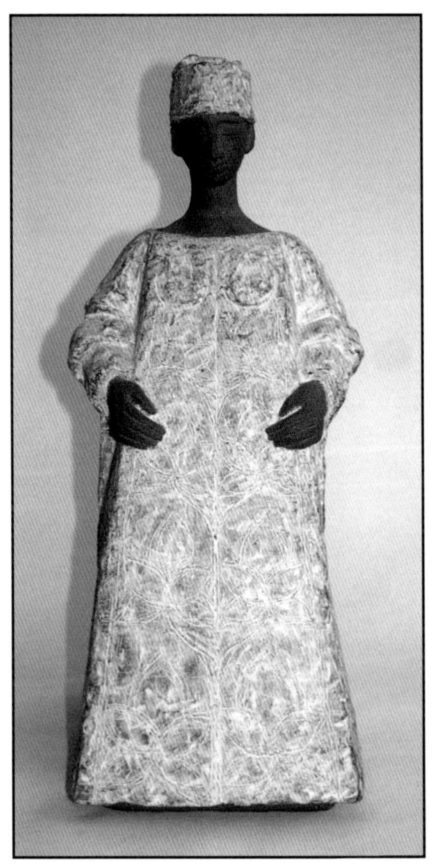

7016
'Africa'
30cms
Stoneware

7029
Grizzly Bear
35cms
**
Stoneware

7031
Ravens
32.5cms
**
Stoneware

7032
Mountain Goat
37.5cms
**

Stoneware

7034
Thrush
**
Stoneware

7036
Pigeon
20cms
Stoneware
**

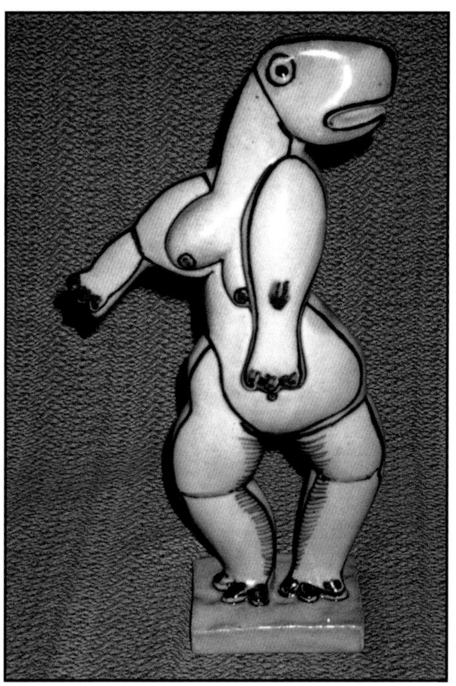

7043
Abstract figurine
Sten Lykke Madsen
34.5cms
***
$300-500

7044
Abstract figurine
Sten Lykke Madsen
22cms
***
$200-400

7045
Abstract figurine
Sten Lykke Madsen
13cms
***
$100-250

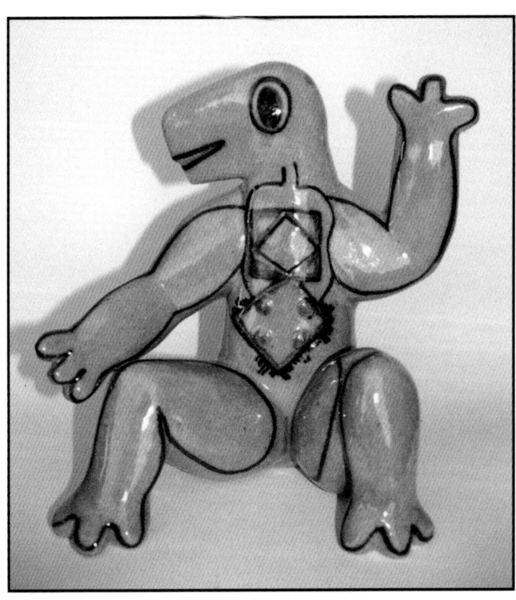

7041
Abstract figurine
Sten Lykke Madsen
20cms
***
$200-400

7042
Abstract figurine
Sten Lykke Madsen
23cms
***
$200-450

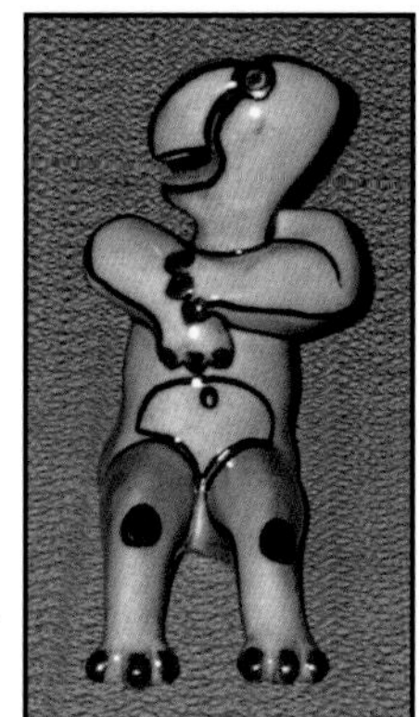

7046
Abstract figurine
Sten Lykke Madsen
21cms
***
$200-400

7047
Abstract figurine
Sten Lykke Madsen
16.5cms
***
$150-350

7048
Abstract figurine
Sten Lykke Madsen
12cms
***
$100-250

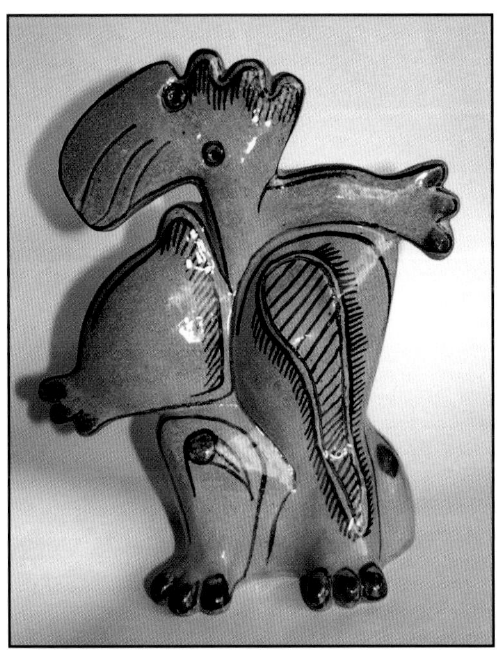

7049
Abstract figurine
Sten Lykke Madsen
26cms
***
$200-450

7051
Abstract figurine
Sten Lykke Madsen
23cms
***
$200-400

7052
Abstract figurine
Sten Lykke Madsen
11cms
***
$100-250

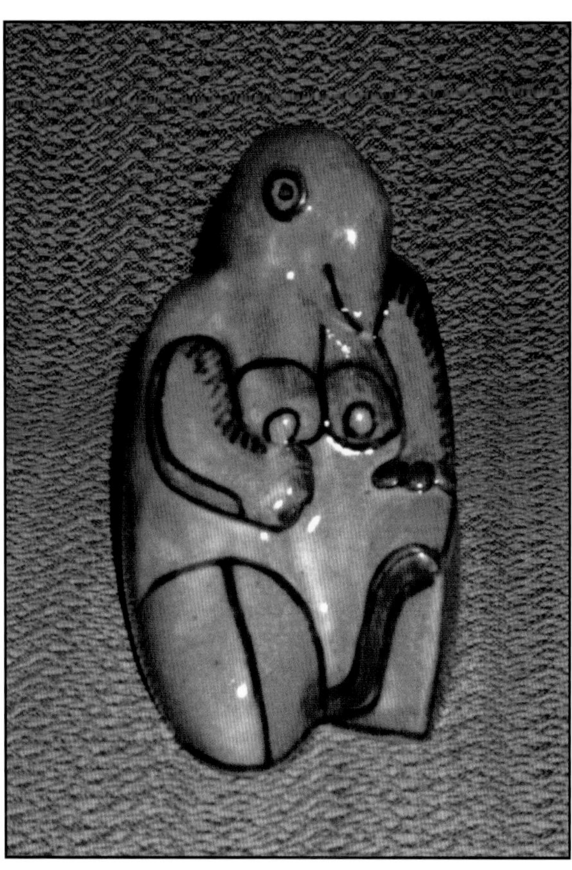

7053
Abstract figurine
Sten Lykke Madsen
12cms
***
$100-250

7054
Bison
35cms
**
Limited edition - 750, also stoneware

7055
Ram's head
35cms
**
Limited edition - 750

7212
Horse
??
***
Stoneware

8023
Skater
Jens Jakob Bregno/Hans Tegner
13.5cms
Overglaze

8024
Restless
Jens Jakob Bregno/Hans Tegner
16cms
Overglaze

8020
Dancing couple
Jens Jakob Bregno/Hans Tegner
14cms
Overglaze

8022
Couple skating
Jens Jakob Bregno/Hans Tegner
14cms
Overglaze

8025
Footman with coat
Jens Jakob Bregno/Hans Tegner
15cms
Overglaze

8026
Footman without coat
Jens Jakob Bregno/Hans Tegner
13.5cms
Overglaze

0027
Skater
Jens Jakob Bregno/Hans Tegner
16cms
Overglaze

8028
Running footman
Jens Jakob Bregno/Hans Tegner
15.5cms
Overglaze

8029
Jumping footman
Jens Jakob Bregno/Hans Tegner
14cms
Overglaze

8030
Lady with dog
Jens Jakob Bregno/Hans Tegner
13.5cms
Overglaze

8031
Lady with racket
Jens Jakob Bregno/Hans Tegner
15cms
Overglaze

8032
Girl with racket
Jens Jakob Bregno/Hans Tegner
16.5cms
Overglaze

8033
Blind Mans Buff
Jens Jakob Bregno/Hans Tegner
15cms
Overglaze

8034
Lady with slippers
Jens Jakob Bregno/Hans Tegner
15.5cms
Overglaze

8035
Lady without slippers
Jens Jakob Bregno/Hans Tegner
15.5cms
Overglaze

8036
Rain
Jens Jakob Bregno/Hans Tegner
16.5cms
Overglaze

8037
Sunshine
Jens Jakob Bregno/Hans Tegner
16cms
Overglaze

8038
Woman watering flowers
Jens Jakob Bregno/Hans Tegner
15.5cms
Overglaze

8039
Man trimming a box tree
Jens Jakob Bregno/Hans Tegner
15cms
Overglaze

8040
Artist at easel
Jens Jakob Bregno/Hans Tegner
13.5cms
Overglaze

8041
Dancing couple tumbling
Jens Jakob Bregno/Hans Tegner
13.5cms
Overglaze

8042
Lady in wind
Jens Jakob Bregno/Hans Tegner
14cms
Overglaze

8043
Man in wind
Jens Jakob Bregno/Hans Tegner
14cms
Overglaze

8044
Lady blowing soap bubbles
Jens Jakob Bregno/Hans Tegner
14cms
Overglaze

8045
Man with apples
Jens Jakob Bregno/Hans Tegner
17.5cms
Overglaze

8046
'Shepherdess & Chimney Sweep'
Jens Jakob Bregno/Hans Tegner
22.5cms
Overglaze

8047
'Emperor's New Clothes'
Jens Jakob Bregno/Hans Tegner
24.5cms
Overglaze

8048
'Little Claus'
Jens Jakob Bregno/Hans Tegner
15.5cms
Overglaze

8049
'The Nightingale'
Jens Jakob Bregno/Hans Tegner
20.5cms
Overglaze

8050
'The Swineherd'
Jens Jakob Bregno/Hans Tegner
23cms
Overglaze

8051
'The Tinder Box'
Jens Jakob Bregno/Hans Tegner
19.5cms
Overglaze

8052
'The Sandman'
Jens Jakob Bregno/Hans
Tegner
21cms
Overglaze

Woman standing - overglaze

26999
Zebra
Stoneware

Woman standing - overglaze

Woman standing -
overglaze

Woman with basket – Blanc de Chine

'Hans Christian Andersen Collection'

The following six pieces were produced in a limited edition of 2500 each.

'Elverhøj' (The Elfin Mound)

'Prinsessen på ærten' (the Princess on the pea pod), 11.5 cms

'Tommelise' (Thumbelina) 11.5 cms

'De vilde svaner' (The wild swans), 12.5 cms

'Den Lille Havfrue' (The little mermaid), 11 cms

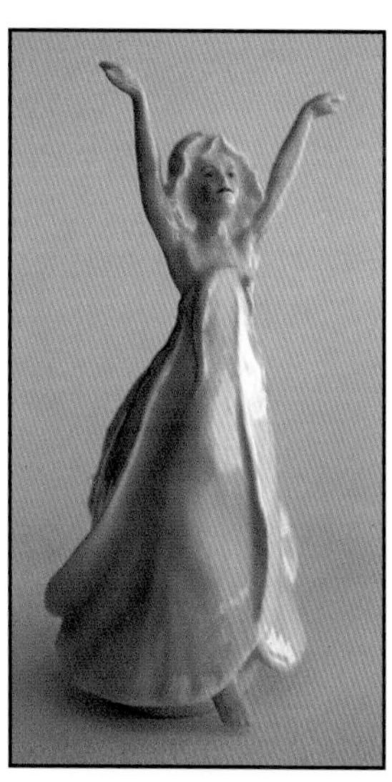

'Den lille Idas blomster' (Little Ida's flowers), 18.5 cms

Marked 'Eneret'

Annual figurine – Bear on rock

Marked 'Eneret'

1986 Elephant

Annual figurines

1990 Chicken

1987 Lamb

1991 Goat

1988 Peewit

1992 Panda

1993 Beagle puppy

1998 Penguin

1995 Hedgehog

1999 Rabbit

1996 Koala

2000 Dolphin

1997 Duckling

Dog – Blanc de Chine – 45cms

Grebe

Cats - pair

Ram - stoneware

Lions – pair - stoneware

Duck

Monkey and young - stoneware

Karl Otto Johansen

Wolf

Rabbit

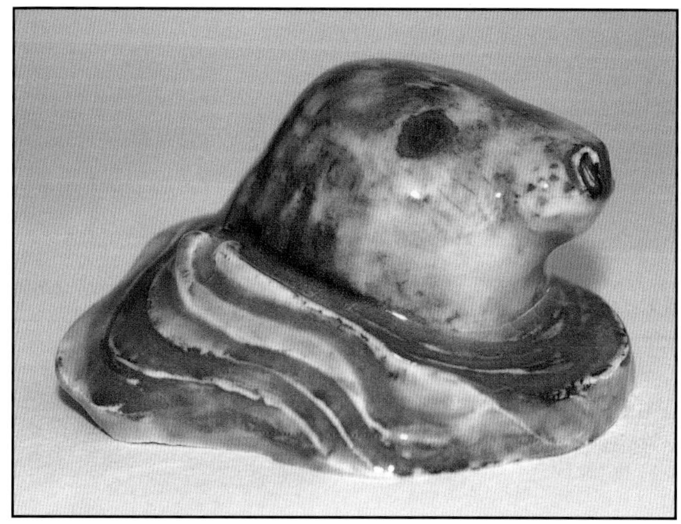
Seal

Rabbit

Abstract

Vases, Commemoratives, & Other Items

The Bing & Grondahl company, like Royal Copenhagen, produced a significant number of vases, commemoratives, and other items, including advertising material. Bearing in mind the diversity of these items, we have not attempted to give price guidelines, as accuracy would be suspect.

Many of these pieces are not numbered or are identified only by decorators' signatures or monograms. The signed pieces, of the leading decorative artists, are highly sought after, and prices reflect their rarity and quality.

2 Vase

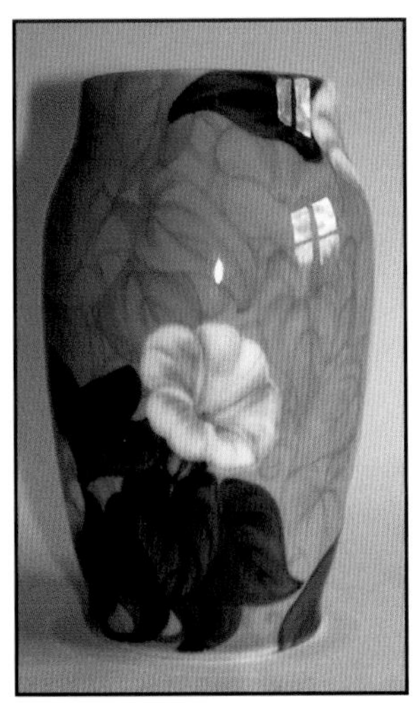

2 Vase - Ingeborg Skrydstrup

4 Vase

4b Vase with pierced top, 17cms

5 Vase, 10cms

8 Vases

7,Vase - Danish China Works

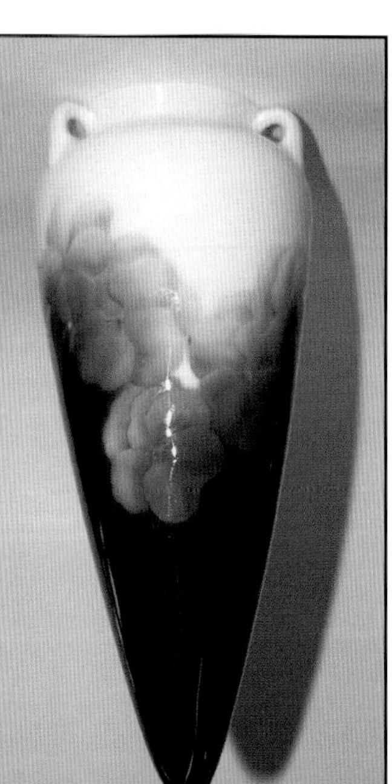

23 Hanging Vase, 15cms

27 Vase, Effie Hegermann-Lindencrone

38 Vase, Effie Hegermann Lindencrone

29 Vase, Fanny Garde

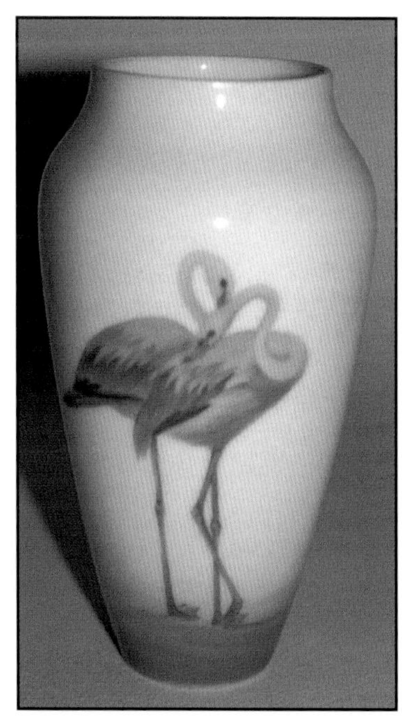

45 Vase, 15cms

47 Vase – Danish China Works, 32cms

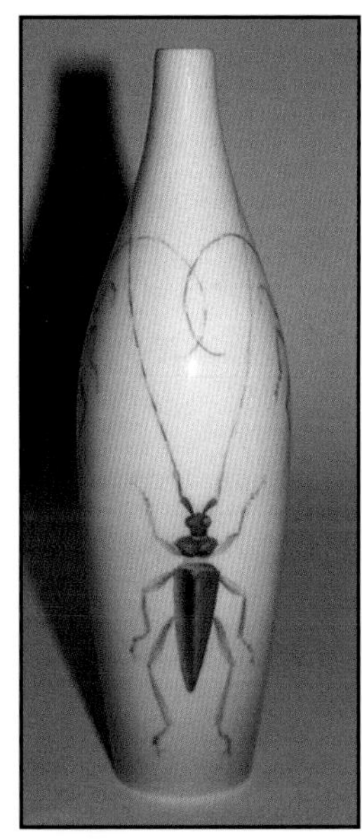

56 Vase, 22cms

58 Vase

51 Plate

59 Vases

61 Vase, 25cms

65 Vase – Danish China Works

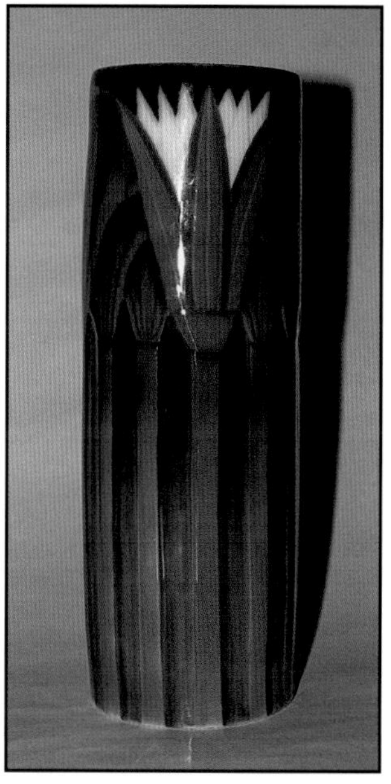

62 Vase – Danish China Works

69 Pomander, 7cms

63 Vase

74 Vase

98 Vase, 363 Vase, 7cms

95 Vase

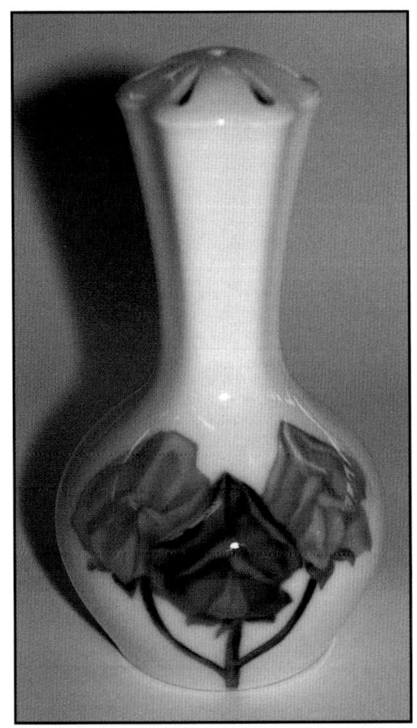

145 Hatpin holder?

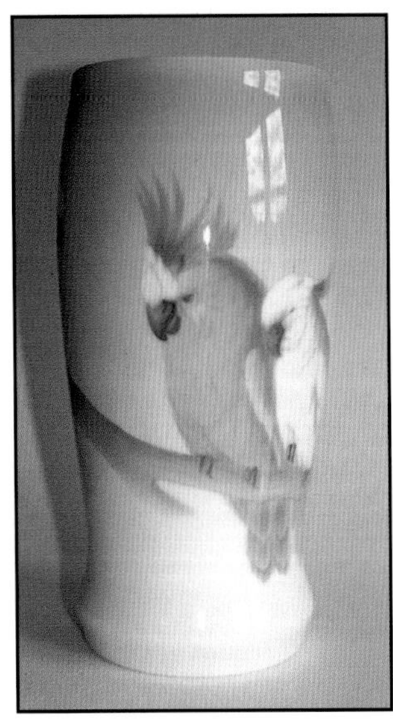

95 Vase

155 Vase, 7cms

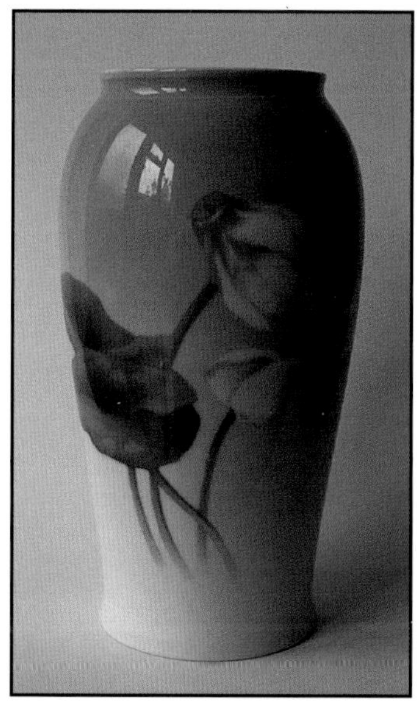

205 Vase

258 Vase

207 Vase, Effie Hegermann-Lindencrone

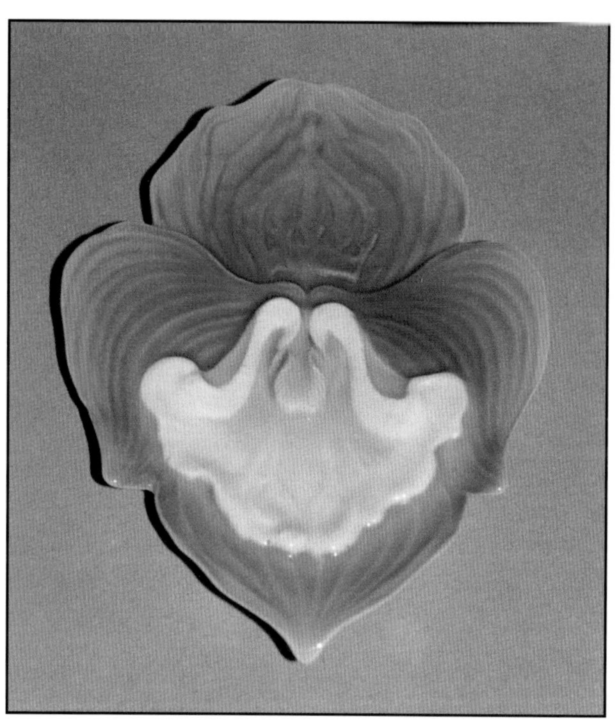

278 Dish with lily

218 Vase

286 Vase, 12cms

288 Vase

290 Dish with lid, Elias Petersen, 7cms

383 Vases

562 Bowl

567 Vase

673 Vase, 12cms

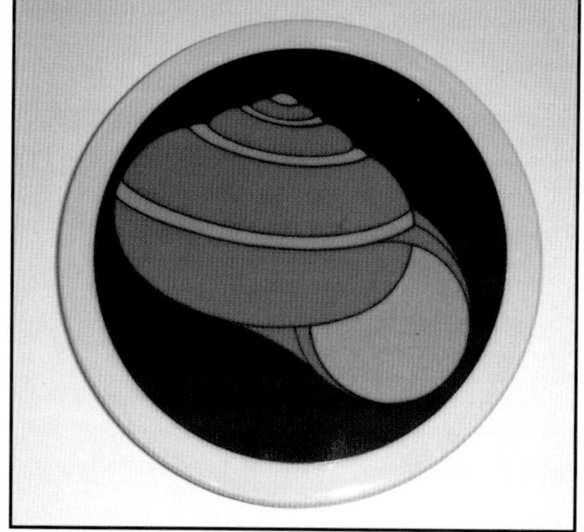

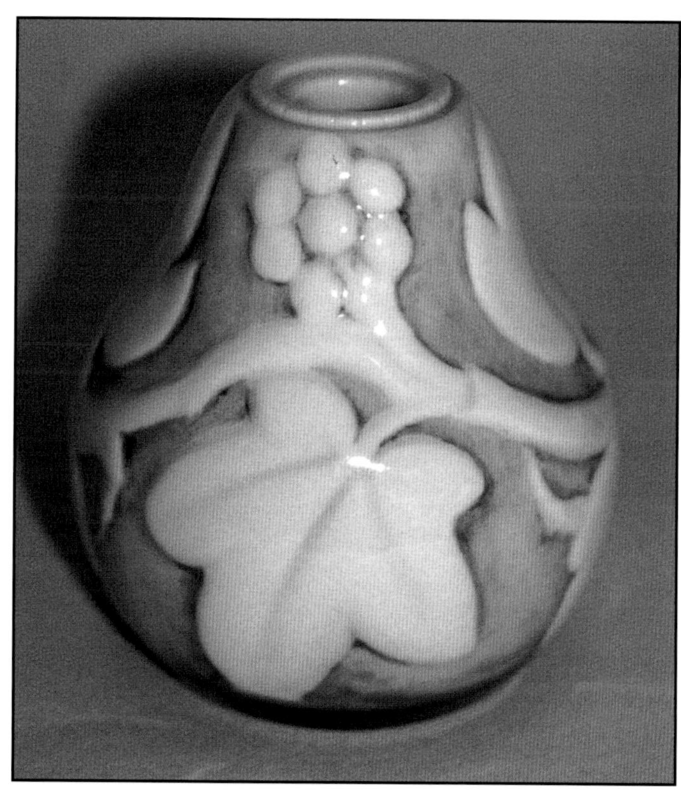

803 Vase

949 Wall plates

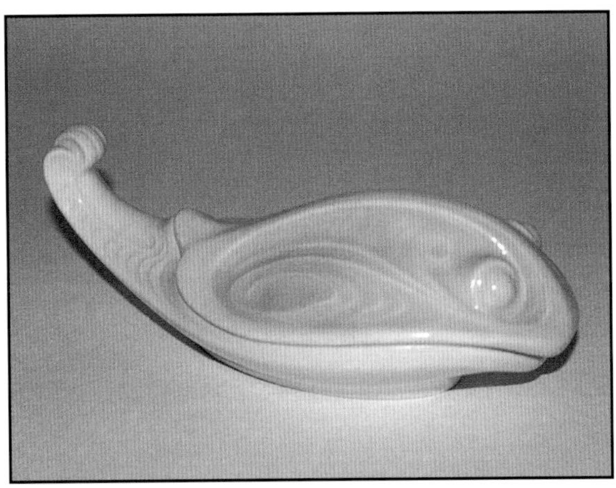

1000 Fish shaped covered dish, Dahl-Jensen

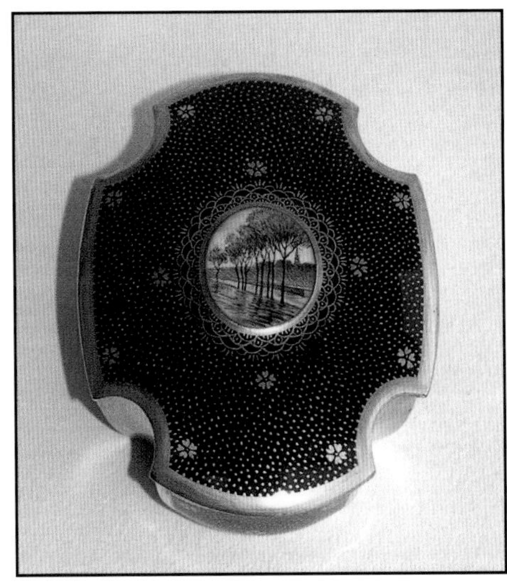

1060 Dish with lid

1020 Vase

1080 Vases

1044 Place holder

3503 Vase

Vase – Danish China Works - Tiger decoration

Vase, A Schou

Vase with faun

Vases

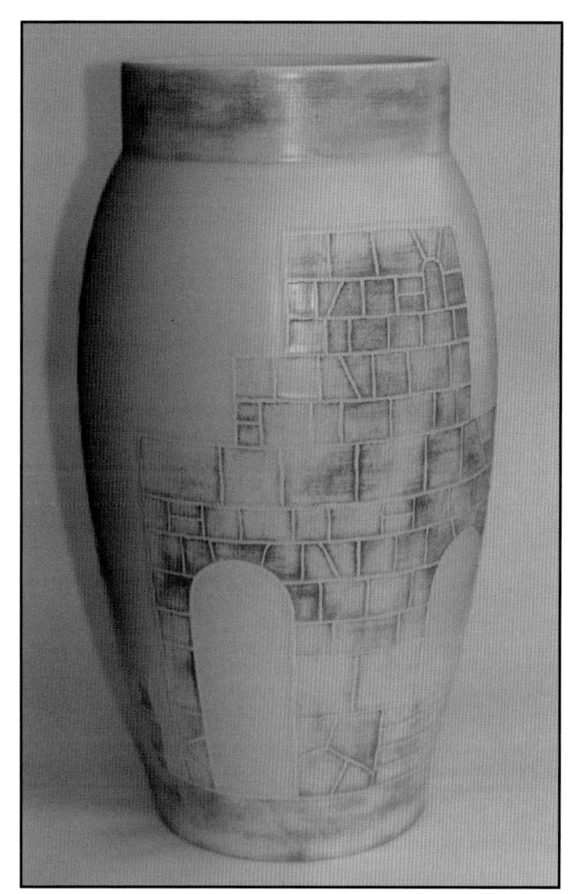

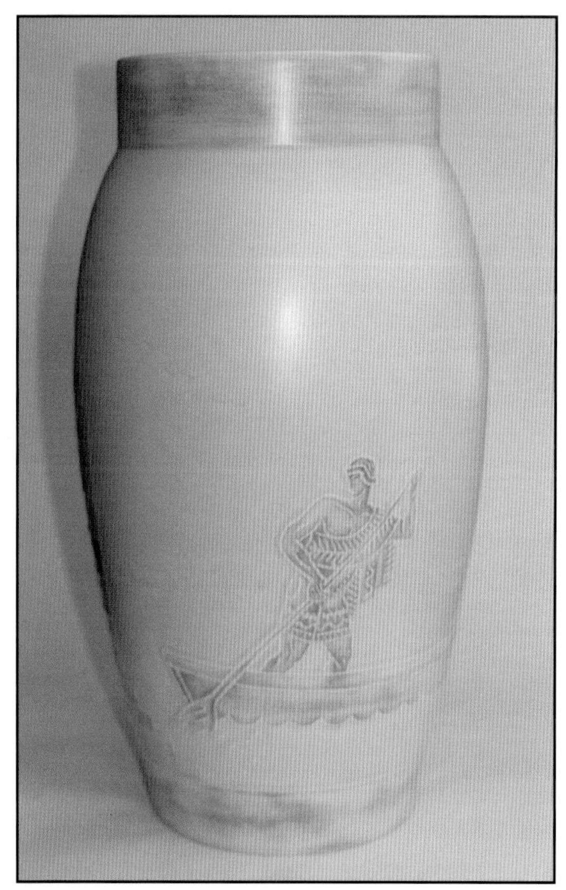

Vase – Cathinka Olsen

1931 Christmas Vase

3719 Egg

Place holders

Commemorative Items

1037 Dish with dragonfly

1187 Dish – celadon

1111 Plate

Plate

1113 Plate

Plate - Bears

Exhibition dishes – designed by Dahl-Jensen

Dish – designed by Dahl-Jensen

Commemorative plate

Advertising, shop and dealer signs

BING & GRØNDAHL
B&G
KJØBENHAVN
ECHT KOPENHAGEN
·B&G·
KIØBENHAVN
BING & GRØNDAHL

BY APPOINTMENT TO THE ROYAL DANISH COURT
BING & GRØNDAHL
B&G

BING & GRØNDAHL
B&G
COPENHAGEN

BY APPOINTMENT TO THE ROYAL DANISH COURT
BING & GRØNDAHL
COPENHAGEN PORCELAIN
COPENHAGEN PORCELAIN
B&G
MADE IN DENMARK

Teapot

Flask with stopper

Dishes with lid

Oil lamp
Dahl-Jensen

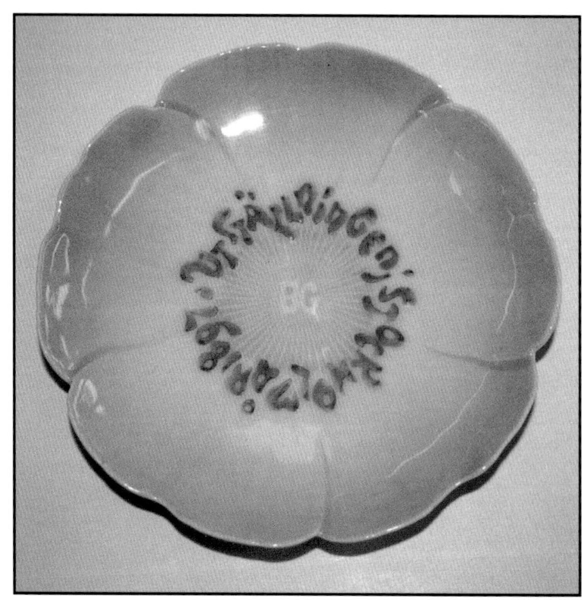

Stockholm 1897 plate

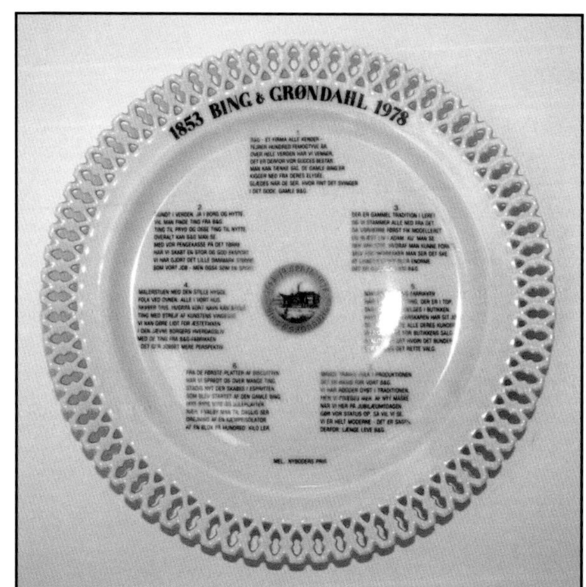

Plate 1853 – 1978

1853-1978 Employees Commemorative Plate

Appendix
List of Numbering Before and After 1987

The first column gives the original Bing & Grondahl number, used before amalgamation in 1987. The second column gives the current Royal Copenhagen number. Sometimes the old Bing & Grondahl number is found with the Royal Copenhagen back stamp, but we believe this was done only during the transition period. Many of the Royal Copenhagen numbers were used previously, for original Royal Copenhagen pieces.

B&G Pieces

B&G#	RC#
1526	400
1552	401
1567	402
1568	403
1574	404
1582	405
1614	406
1619	407
1624	408
1629	409
1633	410
1635	411
1636	412
1642	413
1656	414
1670	415
1684	416
1692	417
1713	418
1728	419
1744	420
1745	421
1747	422
1770	423
1779	424
1785	425
1785	426
1790	427
1808	428
1809	429
1810	430
1821	431
1826	432
1857	433
1875	434
1876	435
1885	436
1902	437
1909	438
1926	439
1951	440
1953	441
1954	442
2017	443
2026	444
2037	445
2161	446
2162	447
2168	448
2169	449
2172	450
2179	451
2181	452
2206	453
2207	454
2208	455
2209	456
2210	457
2217	458
2218	459
2225	460
2233	465
2246	466
2247	467
2262	468
2298	473
2310	474
2316	477
2324	478
2329	479
2481	481
2482	482
2483	483
2484	484
2485	485
2353	486
2354	487
2355	488
2370	489
2372	490
2379	491
2385	492
2425	493
2426	494
2435	495
2453	499
2454	500
2366	502
2235	503
2504	504
2505	505
2506	506
2507	507
2508	508
2509	509
2510	510
2511	511
2514	514
2515	515
2516	516
2517	517
2525	525
2527	527
2530	530
2532	532
2533	533
2535	535
2536	536
2537	537
2538	538
2539	539
2540	540
2468	541
2471	542
2472	543
2544	544
2546	546
2547	547
2548	548
2549	549
2558	558
2560	560
1721	561
2562	562
2564	564
2565	565
2573	573
2575	575
2576	576

Bibliography

Bing, Harald. *Bing & Grondahls Porcelaensfabrik 1853 – 1928.* Copenhagen: 1928.

Bing & Grondahls Porcellainfabrik Kjobenhavn 1890. Copenhagen: 1890.

Brohan-Museum. *Porzellan Kunst und Design 1889 bis 1939.* Berlin: 1993.

Grandjean, Bredo. *Kongelig dansk Porcelain 1884-1980.* Denmark: 1983.

Hecht, Robin. *Scandinavian Art Pottery, Denmark and Sweden.* Atglen, Pennsylvania: Schiffer Publishing Ltd., 2000.

Jakobsen, Gunnar. *Dansk Keramisk Bibliografi 1880-1997.* Host & Son.

Lassen, Erik. *En Kobenhavnsk porcelaensfabriks historie Nyt Nordisk.* Denmark: Forlag Arnold Busck A/S, 1978.

Museum fur Angewandte Kunst. *Kopenhagener Porzellan und Steinzeug.* Cologne: 1991.

Royal Copenhagen Porcelain 1775-2000. Copenhagen: Nyt Nordsk Forlag Arnold Busck A/S, 2000.

Vingedal, S E. *Porslinsmarken*, Forum, 1986.

Index